FAITH VIEWS THE UNIVERSE

A Thomistic Perspective

Pierre Conway, O.P.

Edited by

Mary Michael Spangler, O.P.

University Press of America, Inc.
Lanham • New York • Oxford

**Copyright © 1997 by
Pierre Conway, O.P.**

University Press of America,® Inc.

4720 Boston Way
Lanham, Maryland 20706

12 Hid's Copse Rd.
Cummor Hill, Oxford OX2 9JJ

Library of Congress Cataloging-in-Publication Data

Conway, Pierre
Faith views the universe : a Thomistic perspective / Pierre Conway;
edited by Mary Michael Spangler
p.   cm.
Includes bibliographical references and Index.
1. Religion and science. 2. God--Proof, Cosmological. 3.
Apologetics. 4. Thomists. I. Spangler, Mary Michael. II. Title.
BT1220.C66   1997   261.5'5--dc21   97-20070 CIP

ISBN 0-7618-0786-1 (cloth: alk. ppr.)
ISBN 0-7618-0787-X (pbk: alk. ppr.)

⊖™ The paper used in this publication meets the minimum
requirements of American National Standard for information
Sciences—Permanence of Paper for Printed Library Materials,
ANSI Z39.48—1984

To
Sister Margaret Ann McDowell, O.P.

Contents

Preface

"Sire, I had no need of that hypothesis." So responded the Marquis de la Place to Napoleon when the latter asked how he could write such a big book, his *Mécanique Céleste*, with no mention of God. (Newton, in speaking of his *Principia,* had stated that God might have to intervene someday to rectify irregularities in the orbits of planets. Laplace in his *Mécanique Céleste* demonstrates that these irregularities are cyclical and self-correcting.)

Laplace's statement typifies the position of God in modern science's view of the universe. God is not being attacked. God is simply an hypothesis, duly considered and found uncompelling, in modern science's enterprise to explain the universe, to formulate a theory of everything. For traditional scholastic philosophy textbooks the axiom *Whatever is moved is moved by another* remains indispensable to the proof of the existence of God as First Unmoved Mover. Modern science is based, successfully, on the tacit axiom *Whatever is in motion does not require a mover* implied in the supposition of the first law of motion, first enunciated by Galileo and set by Newton at the head of his *Principia.*

Science does not attack God today. God is simply ignored. His place is occupied by the laws of physics. Enlightenment has moved, in Carl Sagan's words, from a view of God as a venerable old man with a white beard, to whom one prays, to the better understanding that what one is dealing with are the laws of physics, to which one does not pray. (This is also germane to the outlook of Ludwig Feuerbach, upon whose materialism, along with Hegel's dialectics, Marx and Engels based their dialectical materialism, a.k.a. communism.)

For practical purposes, God no longer exists, not only in science, but in Western society as a whole. Current pleadings before the Supreme Court against legalizing assisted suicide make no mention of God, whose Fifth Commandment eliminates any such possibility in advance. In the speculative domain final words about a regretfully nonexistent God are delivered, if at all, not by theologians but by scientists, acknowledged today as being on the cutting edge of human knowledge.

Hence current titles, such as *The Mind of God* (Paul Davies), put out by men of science, mean, in the sense of Stephen Hawking, that when humankind comes to know fully the laws of physics we shall then know the mind of (the fictional) God. The appearance of a book by a Nobel Laureate in physics, Leon Lederman, entitled *The God Particle*, has nothing to do with God. The name *God* is retained in the title because "God sells" (caption of a newspaper article). The book is about an elusive ultimate particle, the Higgs boson, termed by Lederman "the God-damned particle." Lederman's original title was rejected but *God* was retained.

The present book is intended, not to combat science, but to place science in perspective for those of us who have by faith a more encompassing view than that of science and who are in danger of forgetting it in a society with a limited-by-science view. In this view the final theory is to be a mathematical explanation of a purely physical universe.

The more encompassing view, embracing the immaterial along with the material, the unseen with the seen, is expressed for a believer in the Apostles' Creed, affirming the existence of God as "creator of heaven and earth," meaning, not the physical earth and sky, but the immaterial and material creation, with *earth* representing the physical universe and *heaven* encompassing the immaterial reality of the angels and the blessed, and with the human being, by virtue of body and soul, seen as a combination of both.

Consequently, when a believer views the universe, he views a universe vaster than that of science. Yet, as informed by the media or as a student studying science textbooks, he is in danger of letting his total view shrink to the God-absent, purely physical universe, beginning, for the time being, with the big bang and evolving indefinitely in space and time as a closed system forever.

Such a future is addressed on the front page of the *New York Times* (Jan. 16, 1997) relating a meeting of the American Astronomical Society, captioned "At the Other End of the 'Big Bang,' the Finale May Be a Whimper." Looking ahead the astronomers, among whom Dr. Fred

Adams, foresee the universe as finally reduced to an ongoing dark age of small inactive particles. "This is not when the universe will end," Dr. Adams said, "but when any given physical process in the universe will cease to be important." Such an end, however, is not foreseen any time in the near future but trillions of trillions of years (10^{100}) hence. After mentioning an alternative big crunch theory, the article concludes: "In any event, Dr. Adams offered the reassuring thought that the end was not coming any time soon."

For the believer this prognosis, science's best, overlooks the reality that the universe so considered is destined to end at the Second Coming of Christ, which Christ tells us can be at any moment and which is scientifically unpredictable. "Stand ready, because the Son of Man is coming at an hour you [astronomers not excluded] do not expect" (Mt 24:44). Does this mean: "Take down your telescopes"? No. It means: "Stay in the state of grace."

The believer must ask of science: "Where is the Second Coming?" The answer: Science knows nothing of any such Second Coming, which presupposes the existence of an immaterial God and the coming of the Son of God to judge God's world, marking the definitive end and fulfillment of the world as we know it, and the inception of a new and eternal life of the blessed with God, with a renewed physical heaven and earth, now devoid of the corruptible, supplementary (but not necessary) to the human being's happiness with God.

The purpose of the ensuing pages is not, first of all, to enlarge science's unduly restricted view of the universe, but initially to evaluate science itself in terms of its probativeness. Are its premises, when producing predictable and productive results, to be considered true? Or is no more claimable for them than that they satisfy the appearances (an indispensable requisite for any hypothesis) and work? In the latter case one would be scientifically erroneous to regard a scientific hypothesis, because it works, as true. This a scientist, present or future, would wish to guard against.

This evaluation concentrates on the roots themselves of modern science (the starting points), originating with Galileo and Newton, which therefore characterize the whole ensuing and ongoing enterprise. If the roots are dialectical, i.e., without claim of truth, so must be the speculative edifice erected upon them. Since these roots are the starting point of science they must be understandable by all; otherwise science could not be taught. To evaluate roots is radical (from Latin *radix* 'root'). Since the insights brought to bear are present in Aquinas, himself acknowledging them in Aristotle, the undertaking may be called, among different sorts of Thomism, radical Thomism.

The enterprise takes the form of analyzing the basic premises of modern science, as presented in contemporary physics and mathematics textbooks, as to truth value. This is necessary, not to shatter them, but, indispensable as they are for practical purposes, to guard against their being taken as true when they are not. The basic premises of science, when taken as true when they are not, tend to displace the notion of God held both by faith and reason. Science's successfully posited motion without a mover is seen as displacing *Whatever is moved is moved by another.* If science is purely dialectical, no threat arises therefrom. To use a hypothesis, belief in its truth is not a condition.

How establish the premises of science as dialectical, i.e., not necessarily proved or even probable? This is made clear in the origins of modern science with Galileo and Newton, and which remain intrinsic and organic to it today. The outlook of Galileo, continued in Newton, is that nature may be explained mathematically, i.e., in terms of numbers. In Galileo's day everyone already agreed that falling bodies must accelerate at a regular rate, nature being orderly, but what was that rate? Such knowledge was indispensable then for lobbing a Medici patron's cannon ball over an enemy wall, and is just as indispensable today for calculating the initial horizontal velocity of a space vehicle allowing it to fall around the earth.

In order to initiate number into the continuous of motion and time, two steps were necessary, rendering science permanently dialectical and nondemonstrative. First, in geometry all curves in reality must be crunched for calculational purposes to straight lines. (A circumference becomes a multiple of rectilinear radii: $2\pi r$. The curved area of a circle is expressed in squares: πr^2. The volume of a sphere is expressed in cubes: $4/3\pi r^3$.) Second, in arithmetic, the divided of number must be applied to the continuous of space and time where it does not exist. Hence today's mathematical science rests on a permanent (successful) distortion of arithmetic and geometry, a twofold distortion already present in the age-old concept of π.

The algebraic equations of science function when numbers are substituted for the constants and variables. Thus in the equation $v = gt$, formulated by Galileo, when 32 is substituted for g, and 3 for t, one is stating successfully that a given body is falling, after 3 seconds, with a velocity, v, of 32 x 3 = 96 feet per second. In the expression, $E = mc^2$, the energy, E, produced in the transformation of mass into energy, is calculated by multiplying a given number standing for the mass, m, by the square of the number for c, the speed of light, 186,000 miles per second.

All such successful operations presuppose, starting with π, the permanent artificial crunching of the curved into the rectilinear, accompanied by the irrational merging of the discrete (number) into the continuous. (Such a merging is specifically irrational since it only accidentally, if ever, furnishes a rational number.)

What does one say when these artificially numerical equations produce the true predicted results of science? Unproved? No. They work? Yes. One rightly then asks why such artificial, nonobjective equations work—as they do and always will. The answer is that they must somehow be tapped into an objective order in the physical universe, even though the equations themselves are nonobjective. (Thus the successful mathematical calculation of the spot where a projectile, moving in a curved parabola, will land, is based on viewing the objective parabola as constituted from two straight lines, which admittedly it is not and cannot be.)

Does science recognize this objective order in the universe? Yes, and as indispensable to science's operation. However, in acceptance of the Hume-Kant position that nothing is objectively provable, science's spokesmen, such as Whitehead and Wiener, declare this recognition to be the object of an act of faith. (Faith, like demonstration, considers its object as real.) This does not deny that the perception of order is the result of induction. But induction itself, in Hume-Kant terms, must be held as nonprobative. (The believer, however, unconstrained by Hume-Kant, is free to believe that the inductive process itself is valid and objective, and the perception of order in the universe attainable not only by faith but also by reason.)

It is customary to speak of the Copernican revolution as the great recognition, starting with the persecuted Galileo (although actually set forth by an unpersecuted Copernicus a hundred years earlier), that it is the earth that revolves yearly around the sun, not the sun that revolves daily around the earth. But the true revolution is the perception and recognition (conscious or not) that science does not need, once granted order in the universe, objective or true premises to operate.

This is nowhere more clearly expressed than in today's celestial navigation at sea, where longitude and latitude are duly pinpointed on the basis of an earth-centered system, with the sun, moon, planets, and stars in daily revolution. Were one to ask a twentieth-century celestial navigator: "Do you believe the Ptolemaic theory is true?" he would respond: "Of course not." "Then why do you use it?" "Because it works." What is the final criterion for acceptability of a scientific theory today? Truth? No. Because it works? Yes.

The ensuing pages are destined to demonstrate to a reader that successful science is not, in its theories, truth stating, but simply practically effective. Because of its being wed to mathematics in a way that reduces geometry to the rectilinear, and arithmetic to the irrational (i.e., "numbers" unobtainable as the ratio between two whole numbers), any numerically effective summary or TOE is necessarily, while presenting only a partial view of the universe (the material), even in this restricted domain unobjective.

Where then does one go for truth? Both belief and science are at one in recognizing an objective order in the physical universe. For a believer this order can be deduced from the existence of God. The believer can then frame therefrom a concept of the total universe, material and immaterial. For a scientist, starting from this acknowledged order, he can, in the human being's innate pursuit of ultimate truth, ask himself whether any hypothesis concerning its origin is better than God. ("How can you resist speculating on the future of the universe?" asks Dr. James E. Peebles, a theoretical astrophysicist at Princeton University, quoted in the *New York Times* article above. Such speculation must take into consideration whether that future is not God.)

An atheist and a believer can plant tomatoes together, following instructions on the seed packet with equal chances of success. One can operate on *that* it is so without answering *why* it is so. The present book is concerned with establishing that today's science, while successfully utilizing the order in the universe, deductively proceeding from nonobjective hypotheses, still leaves open *why* the universe is orderly. Belief in the order of the physical universe calls for completion by initially belief, and ultimately proof, of an Orderer.

Thanks are due to Sister Mary Michael Spangler, O.P., of Ohio Dominican College for assembling of material, editing, and word-processing; to Mary Kay Clark of Seton Home School for initial encouragement; to Charles Petruzzo of NASA and Patricia Connick of

Ohio Dominican College for technical assistance; to P.R. Masani of the University of Pittsburgh for establishment in his works of science's public adherence to an objective order in the universe; to Thomas Gallagher of Magi Books, Inc., for funding; and to Father Kenneth Baker for permission to reprint "The Theory of Everything," printed in the *Homiletic and Pastoral Review,* June, 1994.

Chapter 1

Faith Views the Universe

A. Origin of life
B. Origin of universe
C. Destiny of universe
D. Order in universe
    1. God as author of all events
    2. Order as used by the scientist
E. Newtonian physics
    1. Galileo's foundational law
    2. Faith of the Christian

Two terms in this title require defining, namely, *faith* and *universe*. The reason for this is that different readers may have different meanings for these words. Hence it is necessary to state from the start the meaning that is given them in this context. Insofar as the term *faith* is concerned, it is used here in its religious meaning. Therefore faith is first of all a personal adherence of the human being to God. At the same time it is a free assent to the whole truth that God has revealed. In this context it is the faith of the Christian, specifically the belief of the Christian who subscribes to the Apostles' Creed as a statement of that faith. Every use of the term will be made therefore with this in mind.

What of the word *universe*? It is necessary to explain its meaning as used here, not because some arcane meaning is employed, but simply because the definition of *universe* for a Christian, not only includes the full extent of its meaning when applied to the universe as physically perceptible, but also extends beyond this to comprise the universe in its immaterial aspect—the universe of angels and the blessed, constituting an integral part of God's creation. Hence, when the Christian faith believes in God as "creator of heaven and earth," the meaning is to be understood, not as referring to the earth and sky as constituting creation, but to the totality of a single creation, both material (earth) and immaterial (heaven). The human being is placed at the juncture of these two elements, having a physical body animated by an immaterial soul. This extended meaning of universe for a Christian does not cause him any difficulty in dealing with the term *universe* as employed in everyday discourse to mean solely the visible universe. Nothing prevents him from considering it as the visible expression of an encompassing and superior invisible reality.

A. Origin of Life

This concept of the universe, of the immaterial animating the limited material from a higher, more encompassing aspect, permits a more coherent visualization of the origin of life as discussed by today's science which, having rightly dismissed spontaneous generation (the origin of the living from the nonliving) as a myth, has now brought back that myth to explain the origin of life in the universe. In effect it is now standard procedure in textbooks and the media to describe, sometimes with illustrations, the origin of life from some kind of a cosmic soup composed of the proper inert elements, such as carbon, hydrogen, and so forth. These elements are often then considered as being activated into life status by a lightning flash. What is this perceptible life status? It would have the qualities of nutrition, growth, and reproduction.

Does science make any claim to have produced life by this means in the laboratory? Not so far. Since there is no eyewitness account of its having happened in such a way in nature, its described initial occurrence is purely speculative. What is the intrinsic difficulty in these hypothetical descriptions? It is the difficulty science brought against spontaneous generation; namely, that for the living to arise of itself from the nonliving is getting something from nothing of itself. There is no reason to believe that one can get something from nothing.

So where does one go from here? To deny that such an event could ever have occurred? No. The answer is found in the true understanding of this concept in Aristotle and Aquinas. They both conceive of the living, even if in a somewhat elemental state, as being able, under certain circumstances, to arise from the nonliving. So in what do they differ from the once derided, and now reintroduced, concept of spontaneous generation employed by modern scientific theory where, given the right mix of inert molecules and, if necessary, a lightning flash, life emerges from the nonliving?

The fact is that Aristotle and Aquinas do not believe in spontaneous generation, the deriving of something from nothing of itself, as speculated in modern thought. Seeing such things as insects and worms appearing to come to life in apparently inert slime, and appreciating that something does not come from nothing of itself, they attributed this fact to an intervention by the universal causality in nature, bypassing the usual secondary causes. Since they viewed the first and universal causes in nature (God and the separated substances, or angels, acting through inert universal physical causes such as the sun) as living, they were coherent and logical in their supposition.

Not so modern science which supposes that, once the inert physical components (carbon, amino acids, and so forth) are properly arranged, then with the adventitious intervention of another inert factor such as a lightning bolt, life takes off. Since life is something completely different from the inert components involved, how can this be considered an adequate answer and explanation of the origin of life?

On the other hand, should the same event be explained as caused by, in addition, ultimate living universal causes such as God, there is no difficulty. The role of these universal causes (such as the sun acting under a living immaterial cause) and their constant action, is epitomized in the words of Aristotle: "Man generates man, with the sun." This role of universal causes is recognized in current science's speculation that the demise of the dinosaurs 60 million years ago was caused by a meteorite striking the earth and raising enough dust to obscure the sun, necessary for life.

Hence a Christian, believing with certitude (since he holds his faith as divinely revealed) in a living God as the creator and maintainer of the universe, has no difficulty should, at a given moment, life appear to arise from properly disposed inert components. The universal living cause can, if it chooses, dispense with secondary causes. However, for those who would wish illogically to maintain the genuine spontaneous generation of modern thinking (the living coming spontaneously from the nonliving with no living ultimate causality required), it is important to note that even then life is not conceived as sufficiently explained by simply *any* inert components. They must be of a certain sort—carbon, amino acids, and so forth—and activated under special conditions, such as a lightning flash. In other words there must be certain preconditions, specific requirements.

What does this signify? One can cite the concept of Empedocles, recalling that today's physics identifies the early Greek philosophers as intellectual ancestors. Comparable to the moderns, Empedocles envisioned the production of life to a right convergence of proper elements. In the place of the cosmic soup envisioned by modern geneticists, Empedocles envisioned a kind of mad whirl of various body parts belonging to various species. These kept connecting and disconnecting until finally the right fit was made. Thus an ox head might be whirling around attached to a human torso. Finally, after many whirls, the human torso would connect with a human head and the ox head with a bovine torso, and life as we know it would be on its way. As with the contemporary descriptions, it is noteworthy that not anything at all is considered to be able to combine with anything at all to produce the viable life we see.

B. Origin of Universe

What is the significance of this? It implies antecedent restriction and specification. This may be fittingly moved onto the universal plane, not simply of the origin of life, but of the origin of the universe. Currently this is ascribed to the big bang theory. (Interestingly, standard encyclopedias, under the heading of *Lemaître, Georges*, ascribe this theory to this said Belgian Catholic priest, later president of the Pontifical Academy of Sciences.) According to this theory, a very minute particle (like the head of a pin?) at a given moment began to explode into fission, producing our present physical universe. If the universe is continuously expanding, as it is believed to be, then one can mentally reverse the process, going back to some minute beginning. (The far-reaching devastation of an atomic bomb, starting from a relatively minute initial mass, indicates that such an explanation is not intrinsically implausible.)

But this initial cosmic pinhead is not simply of any composition whatever, or of no specific nature. Rather, just as its size is deduced from moving backward from present expanding, so its composition is deduced from present elements in the universe, such as hydrogen. To say that the initial pinhead is of some specific composition is to say that it is limited, in the same way that, if something is hydrogen, it cannot be oxygen. (Today's search in atom smashers for the ultimate particle, which will enter into and explain all other particles, is still for a particle which will not simply be a vacuum, a nothing, but a particle with a specific identity of some sort. A *this*, which means it is not a *that*.)

One now encounters the axiom, "Nothing limits itself." This applies to the initial particle of the cosmos which, by virtue of being a certain something and not a blur without identity, is, by that very fact (by being a *this* and hence not a *that*) limited. But nothing limits itself. Hence, if limited, it is limited by another. One can see the inevitability of this axiom by supposing that this initial particle of a specific nature is nevertheless unlimited and simply chooses to appear under this limited form. If truly unlimited, then it cannot be material, since every material being is of some specific material sort. In the realm of the immaterial, it also must be limitless, i.e., infinite, completely actual, eternal. Obviously such qualities are those everyone would concede to God. So the particle would have to be God. But it cannot be, since a divine being could not have any such limited specificity such as the initial particle would have to have. Consequently, such a particle could not be God, but would have to derive from God as a separate creation.

Such a particle as the take-off particle of the big bang—should such have been the mode of the present physical universe's coming into existence—while having its specific or limited form from a limitless God, also requires a cause of its existence. Since it cannot exist except under a certain form, the cause of that form is obviously the cause of its being, i.e., its creator (should the particle have ever existed). Hence the Christian, believing by divine faith in God, the creator of all things, visible and invisible, answers in advance the question science appears to stop short of: "Given the initial big bang particle, where did *it* come from?" Should someone answer, "It was always there," this answer does not account for its limited form, which in turn necessarily bespeaks a limited being. In answering "God," the Christian possesses an answer which is coherent and satisfying.

It is appropriate to mention in passing that the serene Christian belief in a universe created from nothing (i.e., *after* nothing of itself, not *out of* nothing) does not require of itself the concept of a universe created in time, i.e., one going back in time to a certain time at a finite remove from the present. God being omnipotent could have created the universe from all eternity, since he himself exists from all eternity and does not require an initial time lapse in order to create. Hence the beginning of the universe in time is held by the solemn teaching of the Catholic faith, alluding to this as the meaning of the first words of the Book of Genesis: "In the beginning God created heaven and earth." Consequently, although a cosmologist, basing himself on the data of human reason alone, could envision a universe existing from all eternity (since this is within God's power); nevertheless the Christian scientist will not so speculate, knowing by revealed and certain faith that God has created the universe in time.

Here one has a concrete example of the fact that the Christian faith, embodying knowledge of the universe to the extent that God, its creator, chooses to reveal such knowledge independently of the endeavors of human reason, does not find itself in a position of a nervous juxtaposition with science. Rather it dominates science when the creator of the universe chooses to reveal aspects of the universe concerning which science cannot reach a demonstration.

An amusing cartoon in the London *Tablet*, a Catholic periodical, in an article entitled "Science and Divine Design," depicts God answering a query of an angel: "I don't remember how I created the universe. Ask Stephen Hawking." The latter is a well-known astrophysicist who has asserted that once one knows the universe, one will have fathomed "the mind of God." Hawking considers both a timeless and a temporal universe as options. One of the two has already been closed.

The Christian, therefore, with the certitude of a freely chosen faith in a revealing God, will endeavor always to view the universe, material and immaterial (the latter encompassing the former), as proceeding from God by creation from nothing and, consequently, necessarily maintained in being by God in every aspect of its being, and infallibly moving toward the end which God, its absolute creator, intends.

Meanwhile the Christian lives in the world, lives in the present, a present in which the world at large does not necessarily recognize God in any way, whether as its creator, ruler, or end, and wherein the Christian is being given in the media various scenarios of the world's future, none of which imply a divine intervention and a divine finality. Does this Christian have a divinely revealed, and therefore certain, concept of the end to which the world, and with it the universe, is moving? One would be surprised if he did not.

The faith which the Christian freely chooses to hold with certitude as divinely revealed is set down in the Apostles' Creed, in which both the beginning and the end of the universe, or creation, are stated: its beginning by creation by God, its end in eternal happiness.

Having defined a Christian as one who embraces his faith as revealed by God and expressed in the Apostles' Creed, it is appropriate to define also the term *universe*. Naturally one will use the most generally expressed meaning, namely, that of the ensemble of reality that unfolds before us. In its astronomical sense, *Webster's Dictionary* states: "Properly, the entire celestial cosmos; the totality of the observed or postulated physical whole." Antecedently, however, *Webster's* gives an enlightening etymology, followed by an identification of the universe with creation: [fr. *unus* one + *versum* turned, that is, turned into one, combined into one whole] "All created things viewed as constituting one system or whole; the creation; the cosmos."

From the above etymology, one can see that common usage, as enshrined by the dictionary, views the world around us as something "united into one"; hence the institution of the term. One also notes that the basic meaning given the word makes it synonymous with *creation*. *Creation* in turn is not a term limited of itself to the purely visible creation of astronomy, but is applicable to creation as proceeding from God, its unifying source, in both the visible and the invisible realms, the material and the immaterial, with the latter by its superior nature encompassing the former.

C. Destiny of Universe

Having defined *Christian* and *universe* as here used, one then turns to the question of the ultimate destiny of this universe, originating from nothing by the power of God and consequently moving infallibly toward the end intended by God. For the Christian this end is expressed in the last article of the creed: life everlasting. What is meant by "life everlasting"? For the Christian this means to exist forever, eventually with a resurrected body, in the divine being as an adopted child of God, living, therefore, no longer on a human plane, but on a divine plane.

How does the Christian envisage the divinely decreed transition, starting with the creation of the universe by God, as expressed in the first article of the creed, "I believe in God, the Father almighty, creator of heaven and earth," and culminating in the last article, "life everlasting," life with God as an adopted child of God?

The cause of this transition is set forth in the intermediary articles of the creed, starting with the one immediately following the first, namely, "and in Jesus Christ, his only Son, our Lord." Immediately after the Christian profession of faith in the divinity of Jesus as Son of God, there follow the essential facts of the human life of Jesus, become man for our sake. One states one's belief that the Son of God, given the name Jesus, was conceived in his human nature by the Holy Spirit and born of the Virgin Mary. Immediately one passes to the central focus of his human life: "[He] suffered under Pontius Pilate, was crucified, died, and was buried." By this action Jesus, as man, freely paid the ransom for all sins and, by virtue of the divinity to which his humanity was united, purchased for all humanity, with himself as its head, a share in the divine life. After descending into hell, i.e., the limbo where the souls of the just from the beginning of time were awaiting this glorious outcome, Jesus "on the third day rose again from the dead and ascended into heaven," where "he is seated at the right hand of God, the Father almighty."

But Jesus' redemption and conferring of divine life upon those who believe in him is not confined solely to those before him from the beginning of time who were awaiting their redemption in limbo, but is for all those who believe in him up until the last soul that God has intended to create. At this moment the creed states: "From thence [heaven] he will come to judge the living and the dead." Such a day will mark the end of the universe as we know it, the observable universe of cosmology and astronomy. Why? Because there will no longer be any earth dwellers. Those chosen by God as faithful will lead divine lives with, in keeping with the human nature God created, glorified bodies. There will no longer be any need, however, for the motions of the solar system, attuned (as with the sun-caused seasons) to the maintenance of human life, since human life is now in a glorified state. Hence the physical universe will remain simply as a kind of window dressing for the blessed who, since they enjoy the divine life of God, creator of the universe, do not really need it.

When will this day come? Far from being outside of astronomy, it will be the very culmination of astronomy, concluding the predestined life-on-earth period of the children of God. Will it be heralded by decipherable signs in the universe? Signs there will be, but Jesus does not make them so clear that it will be possible to have some kind of a countdown before the end of the world. Such a countdown could be envisaged should astronomy fix on an approaching meteorite or comet destined at a certain remove to crash into the earth. Currently plans are being made to send up a space vehicle organized to launch an atom bomb to deflect the course of the meteorite or comet.

Jesus, the master of the universe, warns that his coming as judge will be essentially unforeseeable by any human calculations. "Be ready. You do not know the day or the hour." Since no scientific readiness is possible—the Second Coming can come before any space preparations, with them, or after them—the only readiness possible is that of the heart and mind, expressed in the effort to remain perpetually in the state of grace. In the words of Jesus, "Let your belts be buckled and lights burning in your hands, ready to welcome your Master when he comes, whether at evening, midnight, or at dawn. Blessed are those servants whom, when the Master comes, he shall find waiting."

Simultaneously Jesus warns that the world as such may not be waiting but going on as though no such sudden termination of the world as we know it were to be expected. "Men will be eating and drinking, buying and selling, marrying and giving in marriage." This implies that there will have been no science-based announcements in the media, since daily routines would cease in the face of such announcements. (Can one see the U.S. Congress remaining in session and making future legislation, should science announce that by evening the world would be destroyed? The words of Christ indicate that the Congress could well be peacefully in session when the end comes unheraldedly.)

Consequently, the Christian will look on his dwelling in the universe as something transient, with the universe itself in its present state as something transient. Subsequent to the (humanly unforeseeable) Coming of Christ and the Last Judgment, there will be "a new heaven and a new earth." This renewed physical universe will simply be an adjunct to the sharing in the divine life by the blessed who will already behold in God everything created, and whose blessedness does not depend upon the corporeal while their humanness will be complete by glorified bodies. Meanwhile each Christian knows that his own span on this earth, followed by a particular judgment, is foreordained by God, with the Last Judgment being the judgment of all humankind. This individual span has its own uncertainty since it may end slowly and peacefully or, still in God's providence, by accident and violently. The same divine admonition remains: "Be ready."

In conclusion, therefore, the Christian looks at the universe as coming totally from the hand of God and being continuously sustained in being and directed by God, upon whom the very being of everything at every moment depends, and which is moving toward a physical end preordained by God not within the reach of human ascertaining. Each is hence called upon to be ready at all times.

D. Order in Universe

An ever-present indication of the physical universe's being a manifestation of God is the order in the universe, an order which is likewise indispensable to human living. In effect, all the arts and sciences (science in general) depend absolutely on the perception by the mind of this order, utilized in human living from fishing to orbiting spaceships. How does this perceiving process take place? It does so naturally. Starting from a single instance, which can have occurred by accident, the mind is ever prompt to speculate on the possibility of an intrinsic order's being present.

Thus aspirin, a classic headache reliever, was derived originally from the bark of the willow tree. There is no need to believe that its discovery as a pain reliever was the result of some deliberate investigation. Conceivably someone could have been chewing on a piece of willow bark for purely casual reasons. Should that person happen to have a headache and notice concomitantly that it is relieved, the idea could well float up that willow bark cures headaches. If not on a first occasion, it is easy to conceive that, if a similar occurrence happened again, the mind of the person involved, remembering the previous occurrence, would begin to see a pattern. Subsequently such a remedy could be suggested to a friend on the basis of one's own experience, and the friend confirm it. Eventually it could be perceived reliably that universally willow bark relieves headaches. A permanent axiom in the art or science of medicine has been discovered and can be usefully taught and transmitted universally. (Such a procedure, originating science, is already described by Aristotle in the beginning of his *Metaphysics*.)

1. God As Author of All Events

It is customary to assume that, if an event can be explained by chance (as with the random mutations of genes postulated as the starting point of felicitous natural selection), the need for postulating an ordering divine intelligence is eliminated. But this is false. The Christian, whose God creates the world from nothing and unavoidably controls all its being absolutely, necessarily sees God as the author both of the order of the universe, from which (to the extent that it is grasped) reliable predictions can be made, and of humanly unpredictable random events, such as those postulated in the theory of natural selection.

This Christian perception would answer the current favored descriptions (based on speculation only) of the origin of life from the nonliving, an origin which is therefore spontaneous generation, since in this case life is not viewed as producing life, but rather it arises from an unplanned but felicitous combination of organic molecules with a happy dash of lightning. As has been seen, there is no difficulty in a living God, creator and maintainer of all being from nothing, producing the living from the nonliving, bypassing the secondary causes which he usually employs. Similarly, in his plan for the evolution of the universe, God can bring about new species from random mutation (e.g., by cosmic rays) of an already existing species as supposed in natural selection.

What must be remembered here is that randomness and chance, which are realities, do not exist for God. For the human being some things are predictable, others are unpredictable, the latter being sometimes happy, sometimes unhappy. But with God all things come about according to his foreseen plan, in the way he has decided, sometimes predictable by the human being, sometimes unpredictable by the human being. In the former case one has events that follow from the perception of the divine order, as, when one takes an aspirin, one predicts relief from a headache, with an assurance that is rarely disappointed. In the latter case one has the man who goes out digging for fishing worms and discovers a buried treasure. This is a real event but humanly unpredictable since it involves a humanly unpredictable combination of causes—the burial of the treasure by someone unknown to the digger, and the digger's decision to dig at that spot for fishing worms. Since no consistency in these causes' combining can be attained, no rules—as in the case of taking aspirin for headaches—can be set up. Such is the reality of chance, randomness, luck, accident, good or bad fortune.

However no such distinction between plan and accident exists with God. One has the example of a hungry employer who sends out one of his employees to purchase a hamburger. Subsequently he dispatches another employee to the same place for a cup of coffee. Predictably the two will meet at the carryout but, at least for the first employee, this meeting is intrinsically unpredictable. But not for the employer. In the same way, all events are predictable to God, since he is their cause and they do not exist without him. But for the human being some of these are predictable, some are not. Which are those that are predictable? They are the events which flow from the operations of causes that are part of the order of the universe and which the human being has perceived.

How are the perceived laws of the universe and chance events related? They are not in conflict—as they might appear to be when a carefully planned event according to the reliable laws of science is annulled by an unforeseen accident, as with the space shuttle Challenger. This leads to a definition of chance: those things which occur in the lesser part in things which occur for the most part. For the most part a man digging for fishing worms will *not* unearth a buried treasure, but in the lesser part (since such things are possible) he may. Hence one perceives that the predictable fulfillment of the laws of nature in some cases is not absolute. (Quantum theory requires one to have the state of mind such that, although when hitherto a dropped stone has always fallen downward, someday it might just fall upward. And so it might. For example, an unforeseen gust of compressed air from below could blow it upward.)

When unforeseen events happen, as they inevitably do—for example, out of ten happily growing tomato plants, one may unpredictably wither because of something gnawing at its roots—this does not mean that the laws of nature maintained in place by God may be suspended in a given case. Whatever is unforeseeably gnawing unpredictably at the roots of the one unlucky tomato plant is following a law of nature for its survival also. Such unforeseen events occur since the laws of nature are not so ordained by God that they will be fulfilled with rigidity. They are so ordained that in a given case they may be impeded by some other law of nature crossing their path.

Clearly God does not allow this to happen in the greater number of cases; otherwise the laws of nature, the perception and utilization of which are indispensable to human living, could not be counted on. As the cosmic scale increases, these laws, once discovered, do appear more rigid. Thus the order maintained by the four basic satellites, or moons, of Jupiter in the revolution around that planet is more precise than human clockwork. It was the refusal to believe in any actual variance in their times of revolution that led, when such an appearance occurred, to realizing the finite speed of light. The apparent slowing down in their times turned out to be traceable to the fact that light, moving at a finite speed, took longer to reach the Earth from Jupiter when the two planets, in the course of their orbits, were farther apart.

The nonabsolute necessity of the predicted fulfillment of the laws of nature (making them fulfilled for the most part rather than always, with accidental or chance exceptions occurring in the lesser part) is traceable to the nature of the material creation which, unlike the immaterial, is essentially corruptible. A flower grows, blooms magnificently—and then fades and perishes. In mathematics, however, which abstracts from the sensory elements of material things, corruption does not occur. A given triangle is invisible from a realistic viewpoint, since its sides have no width—and, being nonmaterial, it is also indestructible.

When a Christian looks at the universe, therefore, he is not choosing between two options, God or chance, the latter being, for example, the postulated randomness which is the supposed source of natural selection (production of new species or viable variants through random mutation of genes). God as believed in by a Christian is the creator of all events in the universe (with or without secondary causes), of the predictable and of the unpredictable (humanly speaking).

Thus should two persons meet, not even knowing previously of each other's existence, and this meeting have far-reaching developments, this unforeseen and unforeseeable event clearly depends absolutely upon God "in whom we live and move and have our being," though truly unpredictable and fortuitous to the two persons. Thus, in God's Providence, the two persons now meeting unpredictably are meeting just as infallibly as if meeting predictably by previous appointment. Thus a blind person may meet a passer-by who offers assistance in crossing the street. Initially unknown to each other, and meeting therefore unpredictably, this could be, in God's plans, the beginning of a fruitful relationship affecting the lives of both.

Consequently, when in the media and in textbooks the doctrine of natural selection arising out of a previous random mutation of genes is posited as a fundamental explanation, this is not disturbing to Christians, since God is the cause, along with the predictable, of the intrinsically (humanly speaking) unpredictable. They would be things that happen (unpredictably) in the lesser part, in those things that (predictably) happen for the most part.

Granted the existence of such chance mutations, falling, like all events, under the power of God, it is plain that they need not be for the best but can rather turn up as fatal defects. In certain cases, however, they can be brought about by God as part of the adapted survival of a species. Thus one has the case of the light-colored English moths which, as the bark of trees became sooty due to the (essentially unpredictable) Industrial Revolution, became an easy mark for predators as the moths alighted on the bark of those trees. Random mutations in the moths, however, produced certain dark-colored individuals, which unpredictably successful minority were to develop into the surviving strain, whereas hitherto, on light bark, their color would have made them victims. An outcome necessarily fulfilling the divine plan, but in a way initially unpredictable by the human being. Natural selection taking place because of (unpredictable) supernatural selection.

2. Order As Used by the Scientist

Where does the Christian's view of a God-created, God-ruled, and God-guided universe mesh with the contemporaneous scientific view of the universe (limited to the purely physical universe, mathematically conceived)? There is identity of outlook on the indispensability of affirming an objective order in the universe (etymologically 'something composed into one'). The Christian, seeing every aspect of the universe as at all times deriving from God, naturally sees this inescapably perceived order as a graceful affirmation of God's immediate presence. A contemporary scientist, should he not believe in God, nevertheless acknowledges objective order in the universe as the sine qua non of science. No order, no science.

While depending entirely on his belief in the discernible order of the universe as an objective fact in order to operate in science, need the scientist go farther and acknowledge God as the necessary cause of that order? Clearly he need not. This is enshrined in the supposed retort of Laplace to Napoleon who asked why God did not appear in his monumental *Mécanique Céleste*: "Sire, I had no need of that hypothesis." (Newton had left room in his system for divine intervention to correct certain supervening irregularities. Laplace showed that the irregularities were cyclical and hence self-correcting.) That belief in God is not necessary in order to profit from the perceived (indispensably perceived for the human race) order of the universe may be seen by the fact that, should a Christian, an agnostic, and an atheist plant tomato seeds in adjoining rows, no advantage is conferred upon the believer.

Nowadays, however, Nobel prizewinners in physics are asked their view on the existence of God along with theologians, even though the former do not need to believe in God to practice science. Their answer may be: "Almost, but not quite." The alternative, considered as not completely eliminated: pure chance—this latter leading to the concept of a universe which is pointless. What must be noted, however, is that the concept of chance presupposes order. If there were no order, there could be no chance—that which happens in the lesser part in things which happen for the most part.

It is noteworthy that, even when explanations of the origins of life, which is clearly ordered (i.e., follows certain consistent patterns), are given as deriving by chance (in contrast to any divine plan), the fortuitous circumstances postulated (never so far perceived as life-producing) are nevertheless ordered. Thus only *certain* inert elements (such as amino acids), not any elements whatsoever, are considered as entering into the origin of life. Likewise *certain* conditions of temperature, humidity, and so forth are postulated as required. A previous order must exist in order for the chance event to occur. Where does this order, requiring specified forms, come from? Even the big bang occurs from a something which must have a certain form. As stated above, it has a limited being, and "nothing limits itself." Hence there must ultimately be an ordering source to account for the specific, limited forms called for to hypothesize the origin of life from chance; that is, not from any living source, as in the normal transmission of life from life.

Why should it be called from chance or randomness? This is simply another way of saying that ultimately there is no plan in the universe; hence whatever comes about must ultimately be due to chance. This would require a lot of explaining since, while science depends absolutely for its predictions on the holding of perceivable cosmic order, there is no way of predicting that *anything* should come about by chance. Thus, when one holds that the mythical monkey seated at the word processor, given enough time (billions of years, if necessary), must sooner or later press the letter *I* (the first letter of the first word of the first book of the Bible), this position eliminates chance and introduces determinism. If the monkey is truly operating on chance, there is no reason *compelling* it ever to strike the letter *I*.

What one has, therefore, is simply the affirmation, without grounds, of an admittedly ordered universe coming about by chance, thereby dispensing the affirmer with having to ask whether such cosmic order does not necessarily require the existence of an Orderer, i.e., God.

Meanwhile, unless one wishes to say that everything is living, thereby eliminating the problem of how the nonliving can produce the living, as in the cosmic-soup-and-lightning-stroke scenario of the origin of life, one is faced with a case of that which science once rightly dismissed: spontaneous generation, the production of something from nothing of itself. (As has been noted above, the spontaneous generation attributed to Aristotle and Aquinas is *not* spontaneous generation but generation from a living universal cause bypassing secondary living causes.) This difficulty is resolved currently in the realm of quantum theory, whose motto might be, "Expect the unexpected," i.e., the stone that one day may fall up instead of down, the pond that may freeze over in midsummer. This theory's solution is to posit gratuitously a far-reaching spontaneity whereby the living might rise spontaneously from the nonliving and, even more fundamentally, being from nonbeing, the world from nothing of itself.

One might ask how such thinking can originate in the world of science, considered as it is today on the cutting edge of human knowledge. How can one have science based on such unproved assertions? The answer is simple: Science does not depend on them. The operation of science depends upon the perceivable grasp of order in the universe. The successful operational hypotheses, such as those of Galileo and Newton upon which modern science is constructed, are reliable because they must be somehow tapped into the real and objective order of the universe. Such is the criterion for their acceptance and use.

Examples are Galileo's supposition of all motion's being basically motion in a straight line (incorporated into Newton's first law of motion) and Galileo's calculation numerically of the acceleration of bodies in free fall, which hypotheses combine to enable the calculation of the speed which a spacecraft must reach in order to orbit the earth. Once these successfully operational hypotheses have been discovered, however, there is no need for their user to acknowledge an Orderer upon which their utilization of the order of the universe depends. As mentioned above, the atheist, using the discovered order in nature which enables the production of a crop of tomatoes, does not find his successful crop dependent upon his believing in God.

Ironically, therefore, while science and human life in general depend upon the perception and utilization of the order of the universe, an acknowledgment of God as the sole cause of this order is not a prerequisite to its utilization. Consequently one is able, subsequent to the confirmed discovery of order in nature, to engage in any speculations one wishes as to the cause of that order. The utilization of the order is not affected. The Christian in advance, by his faith, holds to God as the real and living here-and-now cause and maintainer of the order of the universe upon which human life in general and science in its operation depend. The nonbeliever can turn his back on this explanation, or on any explanation whatever. To get a good crop of tomatoes he needs only to follow the instructions on the seed packet.

To what extent does the order of the universe, indispensable to human life and science, have to be comprehended in order to be profitably utilized? The answer would appear to be: Not very much. Thus, in the case of the Ptolemaic and Copernican theories (one earth-centered, the other sun-centered), both theories, giving different and contradictory explanations of the same appearances reflecting a same order, are successful. While all evidence points to the supposition that the earth is rotating daily on its axis while moving yearly around the sun; nevertheless, for purposes of celestial navigation, it is found preferable to start from the supposition of an immobile earth (not actually held to be true) with the sun, moon, and stars revolving around it daily.

While both systems work, they cannot simultaneously both be true. Supposing the truth of the Copernican theory, i.e., that the earth is in actual yearly motion around the sun, then the Ptolemaic theory of an immobile earth is false. Yet, because it works best, it remains the theory of choice for celestial navigation at sea. The fact that it works even should the earth's immobility be false indicates that the theory is somehow tied into the objective order of the solar system. If it were not, it could not make reliable predictions as to the latitude and longitude—by means of sextants and chronometers and tables—of a ship at sea. So one perceives that, in order for science to produce predictable and reliable results, it must be somehow tied into the admitted objective order of the universe, while its actual scenario or hypothesis (for example, an immobile earth with the sun revolving around it daily) need not be factual.

This is what is meant by saying that science is dialectical—in contrast to demonstrative. The import is that, for its purpose of reliable prediction for human benefit, the hypotheses of science, crafted to explain the appearances as a start, are adopted, not on the basis of their having been proved true, but on the basis of deductions therefrom being corroborated by reality.

Does this mean that science does not care about truth—a perceived correspondence between the intellect and reality? Or thinks truth unattainable? No, the mind looks for such a correspondence with a natural and ineradicable appetite. Hence it looks on its concept of sense reality as objective. Not surprisingly, therefore, in forming a mental concept of the universe, one starts out by thinking of the earth as immobile, since one has no sensation of its moving, with the sun and the heavens revolving around it. (Later, when there were more reasons for considering it in motion than immobile, one would have to recall that for certain sense perceptions, those of the common sensibles—motion, rest, number, size, shape—the testimony of more than one sense may be required.) The Ptolemaic or geocentric theory, since it was constructed on a perception considered factual, and by the multiplication of circular orbits as required by apparently disparate motions of the heavenly bodies (such as sun, moon, planets, and fixed stars) was eventually able to account satisfactorily for the appearance of the heavens, came to be considered essentially factual in itself.

When the Ptolemaic theory was eventually displaced by the more coherent Copernican or heliocentric theory, it did not thereby fade into oblivion. Rather it remains in operation today, no longer looked on as factual but as a more practical (imaginary) theory for celestial navigation at sea. Meanwhile at the time of Galileo when, following his telescopic perceptions, Galileo began to opt for the Copernican theory as factual, his views ran counter not only to Scriptural statements of a motionless earth (in the Psalms) and a moving sun (in Josue), but also to the generally accepted view that this was actually the case.

Copernicus himself, nearly one hundred years before, in his own text was forthright in presenting the heliocentric system as factual and was able to cite ecclesiastical encouragement. No objection to this work was made. There is some conjecture that this may have been due to a spurious preface inserted by Osiander, a disciple of Luther, unbeknownst to Copernicus (who received the *De Revolutionibus Orbium Celestium* on his deathbed), to the effect that all astronomy must be considered pure fancy with respect to the certitude of Scripture. In effect, when the *De Revolutionibus* was subsequently placed on the Index, at the time of the first admonition to Galileo in 1616, this was to be "until corrected," with the corrections consisting in shifting affirmations of fact to the hypothetical.

Today, as noted, it is the Ptolemaic system which remains in effect, not as factual, but as the preferred hypothesis for celestial navigation. Since the Ptolemaic theory had been held as factual and turned out not to be (since there are more telling arguments of fact against it than for it), what of the Copernican theory that succeeded it? Does science hold *it* as factual? As demonstrated and true? The fact is that such a decision need not directly concern today's science. Science admittedly depends for its existence and operation on a belief in the objective order of the universe. The term *belief* is used designedly as signifying a certain adherence of the mind which, since it does not come from a demonstration—demonstration by the intellect being forbidden by Hume and Kant—must come from the will. (Those not accepting of Hume and Kant are free to say that this firm adherence of the mind to acknowledgment of order in nature is compelled by the intellect.)

Supposing that the Copernican system is proved true in the eyes of science, this would not affect the utilization of the Ptolemaic system for navigation, since the latter is used because it works reliably. Supposing that the Copernican system is proved untrue, this likewise would not affect *its* utilization since it is based on the fact that it satisfies the appearances and works. What is held as true, however, and is certainly a condition of human existence, is the objective order of the universe. In keeping with this is the fact that the mind is able to perceive *that* something is true and utilize that knowledge without knowing *why* it is true. Thus one can know *that* aspirin cures headaches and utilize this without knowing *why* this is true, i.e., the actual organic processes that bring this about. Whatever speculations one may make, even if wrong, will not affect the fact that an aspirin can relieve a headache.

In the same vein the utilization in science of the perceived order of the universe does not require a knowledge of the cause of the order of the universe. This means that one can speculate as freely as one wishes, as science currently does, perhaps erroneously, without science's being affected. Any inducement to take such theories seriously would have to arise from showing that the order of the universe cannot be explained otherwise. The faith-held concept of a God-created and ruled universe on the part of a Christian gives a coherent explanation. By comparison, scientific attempts to give a coherent explanation of the order of the universe without the God of Christian faith (which need not agree with the disposed-of God of science) do not achieve intellectual compulsion. This is understandably so if there *is* a God.

Today it is customary for a beginner in today's science, whether in a textbook or in the media, to be told that since the advent of Einstein and relativity our ideas about reality have fundamentally changed. Our ideas about space and time need to be modified. But what do the new ideas represent? Certainly no change in reality, since reality does not change with a shift in ideas. When the Copernican theory succeeded the Ptolemaic theory, the earth did not go from an immobile state to a rotating state. The sun did not stop going daily around the earth and start to stand still. What *did* happen was that, against the appearances which everyone sees and which remain unchanging, new explanations of these appearances were presented, justified on their predictive ability. Such explanations can succeed each other while reality stays the same. What remains unchanged is the perceived objective order of the universe.

Succeeding successful explanations of the appearances of this order indicate, first, that in order to be successful or predictably usable, they must somehow be tapped into the order of the universe; secondly, that they do not necessarily convey mirror images of the order of the universe since one explanation can be succeeded by another quite different from the former and even more successful in explaining the appearances and in working. Hence the dialectical nature of science: its premises or axioms or hypotheses are held, not because they have been shown to be mirror images of the universe but because, having been supposed, they produce predictable results.

Such premises can be shown in some cases to be actually false from a realistic viewpoint, such as those involved in calculating the trajectories of projectiles, or the basic supposition of quantum theory of a moving body's being always at a point. While such suppositions may, and do, produce predictable results, indicating that they are somehow related to the order of the universe, they nevertheless cannot be accepted as representations of that order, not having an actual existence in reality.

How does the Christian faith explain such a condition? It does so by saying that God clearly allows such human explanations of the appearances to work, signifying that they are somehow tied into the more complex order of the universe. One need only be aware that, because they work, they, are not necessarily true, i.e., actual representations of reality. As for a Christian looking at the universe, he sees with everyone else its reality and perceives its order, which it is the very nature of the human being to perceive and utilize. By his faith he knows that God is the cause and end of that order. In addition he is taught by his faith that the existence of God, cause of the order of the universe, can be attained by human reason.

E. Newtonian Physics

When one is greeted with the statement in contemporary physics textbooks that, since Einstein, our whole view of reality has changed—all things are monitored by the speed of light, c; time and space are relative—this does not refer to a supplanting of Newtonian physics, but to an adjustment therein. Was the introduction of Newtonian physics, itself laid on the foundations of Galileo, synonymous with the introduction of the Copernican system, with which Galileo's name is associated? Actually this is not the case, since the acceptance of the Copernican system as best explaining the appearances of the heavens, subsequent to the publishing of Copernicus's book, would have taken place without Galileo and owed its scientific progress to Kepler, a contemporary of Galileo, whose three laws of planetary motion were subsequently seen to be fulfilled by Newton's postulate of universal gravitation. (Newton's postulate of universal gravitation, first applied to the moon, involved the concept applied today to orbiting space vehicles: a body orbiting the earth—moon or spacecraft—is in a state of falling toward the earth due to gravity but moving at a speed such that it falls *around* the earth.)

1. Galileo's Foundational Law

It is for another reason that Galileo, in the introduction of all physics textbooks, is greeted as the founder of modern science, and rightly so. The introductions invariably, and also rightly, posit his inaugural thinking as superseding that of Aristotle. It will be stated incorrectly that Aristotle thought the natural state of a body was to be at rest. For example, a body given a shove eventually comes to a stop. Galileo then conceived of the thought that, should friction be removed and gravity suspended, a body in motion would continue to move indefinitely in a straight line. It is this concept of indefinite motion in a straight line as the basic motion of the physical universe which becomes the first law of motion in Newton's foundational work (initially in Latin): *The Mathematical Principles of Natural Philosophy*. This law remains at the basis of all physics, continuing to be presumed by relativity and quantum theory.

Where did this law come from? (As expressed in Newton's *Principia* it is: "Every body tends to maintain its state of rest or uniform motion in a straight line unless compelled to change its state by forces acting upon it.") It is significant that this foundational law of physics, assumed by all subsequent calculations, is the perfect example of a dialectical or nondemonstrated hypothesis, since it explains the appearances and works without its having been ever perceived or proved. In effect, no circumstances exist where one might perceive a body moving uniformly in a straight line with no forces acting upon it (such as gravity), nor can it be proved indirectly that such a situation *must* exist in order to calculate satisfactorily the trajectory of a projectile (as a spaceship would be considered).

The reason, therefore, for Galileo's introduction of this postulate, neither observed nor proved, upon which all modern science depends for its calculations—and which therefore makes all modern science dialectical—is to be sought elsewhere. Interestingly, although the concept is in keeping with Galileo's genius, he had no choice about making it. Why? Because he could not otherwise explain the universe in *mathematical* terms. Galileo, along with Copernicus, Kepler, Descartes, Newton, was certainly encouraged in his search for mathematical (i.e., numerical) explanations of the order of the universe by his belief that the universe was mathematically ordered by God and that therefore the mathematical structure was there for the finding. However, independently of any belief in God, Galileo was confronted with practical problems such as at what angle a cannon should be pointed to lob a cannon ball over an unfriendly wall, problems which called for mathematical solutions.

The successful search for mathematical (i.e., numerical) answers to practical problems, such as the acceleration in numbers of feet per second of a falling body, established by Galileo, has tended to confirm the outlook that any effective summation of the nature of the physical universe, now dubbed the theory of everything, must be in mathematical terms. In keeping with this, should one wish to understand some major area of contemporary science such as relativity, one discovers that from the start one is expected to cope with mathematical formulas. In other words, an understanding of the appropriate mathematics, involving numerical expressions, becomes indispensable to the understanding of modern physics.

Granted that today's physics, fundamental to today's science, is mathematical and specifically numerical, what is its relation to reality? To what extent is it an image of reality? The answer is that, by the very fact of transforming the view of the universe into a mathematical expression, contemporary science has had to forego an objective presentation of the universe.

It is this aim, namely a mathematical expression of reality, that renders the first law of motion, unproved and unprovable as existing in reality, a necessity. How does this come about? It comes about from the fact that, for the sake of numerical measurement, the real curvature existing in the universe must be reduced to the rectilinear (there being no unit curve for such purposes). Even with this accomplished, however, the numbering of the continuous, at stake in space and time, is not an objective reality—as witnessed by the fact that crucial numbers involved, such as the numerical value of π, are not really numbers, despite their being called irrational numbers, since they cannot be made to conform to any division in reality.

The genesis of the illusory numerical value of π—illusory because it does not exist in the first place, and even when given, is arbitrary, not a constant—illustrates the necessity for inventing the first law of motion, the fruitful product of Galileo's mind, and upon which modern science intrinsically depends. Mathematical minds—or better, human minds in general—recognize that there is no such thing as a unit curve, even for something as regular as a circle. Hence the impossibility of having a unit comparable to foot or inch for measuring the circumference. Since the rectilinear is believed to be so measurable, one sets out to duplicate the circumference by inscribed or circumscribed polygons, whose perimeters will then be measured in place of the circumference. Because of the impossibility of identifying curve and straight line, it is known from the start that no such perimeter measurements will correspond to the circumference of the circle, no matter how many times one multiplies the sides of the polygon employed.

Periodically one will be informed that the value of π, by dint of computers whirling away for hours or days, has been carried out to a few million more places. What does this signify? It recognizes that, since straight line and curve can never coincide, this is a kind of game one can play forever with no end in sight. Meanwhile, for all practical purposes, a value for numerical π, obtained by substituting the perimeter of a polygon of a relatively small number of sides such as 96 for the circumference, is perfectly adequate for all practical scientific calculations. Usually one sees the value as 3.1416.... In keeping with this, *Webster's Dictionary* defines π (falsely) as "the ratio of the circumference of a circle to its diameter," and gives its value to eight places as

3.14159265, while failing to add decimal points indicative of the fact, in this case, that no such number exists.

Since this is a matter of a proportion between straight lines, a perimeter and a diameter, it is worthwhile noting that there is no proof that *any* two straight lines need be proportional. This derives from the fundamental fact that the continuous is not numerical, the latter quality arising as it does from division. While falsely stating π as the ratio of circumference to diameter (which it is not), a larger dictionary may redeem itself by, under the heading *square*, citing the metaphor of squaring the circle (which is what establishing a numerical value, π, represents) as a metaphor for trying to do the impossible. Meanwhile the fact that, even after reducing curvature to the rectilinear in order to have numerical measurement, such measurements do not necessarily yield whole numbers, indicates that not only curves in nature but also the continuous of nature in general which is primarily measured in numbers—for example, distances, times, velocities—is not of itself mathematical. Hence one is justified in referring to the physical universe, the object of science, as unmathematical, in the sense of its not being, in an authentic and realistic sense, mathematically numerable.

What conclusion is therefore to be drawn? It is the conclusion that, while the consideration of the physical universe (the only one known to science) as mathematical, i.e., numerical, is quasi-indispensable for human living and intrinsic to all the arts and sciences in their practical range, it is not, thus considered, a true image of reality, and hence fulfills the appellation of *dialectical*, in the sense of that which explains the appearances and works reliably. The danger involved consists in not recognizing the dialectical, and subsequently identifying it with the demonstrative, i.e., that which is proved true. This failure to distinguish the dialectical from the demonstrative, perceptible, for example, in the first lemma or proof of Newton's *Principia*, leads one to think of the real universe as mathematical when, even in the physical sense, it is not, thereby lulling one into a false concept of the universe, sidetracking one's efforts to arrive at actual truth concerning the universe.

Newton's error, successfully enshrined in the calculus, with its undeniable practical value, consists in believing that, if one has a rectilinear area greater than a given curved area and a rectangular area less than that curved area, there must therefore be a rectilinear area equal to that curved area. This is simply squaring the circle. If he had said *approximates* rather than *equals*, he would be right. By failing to do so, he does not diminish the practical value of the integral calculus. More fundamentally, though, by failing to distinguish between the true and that which works, his view of the universe, as seen by reason alone, becomes incorrect.

Such an error is, however, held in check by a belief in God as creator and ruler of the universe, as was the case with Newton. Without belief in God, however, the failure to distinguish between the dialectically workable (such as the first law of motion, and science as resting on it) and what is directly perceivable or demonstrated (such as that a curve can never become actually identified with a straight line) lays the groundwork for relativism, the denial of any perceivable objective truth. Since science can operate with such an outlook, confining itself to hypotheses and axioms which work while not having to be proved true (and possibly being unable to be proved true) as in the case of the Ptolemaic theory still perfectly operational in a Copernican world, it is up to the student of science to recognize this and, while utilizing science as it now is, not accept any of its axioms and hypotheses as true unless so proved by a reduction to reality, i.e., either directly seen or known necessarily to exist from what is seen.

2. Faith of the Christian

Because science can operate successfully from hypotheses that need never be proven true—and can even be false, as is the Ptolemaic theory if the earth is not immobile—the Christian, looking at the universe (and quite inescapably today the universe as science sees it), has no need for concern should a scientific hypothesis contradict his faith. Why? For the simple reason that the hypothesis, by science's own standards, need not be true.

Thus a Christian, holding to a God continuously responsible for the being of all things, when confronted with the successful hypothesis of the first law of motion that a body once in motion does not require a mover, which contradicts the axiom (employed in the proof of the existence of God from motion) that whatever is moved or is in motion is moved by another, has no reason to be concerned. The hypothesis is used because it works, while rightly making no claim to objective truth. The Christian is at ease because he holds with the certitude of faith that all being—and hence all movement—depends upon God, whether he demonstrates this by reason or not. Supposing that he does, the unbelieving scientist, using his dialectical viewpoint, may properly respond, "I hold that a body in motion does not require a mover because this hypothesis works to produce successful calculations; whether it is true or not is not my concern as a scientist."

What then of the statement found in the beginning of contemporary physics books and accepted by the media to the effect that our view of reality, since Einstein and quantum theory, has profoundly changed, such as by considering time as a fourth dimension? What is correct to say is that our mode of *calculating* reality for practical purposes has undergone whatever changes may be the case, while reality and the appearances of reality remain the same. Thus when a mariner at sea wishes to calculate his longitude by celestial navigation, he refers to what he sees, i.e., the time of sunrise, and compares it with sunrise at Greenwich on the same day, as noted in the tables. His chronometer set on Greenwich time enables him to calculate the time difference between sunrise at Greenwich and sunrise as perceived by him. The difference in time, at one hour per meridian of longitude, will tell him how far west he is from Greenwich. In doing this the mariner of today, whom one can assume as subscribing to the Copernican or heliocentric theory as most probable, has, for navigational purposes, switched to the Ptolemaic or geocentric theory (which he can be assumed as not believing in as factual). For purposes of practical calculation he has momentarily switched theories, but the appearances of reality, from which both theories (contradictory though they be) are derived, have not changed, nor does he change his outlook on reality, being a Ptolemaic at sea and a Copernican on land. Hence contemporary theories such as relativity and quantum theory, accepted for whatever practical success in explaining appearances with subsequent satisfactory prediction they may enjoy, do not thereby imply a change in outlook on the actual physical universe—which remains the same in appearance to layman and professional alike.

Is it at all possible to get a view of this physical universe that is known or proved to be objective? Science does not need one, since it operates on theories whose value is measured on their ability to make reliable predictions in the real order, independently of any truth value for the theories themselves. Thus science is not concerned that the Ptolemaic and Copernican theories are contradictory but uses either one as it chooses. What is rightly taken as constant throughout is the objective order of the universe, to be tied into which, both theories, in differing ways, owe their success in prediction. The fact that at least one of them cannot be true indicates that successful utilization of the order of the universe in scientific theory does not of itself express a reliable mirror image of the universe.

What then of the fact that, upon opening a physics book or endeavoring to understand physics, one immediately encounters a mathematical barricade? The correct implication is that one cannot understand today's physics except mathematically. This condition is dictated by the practical aim of physics, for which number is indispensable. Galileo had to deal with cannon balls. His numerical formulas remain indispensable today at the cutting edge of science for the launching of space satellites and the like. Newton clearly viewed his foundational continuation as mathematical, calling his work *The Mathematical Principles of Natural Philosophy* (English trans.).

The fact that modern science, starting with Galileo and Newton, has successfully used the numerical for practical purposes is underpinned by the fact that Galileo, and possibly Newton, considered the universe itself, ordained by God, as mathematical, i.e., numerically expressible. This outlook, however, is unsustainable even in the practical order. In order to reduce the physical universe to mathematical dimensions, modern science, starting with Galileo, has been obliged to artificially transform reality—reducing curves to the rectilinear (something not mathematically accomplishable), for the sake of numeration (where number does not actually exist, i.e., in the extended). This is symbolized in the numerical construction of π, as elsewhere noted.

So what does one who wants to study the nature of the physical world, as updated in physics, do? Clearly, since the physical world will be immediately proposed to him in numerical measurements which in their turn have required an antecedent artificial reduction of the real world to the rectilinear, starting with vectors, he is getting the real world not as it objectively is, where circumferences cannot be reduced to polygons, and where the radius does not go any times at all into the circumference (the radian), but a world artificially adapted to calculational purposes. Such a route is indispensable for one having to practice physics as it is today where such successful mathematical formulations produce looked-for results.

Such a presentation, however, since it does not present the universe as it actually exists, can only be misleading when accepted as an objective explanation of reality since, for practical purposes with the indispensable utilization of number, reality is not presented as it is. Thus, though a projectile *actually* falls in a curve irreducible to the rectilinear, its real trajectory is, nevertheless, *scientifically*, and successfully, calculated as though it were an impossible combination of straight lines. Hence any true grasp of reality must be attained independently of science's artificial introduction of number, requiring elimination of the curved and the introduction of number where it does not exist (the irrational number). What is the conclusion? Study science and utilize the practical benefits for humanity of the introduction of number (artificially), but be aware that this is a dialectical (works but not thereby true) view of reality, not a demonstrated one (shown to be true either by observation or proof). Since even the physical universe, as apparent to the senses, is not of itself mathematical but only artificially made so for calculatory purposes, a fortiori this is true of the total universe, which comprehends the immaterial as well as the material, with mathematics necessarily confined to the latter.

In the light of what has gone before, what does the Christian see when he looks at the universe? With everyone else he sees what appears. From his faith, which he considers to be divinely revealed and as such certain, he has from the start a comprehensive view of the universe, one that explains its origin, its continuance in being, and its ultimate destiny. He is able to move deductively from his faith, as expounded and focused by the Church, to answers to the questions of daily life as to what is good and bad, right and wrong, not only on a temporal basis but as permanently and irrevocably judged by God. All of this supposes the continuous action of his reason, the faculty by which what appears is analyzed and notions of the order of the universe are obtained. These notions, gleaned inductively and incorporated into the arts and sciences, are indispensable for human living. As incorporated into today's science they represent successful hypotheses able to produce predictable practical results. Their proper use must correspond to the moral law of God.

Meanwhile such successful hypotheses, since their reliable operation does not require proof of truth or acknowledgment of God, cannot be taken as an objective mirror image of reality. Reliable results are their immediate goal. Only if a scientific theory can be demonstrated to be the only possible explanation of discernibly actual facts may the theory be considered as objectively expressing the order of the universe and not simply tied into it in some nonmirroring way. Thus the Ptolemaic theory, since the same perceived inductive facts from which the theory starts are better explained by another theory, the Copernican, cannot be perceived as the only possible explanation and hence true.

Here one notes that, at the time of Galileo, the Ptolemaic theory was seen by many, not only as working (the trait of any successful dialectical theory), but also as demonstrated. This proof was taken from what appeared to be the truth that the earth, as the ultimate center of gravity, had to be the center of the universe. Since with Newton the notion of universal gravity proportionate to mass, making the earth gravitationally subject to the sun, satisfied even better the requirements of truth, the Ptolemaic theory, still usable when desired, could not be held as truth. This also indicates that it was unwarrantedly held as true in the first place.

The human mind is fundamentally looking, not simply for something that works in the practical order, but for the ultimate reason why of things, starting with one's own existence. Since what is true necessarily works, the appetite for truth inclines one to think conversely that what works is true, when this is not necessarily the case. Ironically the very ones who perceived for subsequent thinking the indispensable distinction between what is proved or demonstrated and what works without being proved (the dialectical), namely Aristotle and Aquinas, considered the geocentric to be proved rather than dialectical. The same phenomenon occurs in modern science, dating from Galileo and Newton, where theories that work successfully, such as the first law of motion and the measurement of the circumference in terms of the radius (the radian), even when clearly not true, eventually come to be treated as fact. With this there is the accompanying danger that such theories, when perceived as conceptually against the Christian faith, will be taken as fact. The real situation is: Theory, yes; fact, no.

Modern scientific theory, by not going beyond the dialectical in any theory of everything, cannot be said to present in a demonstrative way any objective notion of the universe. A Christian will learn and use such science for the practical benefits it can confer when utilized according to divine law. While knowing by faith the true nature of the universe, unsupplied by the dialectical nature of science, he is nevertheless encouraged by his very faith to demonstrate the truths of the universe that can be demonstrated. "The heavens proclaim the glory of God" (Ps. 19).

Chapter 2

Introduction to Basic Science

A. First law of motion
B. Basic scientific assumptions
   1. A rectilinear approximation
   2. A numerical approximation
   3. A predictable space orbit
   4. Value of such assumptions
C. Description of motion: kinematics
   1. Rectilinear motion
   2. Vectors for nonrectilinear motion
   3. Projectile motion
D. Rotational motion and gravitation

What is meant here by basic science? By basic, one would mean what is most universally understood in today's science. This would mean a concept of science as equally understood by the man-in-the-street, by science textbooks, and by Nobel Laureates. It will be basic if it successfully identifies the basic premises whence science today begins and upon which the subsequent structure of science is erected and therefore depends.

A. First Law of Motion

Today's science is seen as originating at a watershed between Aristotle and Galileo. The former is viewed (incorrectly) as considering that the natural state of a body is to be at rest. Galileo's supposedly great insight, the one upon which modern science is founded, is to the effect that a body, once in motion, would, friction being removed, continue indefinitely in motion in a straight line. This creative insight is formulated in Newton's *Principia* (the foundational work of modern science) as the first law of motion: Every body perseveres in its state of rest or uniform motion in a straight line unless obliged to change its state by forces impressed upon it.

As to the timeliness and permanence of this first law of motion, first enunciated by Galileo in his *Dialogue on Two New Sciences*, without it space shuttles would not fly. Their orbit is calculated by an application of the first law of motion combined with Galileo's formula for the acceleration of falling bodies.

An analysis of the first law of motion, the indispensable first supposition of all modern science (starting with physics), gives one a grasp of the nature of modern science and the perception that its basic tenets do not claim truth, but are used solely on the basis of their ability to produce consistent predictable results. Because of a certain intellectual carelessness, a successful scientific theory, such as that of relativity, may tend to be taken as truth, even though it, and other similar successful theories, are, in the words of Einstein (relativity's founder), no more than "free creations of the human mind." Consequently one will read in physics texts: "Because of Einstein our whole way of looking at things has changed."

Actually our way of looking at things does not change. It is the same world, seen in the same way by all people, past, present, and future. What has changed, in the transition from Aristotle to modern science with Galileo, is the transition to the confidence that the world may be calculated arithmetically, i.e., in numbers.

The first law of motion—that a body of itself has the tendency, once in motion, to move indefinitely in a straight line—has no claim of experimental proof. Rather it is a necessary presupposition which Galileo had to make if he was to analyze reality mathematically, i.e., arithmetically. Brilliant creation though it was, Galileo had no choice but to make it if he was to pursue his practically rewarding arithmetical analysis of nature. In a word, to look at the world arithmetically, the necessary precondition is to look at it, unrealistically, as composed of the rectilinear. The circumferences of circles are constituted out of straight lines, their areas are expressed as squares, the volumes of spheres expressed as a collection of cubes. What is most surprising is that, while all this is not true, it works!

Needless to say, the reduction of the universe to the rectilinear for arithmetical computational purposes was not done willingly. It was simply unavoidable. This is seen in the necessary attempt, for practical computational purposes, to measure the circumference of a circle in terms of its diameter, leading to the establishment of a numerical constant, denoted π, and most commonly expressed as 3.1416.... This numerical constant, which actually does not exist, is seen to be intrinsic to all modern science and permanently on the cutting edge. This is no doubt so because in dealing with real nature, one is dealing more fundamentally with the curved and spherical. Hence the constant need for π, the rectilinear substitute for curvature.

B. Basic Scientific Assumptions
1. A Rectilinear Approximation

There are actually two approximations involved in the presentation of π as a numerical constant, both of which together account for the whole of the structure of modern science. Hence, meditation on π is meditation on modern science. The first of these approximations, whereby π is calculated, not on the basis of circumference to diameter but on that of the perimeter of an inscribed (or circumscribed) polygon to the diameter, recognizes the basic irreducibility of curve and straight line. There is no question of the circumference being calculated in terms of the diameter at all. Hence the substitution of a rectilinear polygon for the circumference. This basic recognition pervades all of subsequent science. All of reality, whether curved or not, must be reduced, for calculational purposes, to the rectilinear.

Unfortunately, no such recognition is found in physics textbooks. One simply begins with a rectilinear approach, i.e., vectors, used to describe all motions—whether rectilinear or curved. Thus the motion of a car around a curve is represented as a series of changing rectilinear vectors, which is clearly not the case. This will now be true throughout science. Curves will be represented as points on rectilinear graphs. Calculus will calculate the slope of such curves by calculating the rectilinear tangent to such curves at a point. Calculus will likewise calculate the area under a curve as a certain number of squares. Newton supposes in the beginning of his *Principia* that, if there is a rectangular area greater than some area under a curve, and one less than such an area, there is also one equal to such an area. True for the approximations of calculus; false in reality, because of the irreducibility of rectilinear and curved.

As has been seen, the basic imaginary concept of science, that of the universe as rectilinear, is dictated by the irreducibility of curved and straight. Hence the substitution of the rectilinear in science wherever curves exist—which is everywhere. This fundamental approximation, where the imaginary is substituted for the real, is dictated by the need for calculation, such as Galileo's arithmetical calculation of the acceleration of bodies in free fall, where numerical distances are calculated as proportionate to the squares of numerical times.

2. A Numerical Approximation

Such calculation is done on the second imaginary supposition that the rectilinear can be calculated numerically, on the basis of uniform numerical units such as the inch and the foot. But this is clearly not the case with the curved, there being no unit curve to measure all circumferences as there is presumably a unit length (such as inch, foot, and so forth) to measure all straight lines. Hence, to measure numerically for calculational purposes there is no alternative but to reduce the universe to the rectilinear, as science necessarily does.

But here too the second approximation, as that of the curved by the rectilinear, is imaginary, due to numerical incommensurability of the rectilinear. That is, even when nature is reduced to the rectilinear, there are no numbers in nature. This is already illustrated by the fact that all calculations of π, even on a rectilinear basis, become (after the initial crude approximation of an inscribed hexagon for the circumference, giving a value of 3 for π) irrational numbers. That is, they are numbers with values perpetually too great or too small, and hence nonnumbers for what is to be measured. This should not be astonishing, since the supposition (even in the case of two straight lines) of commensurability, i.e., of the possibility of comparing such lines as two integers having each a certain amount of a given numerical unit, is pure supposition, borne out neither by proof nor experience.

In effect, trying to calculate the diagonal of a square in terms of its sides, which is the calculation of the square root of 2, is just as impossible as getting a rational value for π. The reason for this, as stated above, is that there are no numbers in nature. (Hence the dream of a theory of everything, to be mathematically, i.e., numerically, expressed, is pursuit, not of the real, but of the imaginary.) Why are the numbers, such as on a ruler, imaginary projections of the human mind for practical purposes? This may be seen from the fact that different numbers and spacing will be given according to whether one uses inches or centimeters, an arbitrary choice in keeping with the recognition that there are no uniform units as such in nature in the first place.

This may be seen in turn from the fact that the existence of number is not tied to any spatial unity. This is because number represents, not the continuum, but the division of the continuum. Thus the numbers on a ruler do not represent real divisions. The ruler of itself is a one, i.e., an object undivided in itself and divided off from others. Theoretically it can be chopped up into any number of pieces. The count of these pieces does not require any regular chopping. Each piece can be of a different length, leading to any variety of counts one wishes. But each count will be valid. Yet none of these counts is actually present in the real ruler. A count becomes actual only by actual division. Consequently the numbering of physical spatial reality in all three dimensions is not a numbering of units in nature but simply a convenience that works for practical calculational purposes.

3. A Predictable Space Orbit

The combination of these two approximations—or, more properly, imaginings—which are at the heart of modern science is beautifully expressed in contemporary physics books in the description of the mode of calculating the orbits of space shuttles. Diagrams will show the actual curved orbit of the shuttle by a solid line and the imaginary rectilinear orbit, upon which the mathematical calculations are made, by a broken line. The latter involves an imaginary combination of the imaginary first law of motion and the imaginary calculations of numerical distances covered by a body in free fall, both deriving from Galileo. The space shuttle is first launched vertically to a given height predetermined by the combination of calculations in question.

When that height is reached the shuttle levels off and proceeds in a theoretical horizontal straight line with a velocity determined by the arithmetical calculations of free fall. Once the appropriate velocity is reached by the shuttle, the jets are turned off, in keeping with the first law's supposition that a body once in motion does not require further force to keep it in motion. Meanwhile the shuttle is considered, while moving horizontally in a straight line, as also falling vertically toward the center of the earth in a straight line according to the arithmetical formula for free fall established by Galileo. No one claims for an instant that any such self-contradicting simultaneous motions in a straight line are actually happening. But the calculations based thereon work to perfection.

None of this would be possible without Galileo's establishing of an arithmetical formula for the acceleration of a body in free fall—the formula for which can be attained by a thought experiment antecedent to any actual physical experiment, such as that of Galileo utilizing the timed acceleration of balls rolling down inclined planes. Thanks to Galileo, the constant of acceleration for bodies in free fall was seen to be 32 feet per second per second, or 9.8 meters per second per second. In keeping with this, the distance a body would fall in free fall in the first second would be 16 feet, or 4.9 meters. (If the body accelerates from 0 to 32 feet per second in 1 second, the distance covered will be 0 plus 32 divided by 2, i.e., the average distance, 16 feet.) Consequently, in order to fall around the earth, the shuttle must attain an imaginary horizontal velocity sufficient to match 16 feet of curvature of the earth's surface in 1 second. This having been achieved, the vertical fall of the shuttle per second will correspond to the downward curve of the earth's surface in such a way that, although falling, the shuttle remains at the same distance above the earth. It is in circular orbit.

As may be seen, if Galileo, or someone, did not come up with a numerical formula for the acceleration of free fall, space shuttles could not be launched. At the same time, not only are the rectilinear diagrams of the admittedly curved orbit imaginary, but likewise so are the numerical values. In effect, a body in free fall can be considered as though falling alongside a ruler appropriately marked off in feet. In keeping with this, the body, in passing from the distance of 1 foot into 2 feet, would pass over the unextended dividing mark between the two. At a certain moment or instant the body would therefore be at this dividing mark, would be at a point—or so it would seem.

Startlingly, however, a moving body is never at a point. This is for the simple reason that motion is extended while a point is not. A first inkling of the impossibility of motion at a point may be had by asking, when contemplating a beginning of motion from rest: "Where is the first point in motion?" It is clear that motion cannot be detected until the moving body has first covered a certain extended distance, however slight it may be. There is thus no first point in motion, motion being, whether one likes it or not, extended.

Therefore, applying this to the successful calculation of the distances covered by a body in free fall, and its velocity at any given (imaginary) point (instantaneous velocity), one perceives that the application of supposedly commensurable units (such as feet) to such circumstances is imaginary. This is verified by the impossibility of measuring arithmetically the diagonal of a square in terms of the sides, while the geometrical answer—square on the diagonal equal to the sum of the squares on the sides—is certain. One also perceives the accompanying impossibility of a moving body or particle's ever being at a point (the fundamental supposition of quantum theory).

What is the point of the above analysis of the efficacious, but imaginary, basic suppositions of modern science? The analysis is aimed at enabling the student of modern physics, admittedly the basic science, to comprehend in advance the procedures to which he will be introduced, the essence of which will not be revealed in advance to him. The basic aim of modern science is to explain all things numerically. In order to do this, nature must be falsely considered, for numerical computational purposes, as universally rectilinear. (Numbering requires units to measure with, and there is no unit curve.) Hence the base rectilinear position in all calculations of the first law of motion, admittedly not as a fact, but as an indispensable presupposition. Subsequently comes the application of number to the continuous—such as a continuous free fall—although number does not exist in the continuous, except as the continuous is arbitrarily divisible.

Insofar as human constructs are concerned, and everyday life in general—building houses and buying oranges—mathematics, and specifically arithmetic or number, is more or less indispensable. However, mathematics, arithmetic, number cannot be part of the basic explanation of reality, since even something so basic and fundamental as a circle cannot be measured mathematically—all measurements being based on an admittedly totally different substitute figure, a rectilinear polygon. Then even when nature is reduced to the rectilinear for computational purposes, number still does not exist realistically even in the artificially universalized rectilinear, as seen in the impossibility of finding the square root of 2. The same applies to the square root of 3 which enters promptly into the hopeless attempts of finding a nonirrational (i.e., exact) value of π, even when the latter is considered as the ratio, not of circle to diameter, but of rectilinear polygon to diameter.

4. Value of Such Assumptions

What then of the value of modern science? Its value clearly depends on the fact that its imaginary presuppositions, such as the first

law of motion, and the subsequent reduction of all motion to the rectilinear for mathematical purposes, produce marvelous results—modern
technology. Such a procedure is deductive, drawing predictable results
from universal principles. Inductively, however, such principles, such
as the first law of motion, cannot constitute a basis from which to infer
a higher reality; there can be no valid inference from the imaginary as
such to the real. One cannot ask, "Does the first law of motion require
the existence of God?" The first law of motion is not held—with its
denial of any need for a mover of a body once in motion—as a proven
fact, but simply as a fruitful assumption, indispensable for productive
calculations. Consequently, of the basic principles of modern science
one must say: "Use, but do not believe (as fact)." This would apply to
the Holy Grail of physics, a mathematically expressed theory of everything.

Since the technologically productive assumptions of modern science do not, and cannot, claim to be statements of fact; then, when they
come into conflict with articles of faith held as fact by Christians (such
as not only the belief in God, but even, in the scientific domain, the
belief in the creation of the world in time), this is not a threat. Science
is reasoning, not from proven fact, but from productive assumptions.
Thus today celestial navigation at sea utilizes, not the sun-centered
Copernican theory, but the earth-centered Ptolemaic theory. Because it
is a fact? No, simply because it is a more effective assumption.

Nevertheless modern science, although the principles on which it
operates do not claim to be more than productively effective assumptions, necessarily does hold to something intrinsic to science as a fact,
namely, objective order in the universe. Obviously Galileo's laws
upon which space shuttles are launched would not be applied if it were
not firmly believed that they were somehow tapped into objective reality, based on continuing successful experience. Interestingly, and in an
ironic meeting with the Christian faith, theoreticians of modern science
(e.g., Norbert Wiener) maintain that such a holding of objective order
in the universe, presupposed to the successful operation of science,
while it cannot be proved, must nevertheless be firmly believed as fact.

Today, when dialogue is being sought between religion and science,
with the latter now fielding questions about the existence of God, the
unavoidable belief on the part of science of an objective order in the
universe constitutes a common ground with it and religion, the latter
holding the same. From here religion can ask science if there are not

certain inferences that must be drawn from its admission of objective order in the universe.

Meanwhile, today's student of physics—enlightened by the knowledge that all concepts in physics will be treated in terms of the rectilinear (including rotational or circular motion), and that this limits science to practical applications, resolved mathematically—will be prepared to see all his physics problems reduced to finding mathematical (i.e., numerical) answers to concrete situations.

Thus the first, and typical, question in a modern college physics book will consist in finding out if a given runway of a certain amount of meters length is adequate for takeoff by a plane which accelerates at a rate of a certain number of meters per second per second and must reach a certain numerical speed in kilometers per hour before being airborne. The ultimate question in the same excellent text, now having arrived at subatomic particles, is to calculate, numerically, the lifetime of a certain subatomic particle (a meson) of a certain numerically measured width.

C. Description of Motion: Kinematics

Physics will be seen to be about motion. Hence the first part of physics is denominated kinematics, from the Greek verb for 'to move' (also present in our word *cinema*—moving pictures). Galileo quotes Aristotle as saying, "He who ignores motion, ignores nature." First, therefore, one has kinematics, the description of motion, to be followed by dynamics, the study of the causes of motion.

Because of the necessity of reducing nature to the rectilinear in order to calculate it mathematically, i.e., numerically, motion will be studied initially in a straight line. (When curved motion is studied subsequently, it will still be calculated in terms of straight lines.) The aim universally will be to arrive at certain mathematical formulas which, when applied, will give a numerical answer in some concrete case, such as how long, in meters, a runway must be. The components in these formulas will be distance and time, leading to the concepts of speed and velocity. Thus, when one divides the distance a car may have traveled, such as 80 kilometers, by the time elapsed, such as 2 hours, one arrives at the average speed of the car, 40 kilometers per hour.

The concept of velocity adds to the concept of speed the note of direction. Hence, even though a car rounds a curve at a constant speed,

it is considered as changing its velocity. How is this change in direction around a curve, this change in velocity, described? The student
who realizes that for numerical calculation all nature must be reduced
to the rectilinear will not be surprised to see it described as a series of
straight lines, i.e., vectors. All subsequent displacements, curved or
not, will be described in this way: in terms of rectilinear vectors and
compositions thereof.

Hence the curved motion of a projectile, or of a ball falling to the
ground after it has rolled off a table, will be described in terms of a
composite of rectilinear vectors, one horizontal, one vertical. Even
though this is not what is happening—since a curve cannot be composed of the rectilinear—it is only by so imaginatively conceiving it
that the desired numerical answer can be obtained. This result is how
far from the table the ball will fall, based on how much time it will take
in fall, combined with how fast the ball is rolling. The same calculations are involved in a bombing run: how fast the plane is moving;
where, ahead of the plane, is the bomb to land; how long will it take to
fall.

The quantitative value of the rectilinear vector is expressed by its
length. Thus a vector in a diagram representing 10 feet will be drawn
twice as long as one representing 5 feet. One can then calculate a resultant motion, such as the path taken by a boat crossing from shore to
shore of a running stream, as a rectilinear displacement, the resultant of
two vectors. Here one must note that velocity is calculated in terms of
displacement, i.e., the measure of distance covered, not primarily as in
actuality, but as the crow flies. Thus, should I walk 3 miles due east,
then 4 miles due north, a total of 7 miles in actuality; nevertheless, for
purposes of physics, I have moved only in a straight line from my
starting point to my finish point, a displacement of 5 miles, an imaginary distance insofar as representing my real walking is concerned.

However, as in all concepts in physics, this concept is retained and
utilized, not because of any demonstrated truth value (which is not
claimed) but because of its value in arriving at reliable concrete numerical results, such as how far downstream a boat will touch the opposite shore if it heads directly across with the river running at a certain
speed. This can also be used subsequently to calculate at what angle
(calculated trigonometrically) it should be pointed upstream in order to
arrive directly across.

Finally there is the concept of acceleration. As has been seen, velocity adds to the notion of speed the notion of direction. Hence, even

though a car may retain its same speed when going from the straight-
away around a curve, its velocity, in physics, is considered changing
(always rectilinearly) as it departs from its original straight course.
Since change of direction, without change of speed, is denoted a
change in velocity, similarly such a change will be denoted an acceleration. Thus if, in physics, a car moves at constant speed around a
curve, it is calculated (imaginatively, but not realistically) as moving in
a changing series of straight lines (expressed by vectors), constantly
changing velocity (by virtue of changing position), and subsequently
constantly accelerating (by virtue of changing velocity).

Why does physics, the basic science, have to resort to concepts that
fly in the face of actuality, such as a change of direction being considered a change of velocity, and such a change of velocity being then
considered an acceleration, although the speed of the body need not
have changed in any way? The secret, of course, is the unacknow-
ledged necessity of reducing all to the rectilinear, due to the fact that,
for numerical measurement, curves cannot be measured and the universe must be calculated in rectilinear terms. Why should everything
be reduced to numerical measurement? Admittedly it is because it is
only by a reduction to the numerical that substantial physical progress
can be made—even though this reduction can be proved to be unreal.

Meanwhile certain persons have a natural predisposition to this
(imaginary) viewing of the real in terms of numbers, with Galileo being
an example par excellence. Their recognizable successes in the practical order—such as Galileo's mathematical tables for the elevation of
cannons to successfully lob cannon balls to a given distance—tend to
lead one to think that nature is actually mathematical when it is not, the
illusion preserved in today's search for a mathematical, by prescription,
theory of everything. Among the practical consequences to be drawn
from this realization is the need for not trying to comprehend physical
formulas successfully arrived at by science as expressions of reality—a
frustrating pursuit. The only productive attitude, in producing the numerical answers to concrete situations sought by physics, is to learn the
formulas and apply them blindly to get the answers—since they are not
so formulated because they are proved true, but because they work.

One is permitted to ask why God should allow science to produce
formulas and laws which can be seen to be patently unreal but which
nevertheless work, all deriving from the imaginary concept of the universe as rectilinear as initially expressed in the first law of motion. An
inkling of the answer may perhaps be present in science's contempo-

rary recognition that it is far from actually comprehending the mysterious working of the universe and perhaps may never do so. Could God in his benignity have left the universe which he has given to the human being to rule such that a merely superficial comprehension of it in physical laws that work but do not comprehend, suffices for the human being to construct practical products?

That physics, the study of material motion, now in mathematical (numerical) terms, is the basic science may be seen from the fact that a standard college biology book begins with a long chapter on (inert) chemical elements as being indispensable to the understanding of living things. This is in keeping with the unsubstantiated supposition that the living has derived (randomly) from the nonliving. In keeping with this the U.S. government provides subsidies so that radio telescopes around the world may be pointed to outer space to pick up any radio signals from the living out there.

Why should there be anything living out there? This is based on the supposition that, since certain chemical elements are found in living beings, consequently, where such elements are perceived to exist on other bodies than the earth, there might be life. All this without any evidence that life arises spontaneously from the nonliving in the first place. That chemistry in turn is reduced to physics may be seen from the fact that chemical elements are seen as composed of atoms, containing protons and electrons (and now many more subatomic particles), the study of which is admittedly in the domain of physics.

Physics in turn is now governed by mathematics in that all its principles must be couched in mathematical terms, or in terms necessitated by the reduction of all to mathematical answers. The latter is the case of the first law of motion, put in place as the foundation of physics from Galileo and Newton onward, since considering all nature (artificially) as rectilinear is a precondition of measuring it arithmetically, i.e., numerically.

1. Rectilinear Motion

In order to put in place universal mathematical formulas capable of producing, by deduction, predictable practical results, algebra, with the substitution of letters for the numerical, is employed. Certain such algebraic formulas will be seen as laying the groundwork for all subsequent calculations, to be made in rectilinear terms even of the curved. The algebraic formulas in question, to be immediately presented, are able to be validly manipulated into several different forms—with the most used and most successful forms farthest from the original, which, for its part, has a reflection of reality.

The most basic initial algebraic formula is that for average speed:

$$\text{average speed} = \frac{\text{distance traveled}}{\text{time elapsed}}$$

or: $\bar{v} = \dfrac{d}{t}$

where the bar over the v is the standard symbol meaning average. Although v is the algebraic symbol for velocity, standing for speed and direction, in rectilinear motion or motion in a straight line, average speed corresponds simply to the magnitude of the average velocity.

As will be remembered, since in the science of physics one does not measure (for formula purposes dictated by the necessity to make all rectilinear) in terms of actual distance covered, but in terms of displacement (an imaginary rectilinear measure from the finish point back to the starting point), the letter d above stands for such a displacement, whether corresponding to the actual distance or not. In this vein, when a body moves around a circumference in a circle, as in a centrifuge, the distance measured is not along the circumference (impossible) but along rectilinear radians. These are the radius taken as a chord measuring (not really) an arc of the circle, making the circumference of the circle (falsely, for rectilinear calculational purposes) equal to 2π radians.

Next comes the formula for average acceleration, acceleration referring to a change of velocity:

$$\text{average acceleration} = \frac{\text{change of velocity}}{\text{time elapsed}}$$

or: $\bar{a} = \dfrac{v - v_o}{t}$

Here v_o is the initial velocity (which can be zero if the body starts from rest) and v the final velocity.

In addition there are the concepts of instantaneous speed (or velocity) and instantaneous acceleration, which do not mean speed or acceleration at a point, or an instant of time (both of which are impossible), but over a very short time or distance, signified by the Greek letter Δ (delta):

$$v = \frac{\Delta d}{\Delta t} \qquad\qquad a = \frac{\Delta v}{\Delta t}$$

One is now ready to put formulas together with their subsequent useful manipulations. Using the formula for average acceleration above, one can calculate, for example, the average acceleration of a car which starts from rest and after 10 seconds reaches a velocity of 60 km/h (kilometers per hour). (The metric system will be used throughout as being simpler for calculations. The system of inches, feet, and yards is of course equally valid.)

$$\bar{a} = \frac{60 \text{ km/h} - 0 \text{ km/h}}{10 \text{ s}} = \frac{60 \text{ km/h}}{10 \text{ s}} = 6.0 \text{ km/h/s}$$

The average acceleration of the car is 6 kilometers per hour per second.

Usually it is preferred to use only seconds. The reduction of km/h to meters per second per second, m/s^2, is achieved by multiplying by 0.278. According to this, the average acceleration of the car will be 1.66 meters per second per second (m/s^2). The 1.66 is in turn rounded off to 1.7, in keeping with the practice of taking significant figures, the number of figures in the least significant number in the product, which here is 2, corresponding to 60. Here one has evidence that mathematical physics, while achieving marvelous practical results, is not required, for those results, to be that mathematically precise. Little wonder, since it begins by substituting successfully an imaginary rectilinear for the curved. Therefore one has for the above:

$$\bar{a} = \frac{17 \text{ m/s} - 0 \text{ m/s}}{10 \text{ s}} = 1.7 \text{ m/s}^2$$

Above, one knew in advance the final velocity of the car, i.e., after 10 seconds. From this one could calculate its acceleration per second. Conversely, if one knows in advance the acceleration per second, one can calculate the final velocity, or the velocity after a certain time, as follows, using algebraic manipulation:

$$v = v_O + at$$

Thus the final velocity of a car (v) after the car has accelerated at the rate of 2 meters per second per second (a) for 5 seconds (t) will be:

$$v = 0 + 2(5) = 10 \text{ m/s}$$

Similarly, given the rate of acceleration and the time, one can calculate the distance covered in that time. First of all, one would calculate the average velocity, which would be attained by taking the sum of the initial velocity and the final velocity and dividing by 2. (Thus a body in free fall, if it is seen to be traveling at a velocity of 32 feet per second, g, after 1 second, is traveling at an average velocity for that period of $0 + 32/2$ or 16 feet per second.)

$$\bar{v} = \frac{v + v_O}{2}$$

In the case of the car initially mentioned, whose final velocity was 60 km/h, or 17 m/s, its average velocity would be $0 + 17/2$ or 8.5 m/s over a time of 10 seconds. Utilizing the very initial formula, $\bar{v} = d / t$, now transposed to $d = \bar{v}t$, one has, for the distance covered by the car in 10 seconds: $d = 8.5(10) = 85$ m.

At this point, it is possible to engage in further productive algebraic manipulation of the formula $d = \bar{v}t$. First one must remember the formula for finding average velocity:

$$\bar{v} = \frac{v + v_O}{2}$$

Then: $$d = \left(\frac{v + v_O}{2} \right) t$$

One then substitutes for v the formula $v_O + at$, as above, giving:

$$d = \left(\frac{v_0 + at + v_0}{2}\right)t = \frac{2v_0t + at^2}{2}$$

$$d = v_0t + \tfrac{1}{2}at^2$$

When the initial velocity is zero, i.e., a body starts from rest, one has:

$$d = \tfrac{1}{2}at^2$$

When it is a case of an object in free fall, for a one substitutes g, the experimentally established or verified acceleration for a body in free fall due to the attraction of gravity, using s for the distance covered:

$$s = \tfrac{1}{2}gt^2$$

Using this formula and substituting 32 feet per second per second or 9.8 meters per second per second for g, one reliably predicts that such a body will fall 16 feet in 1 second, will have fallen 64 feet after 2 seconds, and so forth. This is the formula established by Galileo using inclined planes, and used in launching space shuttles.

Using the same algebraic manipulation, one can also successfully calculate a final velocity, v, without knowing the time involved by starting from the formula:

$$d = \bar{v}t = \left(\frac{v + v_0}{2}\right)t$$

and substituting, from the formula $v = v_0 + at$, leading to $t = \dfrac{v - v_0}{a}$.

This formula can be substituted for t as follows:

$$d = \left(\frac{v + v_0}{2}\right)\left(\frac{v - v_0}{a}\right) = \frac{v^2 - v_0^2}{2a}$$

To find the final velocity, after a start from rest, and knowing the distance covered, one has:

$$v^2 = v_0^2 + 2ad$$

This formula will be used to solve the first problem* in standard college physics textbooks. The problem is to ascertain whether an airfield with a 100 meter runway, to be constructed in a new community, would be adequate for the takeoff of light planes accelerating at a rate of 12.0 m/s^2 which must reach a takeoff speed of 200 km/h, or, by multiplying by 0.278, 55.6 m/s^2. One solves for v^2:

$$v^2 = v_0^2 + 2(12.0 \text{ m/s}^2)(100 \text{ m}) = 2400 \text{ m}^2/\text{s}^2$$

$$v = \sqrt{2400 m^2/s^2} = 49 \text{ m/s} \qquad \text{(significant figures only)}$$

Since the plane accelerates to 49 m/s^2 only, its acceleration is not sufficient to reach the required 55.6 m/s^2 necessary for takeoff on a 100 meter runway. How long would the runway have to be for such a plane? Here one solves for d, calculating the distance required for the plane to reach a velocity of 55.6 m/s^2 at an acceleration of 12.0 m/s^2. From the above, $d = v^2/2a$:

$$d = \frac{55.6 \text{ m}^2/\text{s}^2}{24} = 128.8 \text{ meters}$$

That is, by the time the plane, accelerating at the rate of 12.0 m/s^2, will have reached the necessary acceleration of 55.6 m/s^2, it will have traveled 128.8 meters. This would be the minimum necessary length of the runway.

In all, one now has the following collection of derived equations (in each of which a is a constant):

$$v = v_0 + at$$
$$d = v_0 t + \tfrac{1}{2}at^2$$
$$v^2 = v_0^2 + 2ad$$
$$\bar{v} = \frac{v + v_0}{2}$$

2. Vectors for Nonrectilinear Motion

Up until now motion in a straight line, including regularly accelerated motion, has been considered. To handle motion that is not continuous in a straight line, vectors are now introduced. In keeping with the necessity of reducing physical reality to the rectilinear as a condition for making it numerical, vectors are used to reduce motion in this way. Thus, should someone first walk 10 miles due east, and then 5 miles due north, this will be described by two vectors drawn to scale. Subsequently one will join the tail of the first vector to the tip of the second vector with a third vector, registering the displacement (i.e., the distance between the starting point and the finish point as the crow flies, not necessarily as actually covered). With the use of a ruler one draws these events to scale. If one uses millimeters for miles, the ruler will indicate a displacement of 11.2 miles. If a protractor is placed on the figure it will indicate an angle of 27° for the displacement.

Here one will note the reduction of the angles of geometry to the numerical, i.e., 360° for a circle. This is in keeping with the goal of mathematical physics, i.e., the reduction of all reality to the numerical, a first condition of which is the reduction of all to the rectilinear, since only the rectilinear can be so divided. When this is done, however, it is purely imaginary, since no such numerical divisions are actually existing in nature. There is no innate numbering of angles in geometry. For practical purposes, however—such as the calculation of what angle a boat must be pointed upstream in order to cross the stream directly—such a numerical mensuration in degrees is indispensable (however unreal).

It is possible for the displacement vector to represent the real motion, as in the case of a boat crossing a running stream. If the boat can move ahead in still water at a rate of 10 miles per hour and is crossing a stream which is flowing by at the rate of 5 miles per hour, the drawing of vectors will be the same as above—with the vectors here representing velocities rather than distances. Again the application of a ruler to the displacement vector will show that the boat is actually moving in a diagonal course at the rate of 11.2 miles per hour. Measurement by a protractor will also show an angle downstream of 27°.

One can now calculate at what angle upstream the boat should be pointed in order to cross directly to the other side. In this case the vectors of the triangular figure (See p. 50.) will now be first the direction of the boat upstream at an angle of 30° with, let one suppose, the same velocity of 10 miles per hour in still water. From the tip of this vector one will have another vector pointing directly downstream with its length drawn to correspond to 5 miles per hour. The final vector, drawn directly across, will represent the actual displacement of the boat at a rate of 8.6 miles per hour directly across the stream.

In the case of rectilinear motion, vectors are not required, since the whole motion is in a straight line. Vectors come into place where several motions or forces in different directions combine, as in the case of a boat crossing a stream with a current flowing. One vector will represent a boat crossing directly at a given speed. Another vector will represent the downward course of the stream. The resultant vector will represent the actual course of the boat as a composite of the two forces, boat and stream.

If one assigns numerical values to the factors involved and draws the vectors to scale (e.g., representing 10 miles per hour in still water for the boat, and 5 mph for the current), the drawn resultant vector will itself represent the actual course of the boat, with its speed, and the angle made with the cross-river direction after a given amount of time (e.g., 2 minutes). A protractor would also reveal the angle θ (theta) of the downward drift.

Independently, however, one can calculate the course by the Pythagorean theorem as the hypotenuse of a right triangle:

$$r = \sqrt{10^2 + 5^2} = \sqrt{100 + 25} = 11.2 \text{ mph}$$

The distance covered in 2 minutes would be $(11.2)(2/60) = 0.37$ mi.

One can also calculate the angle θ on the basis of the data given, using trigonometry. Here the angle could be expressed as:

$$\text{tangent (tan) } \theta = \frac{\text{side opposite}}{\text{side adjacent}} = \frac{o}{a} = \frac{5}{10} = 0.50$$
$$\theta = 27°$$

The additional trigonometric functions are:

$$\text{sine (sin) } \theta = \frac{\text{side opposite}}{\text{hypotenuse}} = \frac{o}{h}$$
$$\text{cosine (cos) } \theta = \frac{\text{side adjacent}}{\text{hypotenuse}} = \frac{a}{h}$$

Tables found in the back of a physics book will allow one to find the
angles corresponding to the numerical calculations.

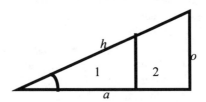

It is clear from the above diagram that as the vectors are extended,
the angle θ remains the same: one is dealing with similar right triangles (1 and 2). Hence if one side is extended, the other sides will be
extended proportionately. Hence in calculating the angle θ in the
above case, it is sufficient to take the velocities per time in a unitary
way before extending the velocities by some given amount of time.

Thus in the case of the boat crossing the river, one can increase the
time required until the boat reaches the other side maintaining its original direction while the angle would remain the same. Multiplying the
value of the resultant 11.2 mph by the time, one would have the distance covered. Multiplying the vector representing the current (5 mph)
by the time, one would also have the distance downstream the boat
would reach on the opposite shore from the point directly across from
the boat's start.

One can now set out to calculate at what angle the same boat, moving at the same still-water speed, 10 mph, should point upstream in
order to move directly across: sin θ = 5/10 = 0.50. This corresponds to
30° in the trigonometric tables and is the angle at which the boat must
point upstream in order to cross directly.

In both of the above cases, the resultant of the two forces involved
is a straight line since the current is carrying the boat downstream at a
constant pace. One can now also discover the rate at which it is crossing directly:

$$\tan \theta = \frac{\text{side opposite}}{\text{side adjacent}}$$

$$\tan 30° = \frac{5}{r}$$

$$r = \frac{5.00}{0.58} = 8.6 \text{ mph}$$

3. Projectile Motion

The problem is not the same, however, in the case of projectiles, such as cannon balls, rifle bullets, space shuttles. All the above cases are subject to two forces, comparable to the forward motion of the boat and the simultaneous downstream motion of the current. In the case of the projectile, however, while the inertial force of the projectile is exercised in a straight line (e.g., along a rifle barrel), this motion is simultaneously subject to the downward acceleration of gravity. This latter force draws the projectile downward in a resultant which admittedly is not a straight line, but a curve, and is so described in physics books. Unlike the boat carried downstream in a steady flow, the projectile falls faster and faster, in a curve.

How then is one to measure the course of a projectile? For example, in the case of a bomb, know where it will land once released from above? (A current physics text cites the problem of a police aircraft flying above a fleeing criminal automobile and having to calculate where and when to release an explosive charge destined to land on the vehicle. See p. 53.)

Galileo, the founder of modern science, just as he first calculated mathematically the acceleration of bodies in free fall (by the use of inclined planes), also calculated mathematically the landing point of projectiles moving in a downward curve.

When one is aiming a rifle at a target, the sights on the barrel line up on the target, with the sight nearest the eye being adjustably raised. This means that, while the line of sight remains directed to the target, the barrel itself is thereby being tilted upward from the line of sight to compensate for the downward curve of the bullet through gravity. If the barrel were pointed directly at the target the bullet, because of gravity, would fall below the bull's eye. Hence the expression, when one is not encompassing enough in some aim: "You have to raise your sights."

A familiar exemplification of this is the monkey and hunter experiment. The case, experimentally reproduced, is envisaged of a monkey hanging from a tree at a certain height. A hunter fires directly along his rifle barrel at it, at which same instant the monkey releases its hold and falls downward. The rifle bullet will nevertheless strike the monkey, since the downward curve of the bullet under gravity is, when considered (artificially) in vertical terms, exactly parallel with the vertical fall of the monkey under gravity.

Galileo, after calculating the acceleration of bodies under the force of gravity by measuring the times on inclined planes on some sort of table top, had then only to let the measuring spheres (at different speeds from starting at different heights on the inclined planes) roll off such a table in a downward curve or parabola and note where they landed. This he did.

But how discover in advance where the landing point would be by a mathematical formula, since science cannot measure curves, there being no unit curve, such as there are unit rectilinear quantities (e.g., the foot and the meter)? Galileo eventually tried calculating the actual curve of a projectile simply as a combination of two rectilinear motions, the one in the horizontal direction and the other in the vertical. And it worked! In diagrams these two (necessarily imaginary) simultaneous and contrary motions are represented as vectors, with the resultant likewise as a rectilinear vector, although admittedly it is a curve.

Much as one would like to think of a curve as something the rectilinear can ultimately merge into—such as the constantly doubled sides of an inscribed regular polygon merging into the circumference of a circle—science, however reluctantly, concedes that there is no chance of this being done. This is evident in science's calculation of π on the basis of a polygon, not the circumference, without any claim that such an eventual merging can ever take place, entailing an extended rectilinear side to be successively divided down to an unextended point.

Before exemplifying how the curved trajectories of projectiles are successfully calculated on an (imaginary) rectilinear basis, which involves the utilization of degrees for an angle θ, it is appropriate to consider the meaning and origin of degrees. Thus one thinks of a circle as having 360°, a triangle (wherein one finds the numbered angle θ of trigonometry) as having 180°, and so forth.

This artificial division of geometrical elements—circles, triangles—into numbers which do not actually exist in them is already evident and utilized, for example, in Eratosthenes' calculation of the length of a degree on the earth's surface in the third century BC. (Here one may note that the rotundity of the earth was thus not waiting to be established by Christopher Columbus as portrayed in the fictional accounts of Washington Irving, still happily passed on to children.)

By noting what angle the sun's rays made with a particular column in Alexandria on a certain day and time that the sun's rays were going perpendicularly down a well at Syene (a known distance to the south), Eratosthenes was able to calculate geometrically the angle in degrees at the center of the earth corresponding to the distance on the surface of the earth from Alexandria to Syene. He arrived at 40,000 stades (a measure derived from the length of a stadium). Unfortunately it is not known what this represents in miles. Aquinas, in his commentary on Aristotle's *On the Heavens*, was able to cite the length, as deriving from similar methods, as 56 2/3 miles. His reference was made some several hundred years before Columbus who, in order to shrink the distance in miles between Spain and the Indies, wrongly chose the shortest available calculation of a degree.

The textbook problem* posed above, involving trigonometry in the calculation of curved trajectories as rectilinear, cites a police aircraft with an explosive to be released while flying at 200 km/h, at 80 m above a criminal car moving at 130 km/h. At what angle with the horizontal within their sights should the car be when the bomb is released?

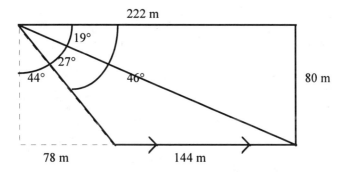

One can first calculate at what angle the plane should discharge the bomb if the car were immobile at a definite spot ahead. This involves knowing how many seconds the bomb would take to fall vertically 80 m, which would be:

$$s = \tfrac{1}{2}gt^2$$
$$s = 4.9t^2$$
$$80 = 4.9t^2$$
$$t = \sqrt{80/4.9} = 4 \text{ s}$$

This means, since Galileo noted that the rate of vertical fall remains the same whether the body is simultaneously moving forward or not, that the released bomb will be traveling in the imagined horizontal for 4 s at 200 km/h or 55.6 m/s. (This was noted in the case of the required takeoff speed for the plane in the first example.)

$$d = (4)(55.6) = 222 \text{ m}$$

This means that an angle θ will be calculated as:

$$\tan \theta_1 = 80/222 = 0.35 = 19°$$

However, since the car below is moving at 130 km/h, consequently the sights will have to be fixed on the car in such a way as to allow it to advance at 130 km/h for 4 s after the bomb's release. How far would the car advance? 130 km/h is equivalent to:

$$(0.278)(130) = 36.1 \text{ m/s}$$

Hence, after the bomb was dropped, the car would travel:

$$(4)(36.1 \text{ m}) = 144 \text{ m}$$

What would be the angle θ for this? One can take the triangle deriving from the subtraction of 144 m from 222 m, whose base would then be 78 m. Calculating the angle θ in this triangle, one would have:

$$\tan \theta_2 = 78/80 = 44°$$

The intervening angle would then be:

$$90° - (44° + 19°) = 27°$$

Hence the bomb must be launched with an angle in the sights of:

$$27° + 19° = 46°$$

(The textbook gives the answer as 45°. The difference in answers could be understood as variance in rounding off, which does not follow any rigid pattern in deciding what are the significant digits.)

D. Rotational Motion and Gravitation

The successful calculation of the curved course of projectiles in terms of an artificial composition of straight lines is now applied to rotational motion.

1. Rotational Motion

It goes without saying that this motion, such as the rotation of a phonograph record or a centrifuge, will be treated in terms of straight lines. Hence, as was done in the initial establishment of a numerical π, the circumference is measured as though composed of the straight lines of a polygon. In this case the straight lines are the radius itself. Since the circumference is calculated as $2\pi r$, twice π times the radius, the radius is considered as going 2π times into the circumference, or $2(3.1416) = 6.28$ times. The radius-length straight lines imaginarily fitted on the actually curved circumference are called radians. There will be 6.28 of these in a circumference. The length of a radian in a given case is determined by the length of the radius in that case. Thus, if the radius of a wheel is 30 cm, the length of a radian will be 30 cm and the length of the circumference, $2\pi r$, will be $(6.28)(30) = 188.4$ cm.

The displacement of a body or particle on the circumference will be measured in terms of radians covered, by an angle θ. (The angle θ corresponding to one radian is $360/6.28 = 57.3°$). The distance covered by a particle in radians will therefore be $\theta \times r$, giving:

$$\theta = \frac{s}{r}$$

The length of a radian is described as an arc length on the circumference although in reality it can be no more than the length of a straight line (i.e., a chord subtending the arc) corresponding to the initial measurements of π, which is in terms of chords. Similarly, the value of a circumference, considered as 6.28, or 2π, radians, actually represents the sum of the chords (less than the sum of corresponding arcs) of an inscribed 24-sided polygon.

As has been seen, the artificial and imaginary measuring of the curved in terms of straight lines does work. The circular motion of a particle is called angular motion, in keeping with the angle θ turned through.

One starts with the problem* of a particular bird (or it could be a spy satellite) whose eye can distinguish objects that subtend an angle θ no smaller than 3 x 10^{-4} rad or 3/10,000 rad. How small an object can the bird see when flying at a height of 100 m?

$$s = r\theta = (100 \text{ m})(3/10,000) = 3 \text{ cm}$$

In comparison with linear distance traveled, one measures angular distance traveled, θ, with the average angular velocity defined as:

$$\bar{\omega} = \frac{\theta}{t}$$

which the particle has rotated in time t (ω is Greek omega.).

Angular velocity is generally measured in radians per second. The angular velocity can be related to the linear speed, v, of a particle and its distance r from the axis of rotation as:

$$v = \frac{r\theta}{t}$$

or, since: $\dfrac{\theta}{t} = \bar{\omega}$

as: $v = r\bar{\omega}$

Angular acceleration, in analogy to ordinary linear acceleration, is defined as the change in angular velocity divided by the time required to make this change:

$$\bar{\alpha} = \frac{\omega - \omega_0}{t}$$

The above represents the average angular acceleration, designated by α (Greek alpha), over a time t.

When ϖ is expressed in rad/s and t in seconds, $\overline{\alpha}$ will be expressed in rad/s^2. When radian measure is used, α is related to the tangential linear acceleration of a particle by $a_T = r\alpha$.

Frequency of rotation, f, refers to the number of complete revolutions (rev) corresponding to an angle of 2π radians. Frequency f is related to angular velocity ω by:

$$f = \frac{\omega}{2\pi}$$

or: $\qquad \omega = 2\pi f$

Example one*: What is the speed of a point on the edge of a 33 rpm phonograph record whose diameter is 30 cm?

$$f = \left(\frac{33 \text{ rev}}{1 \text{ min}}\right)\left(\frac{1 \text{ min}}{60 \text{ s}}\right) = 0.55 \text{ rev/s}$$

$\omega = 2\pi f = (6.28)f = 3.45 \text{ rad/s}$

$v = r\omega = r(3.45) = 15(3.45) = 51.75 = 52 \text{ cm/s} = 0.52 \text{ m/s}$

Example two*: A centrifuge rotor is accelerated from rest to 20,000 rpm in 5 minutes. What is the angular acceleration?

$\omega = (20{,}000 \text{ rev/min})(2\pi \text{ rad/rev} \div 60 \text{ s/min}) = 2100 \text{ rad/s}$

$\alpha = 2100 \text{ rad/s} \div 300 \text{ s} = 7 \text{ rad/s}^2$

How many turns (f) has the centrifuge rotor made during the acceleration period?

average number per minute = 20,000/2 = 10,000
Therefore, in 5 minutes = 50,000

To obtain the formula for centripetal acceleration, one must first consider a particle moving in a circle of radius r, with constant angular velocity ω. This is called uniform circular motion. The angular acceleration is 0, but the linear acceleration is not 0.

The magnitude of its linear velocity, v, is constant and equal to $r\omega$, but the direction of its velocity is continually changing as it moves around the circle. (This goes with the supposition that all motion is basically rectilinear and that curved motion is caused by some constraint pulling the rectilinear motion out of its course.)

Acceleration is the rate of change of velocity, while velocity is the rate of change of position. A change in the direction of velocity constitutes an acceleration just as much as a change in magnitude.

$$a = \frac{\mathbf{v} - \mathbf{v}_0}{\Delta t} = \frac{\Delta \mathbf{v}}{\Delta t}$$

where $\Delta \mathbf{v}$ involves the change in velocity during the short time interval Δt.

One will eventually consider the situation where Δt approaches 0, and thus obtain the instantaneous acceleration. For the purpose of a clear drawing we consider a nonzero time interval:

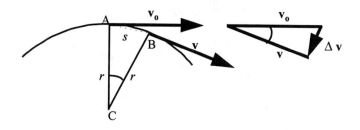

Thus $\Delta \mathbf{v}$ points toward the center of the circle. Since a, by its definition above, is in the same direction as $\Delta \mathbf{v}$, it too must point to the center of the circle. Therefore the acceleration is called centripetal acceleration.

Having determined the direction of the acceleration, one must now determine the magnitude of the centripetal acceleration, a_C.

The vectors $\mathbf{v}_0$, $\mathbf{v}$, and $\Delta \mathbf{v}$ form a triangle that is similar to triangle ABC. This relies on the fact that the angle between $\mathbf{v}_0$ and $\mathbf{v}$ is equal to the angle between the radii. This is true because CA is perpendicular to $\mathbf{v}_0$, and CB is perpendicular to $\mathbf{v}$. Thus we can write:

$$\frac{\Delta v}{v} = \frac{\Delta s}{r}$$

This is an exact equality when Δt approaches 0, since then the arc length Δs equals the chord length AB. Since we want to find the instantaneous acceleration, which is the case when Δt approaches 0, we write this as an equality:

$$\Delta v = \frac{v}{r}\Delta s$$

To get the centripetal acceleration, a_C, we divide Δv by Δt:

$$a_C = \frac{\Delta v}{\Delta t} = \frac{v}{r}\frac{\Delta s}{\Delta t}$$

And since $\Delta s/\Delta t$ is the linear speed, v, of the object:

$$a_C = \frac{v^2}{r}$$

In terms of angular velocity, from $v = r\omega$:

$$a_C = \omega^2 r$$

Example*: What is the magnitude of acceleration of a speck of dust on the edge of a 33 rpm phonograph record whose diameter is 30 cm?

$$a_C = \omega^2 r = (3.5 \text{ rad/s})^2(0.15 \text{ m})$$
$$a_C = \frac{v^2}{r} = \frac{(0.52 \text{ m/s})^2}{0.15 \text{ m}} = 1.8 \text{ m/s}^2$$

Centripetal motion involves the notion of force, e.g., the force necessary to cause a ball on the end of a string to twirl in a circle by virtue of its being pulled constantly to the center of that circle from its "natural" rectilinear course.

This is expressed in Newton's second law of motion: $F = ma$. Force is seen as the product of mass times acceleration. The weight of a body is seen as such a product, i.e., its mass undergoing the acceleration of gravity, 9.8 m/s^2.

The first law of motion, initially enunciated by Galileo, laid the rectilinear foundation of modern science. Since curves, starting with the circumference of the circle, cannot be measured numerically, the curved must be reduced to the rectilinear considered as numerically measurable. (This too is not true, but nevertheless works deceptively in the practical order.)

The necessary reduction of reality to the rectilinear for purposes of numerical measurement (with the rectilinear uncritically supposed, because of natural utilization as numerically measurable), finds its first reward in Galileo's calculation of the vertical acceleration of bodies in free fall, deriving from the measurement on inclined planes. This yields the formulas $v = gt$ and $s = \frac{1}{2}gt^2$, where g stands for an acceleration of 9.8 m per second per second (or 32 ft per second per second), perceived to be the force of gravity attracting bodies in free fall.

The notion of force here which can be described as a push or a pull, is already introduced in the first law as the factor involved in causing a body to go from rest to motion, or motion to rest, or to change its state of motion in a straight line.

Such a factor (e.g., the force of gravity) can now be brought to bear in calculating rectilinearly the curved trajectories of projectiles—from cannon balls to space shuttles—on the basis of a combination of two imaginary rectilinear motions—one horizontal at constant velocity, the other vertical and accelerating due to the pull of gravity.

In the case of a body at rest on a horizontal surface the force of gravity is continuing to exert itself, as may be seen should the surface be removed. The body falls. This pull is registered when the body is weighed. As Galileo perceived, two bodies of the same size, which would fall with equal velocity in a vacuum, need not have the same weight (e.g., if one were of wood and the other of lead).

To harmonize the difference of weight with an identical pull of gravity in both cases, weight is considered to be the product of mass and gravity, with the variation of weight for a same size indicating a variation of mass, called by Newton "quantity of matter." Hence weight is expressed by $w = mg$. Not only is there the force of gravity (a pull) pulling down on a body at rest on a horizontal surface, but another force (a push or a pull) would be required to set such a body in motion.

This state of the body at rest, requiring a force to set it in motion horizontally, is called the state of inertia—a state, real or imaginary, to which is attributed the fact that a force is necessary to reduce a body from rest to motion, and once in motion to reduce it from motion to rest. In both cases one would speak of overcoming the inertia of the body. Hence one has the fact that the first law of motion is sometimes called the law of inertia.

The unitary mass in the SI system (*Système International*) is the kilogram, being the weight of a platinum iridium cylinder preserved near Paris. The basic unit of force is taken as the force required to accelerate a body of 1 kg to 1 m/s². This force is denoted as a Newton. (In keeping with this, the force exerted by one motionless kilogram, *mg*, is 9.8 Newtons—the force of the kilogram pressing down on a horizontal surface, pulled by gravity at an acceleration of 9.8 m/s².) In general such a force is expressed by $F = ma$, the mass of the body in kilograms multiplied by its acceleration in m/s². This is the second law of motion.

Transferring these concepts to circular motion, such as that of a ball being twirled around on the end of a string, a force is considered as acting constantly to pull the ball in from its essentially "natural" rectilinear path as per the first law of motion. Thus an object on a revolving disc, which remains in place (e.g., a horse on a merry-go-round), is considered as being subjected at all times to a pull (a centripetal force) to the center, without which it would depart in a straight line, experimentally verified, tangential to the disc, at its given velocity.

Formulas which work have been derived to calculate the amount of centripetal force required to keep the object in circular motion. The force will be proportional to its mass and linear acceleration: $F = ma$. The centripetal acceleration in turn is a function of the angular velocity (ω) and the distance from the center, r.

Concerning frictional force, Galileo is narrated as conceiving the first law of motion on the basis of imagining what would happen to a moving body if friction could be eliminated. A book given a shove across a table top eventually comes to a stop. To the extent that friction could be eliminated the motion would supposedly continue indefinitely in a straight line. The friction or roughness of the table's surface exercises a force in the direction opposite to the motion of the book.

This is expressed by Newton's third law of motion: Every action of a body on another body is accompanied by an equal and opposite reaction. Thus, when a nail is being driven into a piece of wood, the force of the hammer and nail is ultimately canceled out by the opposite force of the wood. In the same way the outward pull that one feels when twirling a ball on a string is the force reacting to the opposite force pulling the ball constantly inward toward the center.

Hence when a car rounds a curve (although it is conceived of doing so in an imaginary merging series of tangential straight lines), its turning is caused by the opposite frictional force of the road on the turned wheels. That this is the case may be seen by the fact that if the road is icy and to that extent without friction, then, even though the wheels are turned, the car will continue ahead in a straight line, i.e., will skid. Hence to insure the possibility of turning, a certain friction must be opposed. Various coefficients of friction (designated by the Greek letter μ, mu) are thus established for different materials in calculating the force necessary, for example, to start a body moving in a curve from the opposing force of friction.

Example*: A l000-kg car rounds a curve on a flat road of radius 50 m at a speed of 50 km/h (14 m/s). Will the car make the turn if the pavement is dry and the coefficient of static friction is 0.50?

The needed force can be calculated using Newton's second law, $F = ma$, where we use the value of centripetal acceleration, $a_C = v^2/r$, and F must be the total (or net) force. This net force to accelerate the car around the curve is:

$$F = m\underline{v}^2 = \underline{(1000 \text{ kg})(14 \text{ m/s})^2} = 3900 \text{ N}$$
$$\phantom{F = m\underline{v}^2 =} r \qquad\quad (50 \text{ m})$$

Since the road is flat, the normal force on the car, F_N, equals its weight:

$$F_N = mg = (1000 \text{ kg})(9.8 \text{ m/s}^2) = 9800 \text{ N}$$

The maximum force of static friction is thus:

$$F_{fr} = \mu_s F_N = (0.50)(9800 \text{ N}) = 4900 \text{ N}$$

Since only a force of 3900 N is needed to keep the car moving in a circle, the car can make the turn.

At this point it is appropriate for the student or observer of physics to reflect on the actuality of radians, taken as the radius of a circle laid off on its circumference. Since the ratio circumference/diameter, π, is given as 3.1416, and so used in physics texts, there will thus be 2π, or 6.28, radians on a circumference.

Since, starting with π itself, given as the circumference/diameter ratio, there is no possible numerical ratio between a curve and a straight line (a fact recognized by the various calculations of π, all of which are based on comparisons, not between circumference and diameter, but between perimeters of rectilinear polygons and the diameter), it is misleading to make distinctions between radians on the circumference and chords subtending the radians. The reason is that there are no radius-equated radians on the circumference from the start. All measurements, in order to have numerical measurement, are necessarily rectilinear.

In keeping with this, one can calculate the rectilinear measurement that corresponds to the number of radians taken as being laid off on a circle, namely, 6.28 (or 2π). A close approximation is the perimeter of a 24-sided inscribed polygon (starting from a 6-sided hexagon, whose value is 3 in terms of the diameter, and doubling the sides). Therefore the given value of the circumference in radians (6.28) represents the sum of 24 chords, with in each case an arc above considerably in excess of the chord—the sum of the arcs being the true circumference. Further doubling of the sides, while admittedly resembling in shape more and more the circumference—though never formally approaching it, since straight lines, no matter how small, can never merge into a curve—will give values departing more and more from 6.28.

2. Universal Gravitation

What is the reaction one should have to this? Should one say that it cannot be? Obviously not, since such concepts, i.e., that of 6.28 radians or radiuses encircling the circumference, work very well and will be involved in calculating the gravitational influence on the moon, Newton's first step toward universal gravitation.

Rather we must realize that we are living in a universe where its Ruler allows humankind successfully to grasp and formulate laws of that universe which, while tapped into the universal objective order whence they derive their efficacy, clearly are not mirror concepts of reality. This is the meaning of dialectical: to save the appearances and work, without the premises necessarily being proved, or even provable. This leads to a conclusion vis-à-vis modern science: Use, but do not believe that, because the theory works, it must be true. Meanwhile, thanks to revealed faith, a coherent explanation of the presence of graspable order in the universe, indispensable to the existence of science, is always present and in place.

As has been seen, the numerical resolution of all physical problems requires the fundamental concept of all motion's being basically rectilinear, as formulated in the first law of motion. Diagrams of this motion will therefore be necessarily rectilinear. Hence when a ball is twirled on the end of a string, or a car rounds a curve, its motion is conceptualized, curved though it is, as basically rectilinear even though it is not (as is recognized in the case of projectiles).

In keeping with this concept of all motion's being considered basically rectilinear, for a body to move in a curve it must have some force acting on it to deflect it from its conceptually rectilinear motion—a centripetal force, i.e., a force drawing the object (or, in the case of a car rounding a curve, pushing the object) to seek the center (meaning of *centripetal*).

As seen above, this consists in assuming that a body moving in a circle, i.e., the moon, is basically moving in a straight line tangential to the circle and being pulled in the direction of the radius toward the center of the circle. How this can happen supposes that a body is moving in a succession of rectilinear tangents changed to a curve by the centripetal force.

The distance between these successive rectilinear tangents is theoretically diminished so as to arrive at zero, making the motion equated to the curve (which is actually what is perceived), while being able to be calculated linearly (i.e., rectilinearly) as a body whose speed or velocity derives from the number of radians per second it covers, multiplied by the radius (or distance from the center).

Hence, the greater the radius of the curve, the greater the linear distance per radian per second covered. Proportionately, as the radius increases the sharpness of the curve diminishes, requiring less centripetal force to draw the body out of its basically rectilinear motion. All this reflects the first law of motion. Hence a lesser force of gravity is needed to keep the moon orbiting the earth.

Antecedently to Newton, Kepler noted in his second planetary law (following the first law giving the observed fact that planets move in ellipses) that a planet maintaining a steady revolution around the sun and with the same mass, will move more rapidly when nearest the sun. (This is reflected in Kepler's third law, to the effect that the cubes of the mean distances of the planets from the sun are proportional to the squares of their periods.)

The fact of slower motion at a greater distance was later able to be deduced by Newton after he introduced—inspired, according to tradition, by the sight of the fall of an apple—the notion of universal gravitation, whereby all bodies would attract each other, as the earth attracts bodies in free fall, starting with the moon. The moon would now be like the body on the end of a string, the string being gravitation twirled around, not a person, but the earth. From the linear acceleration of the moon around the earth and its known distance from the earth, Newton was able to calculate what the force of gravitation on the moon must be, i.e., 1/3600 of that on earth.

Contemplating the fact that the diminishing of gravitational attraction represented $1/60^2$ and that the moon was 60,000 km from the center of the earth, Newton conceived the idea that the attraction was proportionate to the square of the distance. He also conceived of all bodies attracting each other (not just the earth and the moon), giving rise to the notion that the attraction would be proportionate to the product of the masses divided by the square of the distance.

A century after Newton, Cavendish measured this attraction by measuring the attraction of leaden spheres to each other. From this he was able to derive a constant of gravitation, $G = 6.67 \times 10^{-11}$ N·m^2/kg^2, which, when multiplied by $m_1 m_2 / d^2$, would give the degree of attraction of any two bodies.

Since the degree of attraction of a body on the earth's surface is mg (weight of the object), and the same degree of attraction can be expressed as $G(mm_E / r_E^2)$, one can equate the two, deriving the mass of the earth:

$$mg = G \frac{mm_E}{r_E^2}$$

$$g = G \frac{m_E}{r_E^2}$$

Hence: $m_E = \dfrac{g r_E^2}{G} = (9.8 \text{ m/s}^2)(6.4 \times 10^6 \text{ m})^2 \div G = 6.0 \times 10^{24} \text{ kg}$

The inertial mass of a body is envisioned in Newton's second law, $F = ma$. This is what it takes to move it. The gravitational mass of a body is determined in terms of the force between two bodies. New-ton's and Cavendish's experiments indicated that these are equal for any body—to an accuracy of about one part in 10^{11} (100 trillion).

With this in hand one can calculate the velocity a space shuttle must obtain to orbit the earth through the sole force of gravity. Literally, the shuttle falls around the earth. Combining two formulas for the force acting on a body circling the earth, we have:

$$G\frac{mm_E}{r^2} = m\frac{v^2}{r}$$

Solving for v, we have:

$$v = \sqrt{Gm_E / r}$$

Applying this to a space shuttle orbiting 200 km above the earth, we have $v =$ approximately 27,000 km/h. This velocity is envisaged, for calculational purposes, as a series of rectilinear tangential motions, eventually turning to an imaginary instantaneous change of velocity. This, as noted above, is known to be impossible, starting with the rec-ognized impossibility, in the numerical calculation of π, of bringing by division of the sides, the perimeter of a rectilinear polygon to coincide with the circumference. Hence one comes upon the metaphor used to describe someone trying to do the impossible: He is trying to square the circle.

Since the space shuttle and its occupants are falling together, the occupants experience apparent weightlessness, as would be the case with the occupants of an elevator in free fall, one of whom might re-lease his briefcase. It would fall right along with him. That such a situation is not truly normal for a human being may be seen by the ad-verse effects caused by this artificial weightlessness over a period of time: red blood cells diminish, blood collects in the thorax, bones lose calcium and become brittle, muscles lose their tone.

(Asterisked examples are adapted from relevant chapters in Douglas C. Giancoli, *Physics: Principles with Applications*, 4th ed. [Englewood Cliffs, NJ: Prentice-Hall, 1995].)

Chapter 3

Science's Rectilinear Universe

A. Galileo's rectilinear universe
B. Is motion at a point?
C. Science as workable
D. True and false in physics

In line with the impact made on physics by both Aristotle and Galileo, the classic beginning in today's physics textbooks consists in a comparison between these two thinkers—the latter, with Newton, the founder of modern physics. Galileo is given the credit, rightly, for coming up with the first law of motion, so entitled by Newton in the beginning of his *Principia,* the foundational work of modern science. That physics is itself the foundation of modern science may be seen from the fact that a modern biology text will reduce biology back to chemistry. Chemistry in its turn is reduced back to the particles of physics.

How does motion in a straight line become the inescapable beginning of today's physics? As mentioned above, texts begin with a comparison between Aristotle and Galileo. Of the former it is stated that he considered the natural state of a body to be at rest. Thus a body, if set in motion by a shove, ultimately comes to a stop. Galileo is then seen as envisaging that, if friction were removed, the body, once in motion, could keep on moving indefinitely in a straight line. No mover to move the body would be envisioned.

This is certainly the foundational thought on which all subsequent physics is successfully constructed. Supposing that this was the scenario for Galileo's coming up with the first law of motion, did he have any choice about it if he wished to establish a science of physics as he wished it to be, namely, expressed in mathematical or numerical terms? The answer is that he had no choice.

Meanwhile, before moving on from Aristotle, historical correctness obliges one to note that, while the statement that for Aristotle the natural state of a body was to be at rest constitutes a nice contrast with the statement that Galileo conceived of a body, of itself, tending to move indefinitely in a straight line, the position conveniently attributed to Aristotle is not true. As one consulting his *Physics*, readily available, will note, the ultimate perspective of the universe is that of the perpetual circular movement of the heavenly bodies. Insofar as a relation to realism is concerned, the position of Aristotle is the more coherent.

In effect, since every being in the universe is finite, the universe itself, representing the sum total of all such, is necessarily finite, i.e., only goes so far. In this finite universe, the only motion that can continue indefinitely is circular motion. The conceptualized basic rectilinear motion of Galileo, if looked at realistically, could not be of a nature to continue indefinitely since it would be limited by the finite nature of the universe. Indefiniteness—the only created infinite—is seen by its nature to be contained within the finite. Thus if one takes 10 feet and starts dividing by one-half and counting the divisions cut off, one can go on dividing and counting to infinity. There will always be the possibility of another division beyond the last actually made. This infinity takes place within the finite!

However, the aim is not to disprove the first law of motion, according to which, in Newton's words, a body will persevere in its state of rest or motion uniformly in a straight line unless compelled to change that state by forces acting upon it, but rather to analyze its nature, since all of physics depends upon it. If the first law is dialectical, i.e., works without being perceived directly or proved indirectly, then the whole structure of physics constructed upon it and presupposing it, is dialectical. Physics being the foundational science, this makes the rest of science dialectical.

A. Galileo's Rectilinear Universe

As stated above, whether the first law of motion was a spontaneous concept of Galileo or not, he would have had to lay it down anyway as the indispensable condition for treating the universe mathematically or numerically, as was his intent. This intent continues to be crowned with success. Meanwhile the student of today's physics, arising from Galileo and Newton, will understand it more easily if he realizes that from now on he has entered a world where the curved no longer exists and everything must be computed (successfully) as though all is rectilinear, starting with rectilinear vectors. The reason for this is that the curved cannot be computed numerically, i.e., measured in numerical units, and hence must be reduced, starting with the fictitious numerical π, to the imaginary rectilinear.

Hence when the impact point of a projectile, moving in a curve, is successfully calculated, the curve is real and uncalculated. The successful calculation depends upon a combination of (imaginary) straight lines moving simultaneously in different directions. One useful corollary of this truth is that in physics, given a successful formula (and the only formulas employed are successful formulas), one should not try to visualize the reality in terms of the formula. The successful formula for establishing the point of impact of a projectile moving in a curve is, not an image of the curve, but rather a successful imaginary combination of several rectilinear motions which works. Thus one could sum up today's science tersely in these terms: "What works, but need not be." To use the Ptolemaic theory for celestial navigation at sea, as continues to be done today, it clearly is not necessary to believe that the earth is the center of the solar system.

With this in mind, one is ready to confront the first images of physics which will be, mirroring the first law of motion, of objects moving uniformly in a straight line; for example, a car moving along a road. This rectilinear motion is represented by a vector, an arrow pointing always in a straight line. Since a car, realistically, is always going from somewhere to somewhere, this can be depicted by a line going from **A** to **B**. In realistic terms the distance between **A** and **B** will be conceived of as numbered in feet, miles, with points marking successive divisions of the course, in addition to a starting point at **A** and a finish point at **B**.

Here one should become aware, from the beginning, of the status of mathematics with respect to the physical world (which, for science is equivalent to the universe, although not for a Christian, for whom there is also the encompassing immaterial). Mathematics, basically arithmetic (of the discrete or divided) and geometry (of the continuous or undivided), comes into being by the mind's power to abstract from sense qualities in the material, and consider only the discrete and continuous as such. Thus, should a count of the contents of a lady's purse yield the number 35, what does this signify? It means that there are 35 separated or discrete objects in the purse. No indication is given from the count of what the objects look like, such as their size, shape, or color. This is the abstraction of arithmetic. Each real object in the purse, however, does have a certain shape and size, involving the rectilinear and the curved, and dimensions of length, breadth, and width. When one considers only such aspects, i.e., by abstracting from material composition, color, and so forth, one has the area of geometry.

By virtue of abstraction, the lines are considered without breadth, the planes have no thickness, and the volumes are transparent. Whereas a triangle in reality would have to be put together materially and could break, sag, or wear out, the triangle of geometry, after possibly being drawn by a pencil, is nevertheless visualized as having sides and dimensions that do not strike the senses, with geometric investigations being made on this basis. One need not worry about how to do this, because the mind does it naturally.

Thus, should one manipulate cut-out cardboard squares, rectangles, triangles to perceive the truth of possibly the most celebrated theorem in geometry, the Pythagorean Theorem (the square on the hypotenuse equals the sum of the squares on the other two sides), when one has done this and perceived this universal truth, one is quite aware that its truth is independent of the material of the geometric cut-out figures involved. Its truth, while applying to the material world, is perceived in abstraction from material qualities. This is simply a power which the mind has and uses.

When subsequently one applies the perceived truths of mathematics, composed of arithmetic and geometry (the discrete and the extended), to reality and the visible, one has to bear in mind that mathematics, since it abstracts from sense qualities, is therefore not automatically identical with the physical world. Interestingly, while mathematics is of the very essence of today's physics, with Galileo and Newton being the first to reduce the laws of nature to mathematical expressions that work (expressions dealing with motion and starting with the first law of motion), nevertheless there is no motion in mathematics! Yes, one can take a pencil and draw a line from a point **A** to a point **B** on a piece of paper, and see the pencil moving from **A** to **B**. But these are only helpful images, not the mathematical reality. Thus the drawn line from **A** to **B** is visible, as is the pencil with its sensibly discernible shape. Geometrically, nothing of the above is seen. If nothing is seen, one cannot see motion.

B. Is Motion at a Point?

The need for distinguishing between the abstracted mathematical and the realistic physical in the study of today's mathematical physics may be seen by an investigation of the basic supposition of today's quantum theory as the cutting edge of mathematical physics: one cannot simultaneously measure the position and velocity of a moving body or particle. Such a moving body or particle, by human intuition, is taken to be at a point. Hence the basic supposition of such a condition for a moving body or particle, namely, that it be at a point (the indispensable supposition of quantum theory), is not challenged.

The inquiring mind of a physics student is free to ask the question: Can a moving body or particle ever be at a point? The answer has to be: Mathematically, yes; realistically, no. When we see an unmoving bug on a table, we may give it a nudge to see if it is alive. If it starts moving, we can ask: "Where is the first point in its motion?" Only if it covers a certain extended distance can we tell if the bug is moving. But at what point did this motion begin? Try as we will, we cannot find one. To be scientific we must search for a hypothesis to explain the appearances, that being the beginning of science. One may well have to come to the hypothesis (which may well settle in later as the truth) that a moving body or particle is never at a point in the first place! Not to consider this hypothesis leads to Zeno's deadly Achilles Paradox (which modern mathematics does not solve).

A further verification of the fact that a moving body or particle is never at a point in the first place, however much we might think it to be, is had by a reduction to the impossible: a proposition is shown to be true by the fact that its contradictory is impossible. Thus one starts by supposing that a moving body or particle can be at a point. If it cannot, then the contradictory is true: it can never be at a point. One starts with the recognition that motion is extended, while a point, such as the one where two lines meet, is not extended. One now considers a moving body or particle, or a point on either, to be at a point in space. Since all motion is extended (one remembers that one cannot tell whether a bug has begun to move unless it first covers a certain extended distance), the motion of the body at the point has to be extended. Since it is extended, it can be divided, such as into two halves. During the first half of the motion, the body is at the point in question, as agreed. During the second half of the motion, since it is continuing to move, it moves away from the point. Hence it can no longer be at the point, while being considered at the point. The moving body would therefore simultaneously be and not be at the point in question, which is impossible. Hence for a moving body or particle to be at a point is impossible.

This is made startlingly clear in the Achilles Paradox of Zeno which, with the contemporary supposition of a moving body's being at a point taken as a reality by quantum theory, becomes unsolvable for contemporary mathematics. Achilles is pursuing a Tortoise. The Tortoise has a 10-foot head start and they start off together, with Achilles running twice as fast as the ambling Tortoise. If the race is run in reality, Achilles soon catches the Tortoise, and at a predictable point. (While there is no motion at a point, motion starts from a point and ends at a point.)

Modern mathematics, and with it physics, accepts Zeno's description of the race. Achilles first runs to the point from which the Tortoise has started, 10 feet ahead. Meanwhile the Tortoise has covered half that distance, to a point 5 feet ahead. By the time Achilles has covered those 5 feet, the Tortoise is now 2½ feet ahead. The race is in the form of an infinite geometric series whose ratio is ½. Whereas the actually run race would see Achilles overtaking the Tortoise at a point 20 feet beyond the start, easily calculated in terms of motion as continuous; Achilles can never reach the Tortoise on the supposition of modern mathematics and science of motion at a point.

In subsequent discussion of the theory of limits, it will be stated that this progression comes as close as one wishes to the limit in question (which, in the race as stated above, is 20 feet). But actually this is false, since Achilles, and everyone else, wishes to reach the limit, something made impossible by modern mathematics' and physics' acceptance of Zeno's and our own intuitive description of motion at a point. If, no matter how long one progresses, one cannot reach the limit, as in this case, one is actually, from the start and no matter how long one continues, not getting any closer to the limit. One can think of lowering a rope from a helicopter to be clutched by someone in the water. Realistically it is possible to suppose that the rope cannot be made long enough. For purposes of rescue, the tip of the rope which can never reach the drowning man's hand is not any closer when it is only a ½ inch away than when it is 10 feet away.

This brings out the fact that if there is an irreducibility of form, as between a straight line and a curve, one form never gets any closer to the other. Thus in the calculation of nonexistent numerical π (as the ratio between circumference and diameter) it does not matter how long one goes on multiplying the sides of an inscribed polygon in order to coincide with the circumference, this will never happen. The reason is that a straight line, by continuous division, can never be divided down to an unextended point, the condition required for the polygon to merge with the circumference.

The Achilles Paradox does not exist in reality because, if the conditions for the race are set up as above, Achilles will promptly overtake the Tortoise at a predictable point (a stopping point, not a point in motion). Their race will be represented as the ratio of two continuous motions, starting at a point and finishing at a point, but never being at a point in motion. The unknown, x, represents how far the Tortoise goes before he is tagged by Achilles. The ratio of the distances covered will be that of $10 + x$ (Achilles) to x (Tortoise). Since Achilles runs twice as fast, that ratio is 2 to 1. Factoring out, $x = 10$. Achilles overtakes the Tortoise, and the race is ended at a point $10 + x$ from Achilles' start, namely, at 20 feet. If the race is run as presented in mathematics textbooks, namely, as a series of motions from point to point, one should not wait for the end—as Achilles will run forever.

All of this is in connection with the necessarily rectilinear beginning of classic physics textbooks which begin with Aristotle somewhat doltishly coming to rest and Galileo moving indefinitely in a straight line, as represented, for example, by a car going from **A** to **B**, while passing through a midpoint **M**. While it can start from rest at **A**, and come to a stop at **B**, and does pass a point **M**, it has been demonstrated that, against all our intuitions, it can never be at a point **M**.

C. Science As Workable

As may be seen, the human mind's ability to rise from the sensible order to the mathematical order is indispensable for human living. This is done by the mind's ability to abstract, not only from the singular in order to envision the universal, but also, within the universal, to be able to abstract from sense qualities, producing mathematics. Hence a bottle of aspirin, of admittedly great use, represents a transition from the singular to the universal, in that, from certain singular events of human experience, leading to the perception of pain-relieving qualities in some certain substance (such as the bark of the willow tree), one has perceived a connection that is part of the order of the universe, i.e., is on a universal scale. One can now manufacture doses of the substance for everyone, knowing that each dose will have the pain-relieving qualities.

As humanity benefits from these universally valid perceptions of order in nature, it also benefits from its ability, within the material, to abstract from the sensible. Hence, for someone using aspirin the question will arise: How many? Because of the human mind's ability to count, the answer might be: One a day. Subsequently one goes to the pharmacy and purchases a bottle with 100 tablets to last for 3 months. One is now in the realm of mathematics, with arithmetic representing the ability to measure discrete quantity in terms of number. The count of number requires only of the object counted that it be discrete, i.e., undivided in itself and separated from others. Thus the number 100 applied to the count of aspirin in the bottle is the same number as applied to 100 chickens or 100 of anything, seen only as physical objects separated from each other. There is, however, no such thing as a number 100 existing in a separated state. The counting of 100 represents simply a one-by-one count of separated objects independently of size and shape and material.

Size and shape and material are also able to be viewed in the abstract on the part of the continuous, giving rise to geometry, the companion of arithmetic. Thus the aspirin tablets in the bottle will necessarily have a certain size and shape. Capsules may be considered larger in size than tablets; the former can be described as having an oblong shape, the latter as having a circular shape. The material seen may be, for example, white. Because of the mind's abstractive powers, it can consider size, shape, in the abstract, arriving at certain universal truths concerning the curved and the rectilinear in all three dimensions of length, breadth, and width. For example, giving its sides an arbitrary length $(a + b)$, one can, in three slices, slice up a cube of mozzarella cheese along the divisions between a and b. This will produce the following components of $(a + b)^3$: $a^3 + 3a^2b + 3ab^2 + b^3$. This perception will hold good whether one is slicing mozzarella or marble.

At the same time, because geometry, as arithmetic, abstracts from the sensible, the objects geometrically assessed are, physically speaking, invisible. Thus when one contemplates the properties of a cube in a cube of mozzarella cheese, one abstracts from the color or matter. Likewise the edges, surfaces, volumes are invisible: the lines have no width, the surfaces no depth, the volumes are empty. This is why, strangely enough, there is no motion in mathematics. Motion, to be perceived, needs to be seen by the senses; the elements of arithmetic and geometry abstract from the senses. One cannot see a geometrical triangle.

What about when one draws a triangle to study its properties? Here the lines depicting the sides are visible, but they are not the geometric sides themselves, which have neither breadth nor depth. Hence such diagrams are simply helps to the contemplation of the geometrical triangle as such, concerning which the mind can learn certain truths, such as that the sum of its angles is equal to two right angles.

As has been noted, Galileo was obliged, because of his goal of numerical computation, to consider all motion as a development of a basic, unproved motion in a straight line. This was because the numerical computation of motion, distance, and time requires the possibility of universally applicable units, such as feet and yards, minutes and hours. But no such units exist for curves. One cannot find a unit curve with which to measure the curve on the edge of a dime and the curve on the edge of a quarter. But even when everything is reduced to the rectilinear for numerical measuring purposes, it is clear that such numerical measuring in terms of extended units is not part of nature, but is manmade.

Even when all is reduced to the rectilinear, there is no guarantee that some rectilinear unit may be found to measure two straight lines. Thus there is no possibility of finding a common unit to measure two entities as closely related as the side of a square and its diagonal, i.e., calculating the square root of 2. Hence it must be recognized that extended rectilinear realities—straight lines, planes, cubes—are not necessarily commensurable, i.e., able to be measured as the ratio of two whole numbers. The meaning of the perpetually trailing decimal points in irrational numbers, such as those present in the ongoing calculations of numerical π, is the admission that no such number is to be found. All values are either too great or too small for what is being measured.

Despite all this, such admittedly inaccurate calculations work. Because they work, science works. Thus, when the fictitious value, numerical π, masquerading as the intrinsically impossible ratio of a curve (the circumference) to a straight line (the diameter)—while it is actu-

ally the (incommensurable) ratio of the perimeter of a rectilinear polygon of an arbitrary number of sides—is employed in scientific calculations, it need be carried to a relatively small number of places and then
rounded off as a whole number (by dropping the decimal points).
Admittedly, then, even in terms of the rectilinear, one is not pretending
to have numerical accuracy.

That science works without being mathematically or numerically
accurate may be seen by the standard practice in physics of rounding
off calculations to significant figures. Because a 12-inch ruler cannot
be guaranteed to correspond exactly to some standard 12-inch length,
and one proceeds to measure a box as 5½ inches long and 3¼ inches
wide, the result would be 17 7/8 inches^2 or 17.875 inches^2. The smallest division on the ruler may be 1/8 inch, or 0.125 inches. The latter
would represent 3 significant figures. One would not keep more than
this amount of significant figures in the final answer, which would
therefore be rounded off to 17.8 inches^2, with the understanding that
uncertainty extends to one or two digits above and below the last digit
specified. Hence the measurement would be stated as 17.8 ± 0.1 in^2.
Likewise, even considering the ruler as absolutely accurate, if the object to be measured overlapped the smallest measuring division (here
1/8 inch), there would be uncertainty, requiring that one confine oneself to significant figures without pretense of absolute accuracy. Yet
physics works.

As can be seen, even while it can be demonstrated that a moving
body cannot be actually at a point—in keeping with the fact that motion is extended while a point is not—this can be demonstrated visually
by returning to the divisions on a ruler, such as between inch 1 and
inch 2. To go from the first inch to the second inch, one must traverse
a no man's land, the width of the dividing line between the two, which
must be broad enough to be seen. Hence, even should the 12-inch
length be accurate, the 1-inch lengths cannot be, since they are separated by divisions that themselves have length.

One can see, therefore, that the rendering numerable of the physical
universe, as inaugurated by Galileo and Newton, and as constituting
modern mathematical physics, is, while responsible for endless material benefits and progress for society, nevertheless something artificial.
The universe, although it can be calculated mathematically, i.e., in
terms of number, is not itself mathematical. This is evident in the very
first accomplishments of Galileo, namely, the calculation of the curve
of a projectile—as applicable today for space vehicles as it was initially

for cannon balls. The curve itself is never calculated. What is calculated is an imaginary combination of straight lines which works to perfection. Consequently the student of physics will not take such calculations as actual calculations of reality, but will use them for practical purposes, while studying reality as it actually is and looking for its causes.

Failure to make this distinction between the real and that which is artificial but works (the dialectical), can lead to a dead-end contemplation of that which does not exist as though it does. Such a fateful merger of the unreal and the real was latent in Galileo who, by virtue of taking abstract mathematical concepts as existing as such (with the data of the senses viewed as simply subjective sensations), contemplated a mathematical world that did not exist. A fruitful distinction between the real and the usefully artificial is present in Aquinas who, while knowing that the real extended was not actually divided into countable segments as Galileo perhaps believed, nevertheless recognized the practical value of such a concept, such as the division of a circle into 360 degrees where no such division actually exists.

Thus in his Exposition of Aristotle's *On the Heavens*, he gives the latest calculation of the length of a degree, namely, 56 2/3 miles. Interestingly, his figure for the length of a degree is considered more accurate than that proposed by Columbus several centuries later, when appealing for support for a sea voyage to Cathay. Once it had been settled on a map how many degrees existed between Spain and China, the final distance would depend on the length of a degree. Convinced of the feasibility of his trip, Columbus, in making his choice among several circulating degree lengths, chose the shortest available, thereby shortening the distance to be covered. In so doing, he was wrong, but an unforeseen continent saved him.

D. True and False in Physics

As noted above, numerical measurement is essential in the world of practical technology. Thus, in order for a satellite to orbit the earth, the calculation of free fall in terms of an accelerating number of feet or meters per second is needed. For the sake of such numerical measurement, science and art—temporarily at least—must set aside the pursuit of ultimate truth. This fact is summed up presciently by Einstein when he says that what is true in physics is false in mathematics, and conversely. How is this illustrated? One may again take the case of the orbiting satellite. If one consults a physics textbook, one perceives that the diagram describes in solid lines the physical orbit for what it truly is—a curve. Simultaneously the rectilinear mathematical calculation of the orbit as a combination of straight lines is given in broken lines; since, while this is the mode in which the calculation is successfully made, it is not actually happening. The actual orbit: true in physics, false in mathematics.

The immediate corollary of the above striking contrast is that, in its efforts to arrive at an ultimate formulation for the universe, mathematical physics disqualifies itself from the start. The reason is that the mathematics it uses in its description of nature, while eminently useful and fruitful in practical results, is admittedly false as an objective representation of nature. The universe of mathematical physics is an unrealistically, but successfully, square universe with numbers that don't actually fit—but are close enough for practical purposes. Why all of this? It is obviously because the real universe is not mathematical in the sense of mathematical physics and consequently must be transformed, for practical purposes of production, into an imaginary rectilinear universe, numerically measurable.

What is amiss here? Nothing. One cannot produce practical and true results in reality without employing objectively false mathematical concepts: straight lines for curves; numbers where there are no numbers. This procedure is not alien to science and art but represents the procedure known as saving the appearances. Its value lies in coming up with a hypothesis retained for its ability to predict objective practical results, independently of any establishment of objective truth. Once the necessities of life are procured, science is then more able to proceed to search for ultimate truth. Such truth is nonmathematical, since mathematics is confined to the material order, which the ultimate clearly is not. Even in the material order, mathematical physics erects its productive structure on an imaginary base, that of the rectilinear, as required for all things to be able to be artificially measured by number.

The fact that henceforth, in mathematical physics, the curves of reality will be evaluated as straight lines—and the areas under curves as squares, the basic concept of calculus—is already present in the first lemma or proof of Newton's *Principia*. This proof illustrates how, if there be a rectangle greater than a curved area, and one less, there must be a rectangle equal to the curved area. Such a proof is false in mathematics, while true in physics—where the rectilinear can be substituted in practice for what is not rectilinear, namely, the curved.

Einstein stated that what is true in physics is false in mathematics, and conversely, what is true in mathematics is false in physics. The first has been illustrated from the foundations of mathematical physics where the demand for numerical measurement of the nonnumerical continuous requires the calculation of true curves in terms of false straight lines. The second is illustrated by the basic suppositions of relativity and quantum theory.

An enshrined concept of relativity is that, as velocity increases, time goes slower. Hence astronauts in space, moving at velocities tending even remotely towards the presumed top speed (that of light), are clocked as coming back to earth as somewhat younger (less time elapsed) than the earth dwellers they left behind. This is illustrated in physics textbooks by diagrams depicting the trajectory of a light beam as emitted and reflected vertically in the cabin of the spacecraft, while seen as having a diagonal course (caused by the spacecraft's movement) by an earth observer. Mathematically, it is possible to depict the same trajectory as two, even though physically there is only one. The imaginary depiction of the same trajectory as two is legitimate in mathematics and hence true, even though physically there is only one—the longer one viewed by the earth observer. The shorter one, vertically up and down and viewed by the spacecraft passenger, is an illusion, the same illusion as that a coin dropped in a moving car falls vertically, when in reality it is falling forward in a parabola. True in mathematics, false in physics.

No matter how much time can be stretched or shrunk by mathematical standards, using the speed of light as the ultimate time scale, all such calculations presuppose time as we know it. In fact, the speed of light is not the ultimate time scale, since its numerical identity depends upon the presumed constancy of extraneous units. Today these units are the vibrations of cesium atoms. Originally the finiteness of light was discovered by comparing time variations between the appearances of a moon of Jupiter with respective distances to the earth. Such time variations were and are measured by the earth's rotation, the numbering of which gives us time as we know it. This familiar time is the measure of motion, the counting of the earth's rotations and the subdivision of such daily rotation into hours, minutes, and seconds.

As noted above, what is true in mathematics may be false in physics. Aware of this, one must be careful not to confuse something which is mathematically feasible with physical reality. Thus problems are seen as arising from the so-called weightlessness of occupants of orbiting satellites. While mathematically they are weightless, since their motion in free fall presents no obstacle to gravity, physically they are not. Physically the mass of the body is constructed with a foreseen resistance upward from earth. When that resistance is removed in weightlessness, the inner structure of the body sags downward for want of the normal upward muscular counteraction. This is seen as leading to physical malfunctions.

Relativity also allows for the concept that, in cases of high velocity, it is possible to perceive simultaneously the front and the side of a rectangular structure. Physics textbooks supply diagrams to this effect. In order to make it mathematically possible, one supposes that for an observer to move past an immobile building at something approaching the speed of light is equivalent to the building moving at the same speed past the observer in the opposite direction. This is possible to imagine mathematically, since mathematics abstracts from motion. This abstraction is caused by the fact that it abstracts from all sense qualities: if nothing sensed, then no perception of motion. Not only will light from the front of the fast-moving building strike the observer, but also light from the end of the side of the building originating from the building's previous position. It has a longer distance to go and needs more time, but will diagonally strike the observer simultaneously with light from the front since, starting from the previous position of the building, it has had more time.

This concept is mathematically true, but physically false. Why? Because physically the motion of an observer past a building is not equivalent to the motion of the building past the observer. This can be illustrated by letting the building (**A**) be the end of a nail file held in the right hand, and the observer (**B**) a finger nail on the left hand. As one files one's nail, one can have either **A** moving toward **B** (right hand files immobile nail), or **B** moving toward **A** (file is motionless and nail moves toward tip of file). While these two motions may be considered identical in mathematics (which abstracts from motion) and so represented in mathematical physics, they are not physically identical, or so found in reality. In the first case, the right hand moves and the left remains motionless; in the second, the left hand moves and the right remains motionless. Physically and realistically these moves cannot be equated. True in mathematics; false in physics.

The same is the case with quantum theory. Where relativity theory gravitates around the speed of light as the ultimate reference point, quantum theory does the same for motion at a point—likewise mathematically conceivable while physically impossible. Textbooks invariably introduce the subject with the axiomatic notion that, given a moving body at a certain point, it is impossible simultaneously to calculate both its position and its velocity. This axiomatic notion appeared introductorily in a recent *Washington Post* book review of a work on Werner Heisenberg, Nobel Laureate, and the author of the principle of indeterminism which bears his name.

The basic, supposed uncertainty of the physical universe is seen as arising from the impossibility of simultaneously measuring position and velocity. To measure the first, one slows down velocity; to measure the second, one must neglect position. In either case, because of this indispensable interference for measurement, what the subsequent position of the particle would have been becomes unknowable, and predictions must be reduced to statistics—with the basic formula being Heisenberg's. Meanwhile we are expected to consider ourselves henceforth as living in a basically uncertain, random universe. Mathematically, maybe; realistically, no.

In effect, a moving body or particle is never at a point at any time. (It may be mathematically so conceived, with the subsequent necessity of extricating oneself from the Achilles Paradox—which mathematics textbooks are unsuccessful in doing.) Granted whatever practical benefits are derived from quantum theory, the fact remains that its starting point—motion at a point—is imaginary. Why? Because motion is intrinsically extended, while a point is unextended. This is immediately perceived when one asks: "Where is the starting point of motion?" One sees that one can never be aware that a body is in motion until it moves a certain distance! But before it reached that distance, it was already moving. One can keep retreating toward the starting point (where the body is immobile and not yet in motion), but clearly there is no perceived initial movement without extended distance covered. Hence, try as one will, one can find no first point in motion. Obviously the answer is that motion and a point—the extended and the unextended—are irreducible. This despite our spontaneous intuition to the contrary.

The above benign but physically erroneous intuition is the basis for the indispensable mathematical measurements of mathematical physics as initiated by Galileo. His discovery of a mathematical formula for the acceleration of free fall, $v = gt$, is derived from letting metal balls roll down inclined planes graduated in feet or the equivalent, with the distances covered measured in seconds. This supposes that a moving body, when passing from foot 1 to foot 2 on an inclined plane, must at a certain instant be opposite the point marking the division between foot 1 and foot 2. The *point* in motion is seen as corresponding to the nonextended *instant* in time where time, after moving through extended second 1 and passing on to extended second 2, passes through one period of extended time to another period of extended time via an unextended dividing instant.

This concept of motion through unextended dividing points, the motion considered to be *at* such points as it progresses from one extended unit to another, corresponding to *instants* in the continuous flow of time, is the very key of the practical fruitfulness of mathematical physics and is indispensable for human productivity in the mechanical arts as a prerequisite to material progress beyond the minimal in human life. Such a concept of motion is clearly mathematically conceivable, but physically false. In other words, what mathematical physics uses successfully as happening in the physical world, is not actually happening.

So much having been said about the purely dialectical status of mathematics in modern physics, involving the artificial reduction of the real to the rectilinear and the introduction of number into the continuous where it does not actually exist, one is now able to take an enlightened approach to the immediately mathematicized exposition of textbook physics.

Chapter 4

Science Is Dialectical

This chapter will explain the common meaning of science. Following this, the basic understanding of dialectical knowledge will be applied to the theories of modern science.

A. Science's Common Meaning

One would endeavor to have here a meaning of science acceptable to all and used by all. Hence it must be generic and based on what is usually meant. Reflection indicates that when it is used it refers basically to a body of principles which is arrived at inductively by the human mind, and which is open-ended with respect to continuing additions. The principles arrived at inductively, generalizations from initial individual experiences, are retained because they are productive for human life.

Thus an early ancestor could be the founder of the art or science of fishing when he perceived that a given fish rose to a given bait, possibly a piece of bread. Because of memory, he will think of trying this bait again. If it works and continues to do so, he will have experience.

Thus he may say, "I know by experience these fish will bite for bread." Finally he may visualize an intrinsic, and hence universal, connection between these fish and this bait, and enunciate: "All fish of this sort will bite for bread." He has now founded the art of fishing, and while adding other similar principles inductively derived from observation of singular events, experience, and reliable generalization, he can codify this art. He may then write a letter to his inexperienced cousin on the other side of the mountain, telling him: "When you go fishing, use this bait to catch these fish." With the art of fishing before him, this cousin can now go ahead and be successful by following the instructions without any previous experience. All art—or science, to use another name—is teachable.

A reader of Aristotle will recognize that the above is simply a paraphrase of the opening words of the *Metaphysics*, which lines lay down the genesis of art and science. There he is treating of the discovery of a universal remedy for some given malady, starting from an initial single discovery, which could be by accident. In this vein it appears that aspirin as a remedy for headache arose from such an initial, possibly chance discovery of the analgesic effect of the bark of the willow tree.

Therefore science, as we most generally speak of it today, would seem to be the body of universal principles which are inductively discovered and which are retained and handed down on the basis of their being able to furnish predictable and reliable results of a materially perceivable nature, beneficial to human life.

Would this be true, for example, of relativity as science? Einstein in his thinking, suggested by observation, arrived at the thought that the speed of light, c, remained constant, regardless of the motion of the source or of the observer. This involved subsequent generalizations suggesting that mass and energy were transformable into each other, resulting in the formula $E = mc^2$. For the benefit of life—in this case, the defense of the United States—it was decided to put this formula to the test in the building of an atomic bomb. History relates that the predictions were reliable. The formula itself, $E = mc^2$, the basis for atomic energy, has now become one of the cornerstones of science. As with the ancestor discovering good bait, the mass-into-energy formula is similarly the product of observation, leading to a universal principle, which in turn is reliably applicable and utilized for human benefit. (It is to be noted that with all human science the tested applications can be used well or ill. Thus science produces nerve gas.)

As can be clear, science, understood as a body of general principles arrived at by initial sense perception of singular events leading up to generalization, successful in producing reliable results for human living (rather than being a specialized area of the human mind), is simply a refinement of essential human thought as it proceeds from the perceived singular to the universal. The refinement consists principally in the testing. Thus one might know a red-haired person who tends to be somewhat short-tempered. If one meets other red-haired persons with similar temperaments, one will tend to generalize for all red-haired persons. To really be sure, however, so that such an axiom could find its way into a psychology or biology textbook, testing of a fairly broad swath of candidates would be indicated. Such an initial hypothesis might then be confirmed or refuted. This subsequent confirmation or refutation, however, does not affect the validity of the initial hypothesis which will or will not accord with reality whether any subsequent testing takes place or not.

One might ask why it is basic for a human being to be, by his very nature, always moving from singular perceptions to universal principles, ultimately connected with his good, with or without the codified refinement thereof which is called science. The answer is simple. One need only ask: "Why does a robin know how to build a nest without any instruction from fellow robins, while a man would have a hard time building a house without someone instructing him, utilizing the accumulated acquired art of house building?" The answer is: "Because a robin is programmed, and the human being is not." Thus bees construct honeycombs, using hexagonal apertures. Should science set out to meet the same demands as those of the honeycomb, seeking maximum efficiency, it would be discovered that the ultimate construction would be identical with that of the bees.

Does this place the human being at a disadvantage, since he has none of the built-in skills with which animals are born? Clearly not. By the use of his mind and his hands he can duplicate the programmed skills of different species of animals, whereas they are limited to the skills proper to their species. Thus a polar bear cannot take off his coat and bask in the Florida sun, whereas a human being can add on a coat when he goes north, and take it off when he goes south. Even more. Because of his power of reason, going from the experienced singular to the universal, he is able to reason from the material to the immaterial, an incomparably superior state of being.

B. Science As Dialectical
1. Its Workability

Subsequently, what is meant by saying that science is dialectical? The meaning of this term as used here is in contrast to *demonstrative*. In this context *demonstrative* stands for what is proved as true, whereas *dialectical* stands for what works but need not be true. A universally available example of this distinction is that between the Ptolemaic or geocentric theory and the Copernican or heliocentric theory. The former theory, of the sun, moon, and stars going daily around an immobile earth, was displaced by the Copernican theory explaining these appearances by the daily rotation of the earth on its axis. This latter supposition, along with the supposition of the annual revolution of the earth around the sun, was first published in 1543 by Copernicus, whose *On the Revolutions of the Heavenly Orbs* was presented to him on his deathbed. Subsequently this supposition has come to be taken as proven fact.

Does this mean that science has discarded the Ptolemaic or earth-centered theory? Not at all. Navigation at sea utilizing the stars continues to be plotted according to the Ptolemaic theory, i.e., with calculations supposing an immobile earth with the heavens revolving daily around it. What is the significance of this? Simply that for science the utilization of a theory does not depend upon whether it has been proven true, but upon whether it works. For purposes of celestial navigation the Ptolemaic theory works better than the Copernican theory, so it is used. To do so, need one believe the Ptolemaic theory is true? Obviously one does not and need not. Such utilization is termed here *dialectical*, i.e., utilization of a theory because the theory works with no claim that the theory need be true. May this characteristic be applied to all of science as is understood today? Yes, since science utilizes theories, once they have been elaborated and tested, not on the basis that they have been proved true, but on the basis that they work reliably and predictably. Hence science will use the Ptolemaic or Copernican theory alternately according to what outlook delivers best the desired results in a given case.

Does this mean that science is indifferent to truth, or believes that truth does not exist? No. It simply indicates that science is aware that, for a theory to work, it need not be first of all proved as an expression of reality. Thus, when the Ptolemaic or earth-centered theory of the solar system was supplanted by the Copernican or sun-centered theory, with the latter now being considered as factual and the former nonfactual, one went right on navigating at sea with the Ptolemaic theory. Why? Because it worked—and, for celestial navigation purposes, better than the Copernican theory. The above indicates that, for science as we know it, utilization of a theory depends, not on truth as a criterion, but on whether it works, abstracting from the question of truth.

What does it mean that a theory, law, or principle in science works? It means that reliable and constant predictions can be made on the basis of that theory, law, or principle. Thus, using the cornerstone law of physics, the first law of motion, and the law for computing the acceleration of bodies in free fall, both established by Galileo, one can reliably predict where any projectile, whether a cannon ball or a spacecraft (whose orbit is calculated as a fall around the earth), will fall or land.

2. Its Need for Order

The rectilinear suppositions of these two laws clearly do not correspond to the actual fact of the curved trajectory of the projectile, yet their combination works reliably. Spacecraft orbit successfully. What therefore must be true in order for this to happen? Science recognizes that successful and reliable theories must necessarily be tapped into, in some way, an objective order and constancy in the universe. If such an order did not exist, there would be no science. The reason is that all the canons of science, setting forth reliable principles, presuppose that those principles derive their reliability from being tied into a real and objective order in the universe.

How does this relate to science's being called dialectical, in contrast to demonstrative, i.e., being based on theories which save the appearances (a necessary prelude to any acceptable theory) and work reliably, in contrast to being based on theories claimed to be proved as true? One can say, "There must be something true about this dialectical science. Otherwise, how could it work?" Such an observation indicates that the human mind grasps that the success of science presupposes the existence of an objective order and constancy in the universe, one that the mind can perceive and rely upon.

3. Its Reliance on Faith

How does this objective order and constancy of the universe, from the tapping into which science (with its reliable principles) derives, come to be known? The spokesmen for science, adhering to the principle of Hume and Kant that the mind cannot prove anything about the nature of things (if there is a nature), state that the objective order and constancy is, therefore and necessarily, a matter of faith. Why of faith? Because whatever is held as true (as the objective order and constancy of the universe must be held in order to have science, whose reliability depends totally on that order's being true and constant), if this holding does not derive from proof, must be held on faith.

Just as the object of proof is held as true, i.e., objectively existing, so too is the object of faith or belief. Hence whatever is proposed to someone, if not directly seen or proved, but to be believed, is nevertheless proposed as existing. If one chooses to believe, it will be by an act of the will, holding to the proposition proposed to the intellect. Thus if someone wishes you to accept that he has money in the bank and you do not directly see it, nor can it be definitively proved by some indirect process; yet you choose to believe it, it will be by an act of the will. The reason is that the intellect, while understanding the proposition, is not compelled by facts to adhere to it. If one does adhere, it will probably be because of the weight of some reliable, though nonprobative, authority such as a mutual friend vouching for the reliability of the proposer on the basis of long acquaintance.

Does any such supportive authority exist for science as it makes its act of faith in the reliable and constant objective order in the universe? It does not seem so. If one were to ask science, the answer would seem to be: "What we call science today has developed from the conviction in the human mind from the very start, a conviction based on experience, that there is order in the universe, an order which is grasped and utilized for the good of the human being."

How firm is this, at least tacit, belief in a graspable and reliable objective order in the universe which is at the basis of science? Obviously it is more or less total, i.e., with the mind adhering to it without fear of the contrary. In contrast opinion is characterized by the fact that while the mind adheres to one side of a contrary such as that it will not rain when good weather is predicted; nevertheless the contrary, that it may rain, is not fully dismissed. However, with the laws of science as working, for example, in the launching of a spacecraft, one is at peace with them, not fearing that they might suddenly be placed in suspense.

At the same time, however, this serenity cannot be absolute unless one perceives the laws in question as unable to be changed, i.e., necessary or unable not to be. If there is an Orderer in the universe, a possibility which science cannot exclude since it presents no proof that such an Orderer cannot exist; the necessity of the laws of nature is not absolute, however reliable these laws may be. The reason is that their maintained functioning ultimately depends upon the will of the Orderer.

Meanwhile, while science advances the necessity for the belief in a graspable and reliable order in the universe (the order upon which science indispensably depends for reliance on the predictions in utilization that are made), it is allowable to ask whether this firm adherence may be, not the will holding the intellect to a proposition, but simply an inductive perception. This perception is the same as that upon which the discovery of the individual laws of science is based. Science may say that, even though the perception of a reliable and constant order in the universe is necessarily inductive (i.e., derived from singular observations of such an order, subsequently taken as being universal in nature); nevertheless, since induction itself is not proved as probative, the final adherence to the presence of such an order must be an act of faith.

One is not, however, obliged to agree with this. One is free to think that the inductive process is innate in humanity and that the serene adherence to the presence of reliable and graspable order in nature is due, not to the will's causing the mind to adhere to such a proposition, but rather to the mind's own perception attained by this power's natural and reliable process of arriving inductively at the universal in nature by means of abstraction from singulars.

4. Its Reliable Predictions

As has been stated, the successful procedure of contemporary science as we know and see it in operation is to proceed from reliable and tested theories or laws which save the appearances and produce predictably reliable results. Here it is easily noted that the indispensable saving of the appearances is only a first condition for any successful scientific theory. That is, the theory must be able to present an explanation of what appears, such as the Ptolemaic earth-centered theory gives an explanation of the sun's appearing in the morning and setting in the evening. Nevertheless, this first requisite is not enough. The theory or law must also be confirmed by reliable predictions, since the fact that a theory saves the appearances does not necessarily mean that it will have such a capacity. This is because several explanations may be able to be given of the same appearance. It can be possible that none of them may be true. Thus if a favored horse fails to win a race, various explanations may be given; for example, that the horse had a stomachache that day, or that his jockey held him back. These do not have to be true. There could be instead a real, unthought-of explanation; namely, that the horse's strength was simply not up to it.

For a theory, hypothesis, or law to be relied upon, it must have a track record of making reliable predictions. What does this indicate? It indicates that the theory, hypothesis, or law is somehow tapped into the perceived-by-science order in the universe. By virtue of this tapping in, predictions from the theory, hypothesis, or law can be reliably predicted to come about.

But does this ascertained tapping-in mean that the theory itself is reflecting reality? Clearly this need not be the case. Thus, returning to the Ptolemaic and Copernican theories, both explain the appearances and both make reliable predictions. But in the meantime both explanations cannot be true explanations of what is occurring in reality, since they cancel each other out. In one the earth stands still and the sun moves; in the other the sun stands still and the earth moves. When a switch was made from the former to the latter in what is sometimes referred to as the Copernican Revolution, it is obvious that the order itself of the solar system did not change, but rather a new explanation of the appearances was adopted.

Even should this latter explanation be taken as factual, making the former one nonfactual, this does not detract from the reliability of the former. Thus it continues to be used for celestial navigation at sea, indicating that it is somehow tapped into the order of the universe.

These considerations indicate the sense of the statement that science is dialectical. Science's efficacy, as we know it today, depends intrinsically upon its theories being somehow tapped into the objective order of the universe, as indicated by their reliability of prediction. At the same time the theories themselves, while obviously inspired by reality, are not necessarily mirror images of reality. This means that they need not be true of reality. Consequently, should a successful theory contradict something held by someone as an aspect of reality; then, since

the said theory is not necessarily true, it need not be considered as producing an objective objection to the other viewpoint.

In this respect, the axiom *Whatever is moved, i.e., is in motion, is
moved by another* (indispensable to the Aristotelian-Thomistic proof of
the existence of God through motion), while being contradicted by the
continuingly successful first law of motion which supposes that a body
or particle does not require a mover to remain in motion, is not thereby
affected. The first law of motion is held by science, not as a self-
evident or proven fact, but as a supposition that works. Hence the
theories of science, no matter how successful and reliable, are mistak-
enly taken as thereby true and representative of reality. They are held
because they explain the appearances and work. Self-evidence or proof
of reality is not involved. Hence one has the denomination of science
as we know it today as dialectical, not demonstrative. Armed with this
knowledge, one will have a better appreciation of the objective status
of science as it is presented in today's media and textbooks. One's
motto might be: "Use, but do not believe."

5. Its Use of Number

A perfect example to illustrate that science is dialectical, i.e., that
although it achieves desired practical and concrete results, the theories,
hypotheses, and laws from which it proceeds do not claim to be proved
and consequently should not be held as true, is the case of π. A recent
newsmagazine described enthusiastically the procedure whereby a Nobel prizewinner, then director of Fermilab, teaches Chicago students
the value of π. (A definition of π, as the ratio of the circumference of a
circle to its diameter, may be found in any dictionary.) The Nobel
prizewinner has the students discover the numerical value of π, ubiqui-
tously used in scientific calculations, by wrapping a piece of string
around a can and then measuring off that length in terms of the diameter of the can, which brings one to 3 and a little over. The students
now understand π. But what is the π that they understand? It is a fiction.

Should the students ever reach the point in mathematics of actually
learning how π is calculated, they will become aware that the mythical
π, an indispensable numerical value for science, is not obtained by
measuring the circumference of a circle by means of a rectilinear
length (the circumference of the can measured by a piece of string subsequently stretched out straight). It is obtained by comparing, not a

circumference, but the perimeter of a rectilinear inscribed or circumscribed polygon to the diameter. It is the ratio of the perimeter of a
rectilinear polygon to the diameter that gives the value of π. Even this
value, that of a rectilinear perimeter which is not equated to the circumference, is not a constant; since it varies with the number of sides arbitrarily chosen to more closely approximate the appearance of the polygon with the circumference.

The value π, then, is a fundamental and outstanding example of the
dialectical nature of science (all science being now mathematical). It
works very well as the ratio of the circumference to the diameter, but it
is not such a ratio. Hence, in the interest of truth, it should not be taken
as such. Hence it is to be used, but not believed as described. Since
truth has been mentioned, it is not amiss to come up with a definition
of truth. A comprehensible definition is the correspondence between
the intellect and the thing. In this case, π, as calculated in the intellect
in terms of the ratio of the perimeter of a polygon to the diameter, does
not correspond with the reality, the ratio of the circumference to the
diameter. Consequently π, understood in the former fashion, is false
when taken as corresponding to reality. This false conceptualization is
avoided and truth is maintained should the student appreciate that the
marvelous π is simply a useful fiction—a fiction which is intrinsic to
all modern science and a key numerical constant leading to its techno-
logical advances.

Having discussed π as a perfect example of the dialectical nature of
modern science, whose products are real but whose theories not necessarily so, one can speculate why this numerical value should come
about in the first place. As will be seen, it comes about through the
innate and proper tendency of the human mind to measure, which in
turn means to reduce something to unity. Thus the individual human
being, before the diversity and multiplicity of reality, endeavors to
formulate a single concept that will embrace and coordinate it all.
Such a concept is that of God, as creator, sustainer, and ruler of all
things. The same process is at work if a farmer counts his chickens. If
he arrives at a certain number, say 15, he has done this by measuring
the initially unnumbered multiplicity by unity. Here each successive
unity, as he counts, has a special name enabling one to situate it in a
certain stage in the order. Hence number is aptly defined as multiplicity measured by unity.

For practical purposes, number is quasi-indispensable. Should a
mother need some oranges, she would not simply tell her child: "Go to

the store and get some oranges." This could apply to two or a million. So she first counts off in her mind how many she needs, measuring multiplicity by unity, and comes up with a certain number, say 5, and so states to her child. In the same vein, if a man were planning to build a house requiring lumber, he would not simply say to himself, "I need some lumber," and let it go at that. To get anything accomplished, he would have to calculate the amount of lumber needed, using numbers.

It is such a necessity that is responsible for π. The examination of that necessity reveals how totally dialectical modern science is, a dialectical state brought about by the fact of introducing number into the whole of nature, where, as will be seen, it does not actually exist.

Why does one try to measure numerically the circumference of a circle in terms of the diameter, i.e., arrive at the numerical value denoted π, the fictitious ratio of circumference to diameter? It is because of practical necessity. Thus the Chicago students, schooled by the Nobel prizewinner in physics, having ascertained the circumference of a can in terms of the diameter by wrapping a piece of string around the can and then measuring the string rectilinearly in terms of the diameter, have a workable formula. Thus, if they are asked to calculate how long a sheet of material must be to furnish twice as great a circumference, they can accomplish this by taking twice the original diameter and multiplying by π.

Meanwhile, what if one of the Chicago students (who would deserve to be a future Nobel prizewinner) should ask the incredible question: "Why should the circumference have to be measured in terms of the diameter in the first place? Why can it not just be measured off in units directly, as is the diameter?" The shattering answer is that mathematics, and consequently the mathematical physics of today, has no way of numerically measuring curves, there being no such thing as a unit curve. But there do appear to be rectilinear units, such as the inches on a ruler.

Consequently, in order to measure the circumference of a circle, one must reduce it to a rectilinear approximation, such as an inscribed or circumscribed rectilinear polygon. This is what is done in arriving at the mythical π. The perimeter of a rectilinear polygon is substituted for the curved circumference. This then pervades the whole of science wherever curves are involved, which is everywhere. Since science does not measure the realities but the accommodations that work, consequently science, successful as it is in producing results, is dialectical.

That is, it satisfies the appearances and produces results, while its premises do not correspond with reality, reliable though they may be.

The well-informed student will now be prepared henceforth to know what is going on in mathematical physics, the basic science. All expressions of the curved will be in terms of the rectilinear, although this truth may nowhere be explicitly stated. Hence the parabolic curve of a projectile, of which a spacecraft is one, will be calculated in terms of rectilinear vectors which are imaginary (since the orbit is a curve) and work.

But the imaginary does not stop here. The reason for shifting the curved to the imaginary rectilinear is that there is no unit curve allowing indispensable numerical measurement. Such measurement is indispensable for practical purposes, such as knowing how fast horizontally a spacecraft must move to go into orbit. Once everything has been reduced to a countable rectilinear—as calculus reduces the area under a curve to a certain amount of imaginary squares—it is necessary to note that, even when the geometry of the universe has been reduced to the imaginary rectilinear, number does not actually exist in it.

A hint of this is found in the fact that no satisfactory numerical value can ever be found even for the polygonal π. Every value is found to be either too great or too small (which allows the so-called calculations of π by computers to go on and on in futile endless millions). The built-in example of this is the impossibility of giving a numerical value to the diagonal of a square of side 1, i.e., calculating the square root of 2. In effect it cannot be proved or established that any two straight lines should be commensurable, i.e., representable as the ratio of two whole numbers, such as 3/4.

The reason for this is that the continuous is only imaginarily numerable, despite our intuitions to the contrary. The reason in turn for this is that number is discrete, of things cut off from each other. Thus the basic meaning of a one, the principle of number, is something undivided in itself and divided off from others. Hence the numbering of the continuous (of lengths, times, speeds, and so forth), while practical, is nonetheless nonreal.

Even when one numbers days by counting the rotations of the earth on its axis, and can suppose some point that a point on the earth passes each day to make the count, it does not really happen that one day ends at this point and a new day begins there. The reason is that, although the earth passes this point, it is never at the point, there being no points in motion, as previously demonstrated. Hence when a falling body is measured as falling so many feet in so many seconds, it is never at a point dividing one foot from another, corresponding to an instant between seconds. The division, while it works, is imaginary. This is science as dialectical—the imaginary producing results in the real.

The forthrightly dialectical nature of today's science is affirmed in the continuing preferential utilization of the Ptolemaic theory for celestial navigation at sea. Does this exclude proven truth, even mathematical truth, from science? No. Aquinas, in the first article of his *Summa Theologiae*, mentions a scientific mathematical proof, using geometry: the earth has to be round because a short trip to the north causes stars seen to the south to disappear, adequately explained by rectilinear vision and curved earth.

Today's science, however, remains essentially dialectical since its stipulation of numerical answers throughout requires from the start that the curved be reduced to the rectilinear and arithmetic to the irrational, i.e., incommensurable. Because science works in the objective order, it is natural (by virtue of the fallacy of consequence) for its indispensable dialectical presuppositions to be unguardedly taken as objective also.

Thus Steven Weinberg, theoretical physicist and Nobel Laureate, when recently declaring his commitment to objective reality, specifies his commitment to π as a constant, when such a constant, involving the admittedly impossible squaring of the circle, is purely dialectical. He refers to "the discovery, going back to the work of Newton that nature is strictly governed by impersonal mathematical laws." Elsewhere he states: "For those who have not lived with the laws of physics, I can offer the obvious argument [for their objectivity] that the laws of physics as we know them work, and there is no other known way of looking at nature that works in anything like the same sense.... The meaning of a mathematically defined quantity like *pi* cannot be affected by discoveries in physics, and in any case both *pi* and *G* continue to appear as universal constants in the equations of general relativity" ("Sokal's Hoax," *The New York Review*, August 8, 1996).

Galileo's conviction of the central role of mathematics in understanding nature appears quite soon in his dismissing of the proper sensibles (along with his contemporary, Descartes) in favor of the common sensibles. The former are objects proper to the five senses—sight, hearing, touch, taste, smell. The latter are objects common to more than one sense—motion, rest, number, shape, size. While only the eye perceives color, the perception of size can be common to more than one sense—size estimated by the eye, and also by touch.

The subject matter of mathematics falls under the common sensibles, in that shapes give rise to geometry, number to arithmetic. However, as the subject matter for mathematics, shape and number are in abstraction from the physical world. The given geometrical shape of a snub nose can exist only in a particular actual snub nose. When separated, it is an abstraction, not existing in reality. Its abstract, purely mathematical status is caused by the mind's ability to apprehend an actual physical being and consider one aspect, such as its shape, while leaving other aspects, such as the actual physical nose, aside.

The mind begins with the sense experience of an actual orange. Only subsequently can the mind consider the shape of the orange separately as an object of geometry. Without the initial experience involving the proper sensibles there will be no consideration of shape: no sensed orange, no sphere.

Galileo, however, sees the common sensibles—shape, size, number, motion, rest—as actually existing as such, with the proper sensibles simply supplying a kind of inconsequential clothing in a secondary role. He describes how the book of nature is written in such terms: "I believe the book of philosophy (taken in the broader sense of natural philosophy) to be that which perpetually stands open to us, before our eyes; but because it is written in characters other than those of our alphabet, it cannot be read by all; the characters of such a book are triangles, squares, circles, spheres, pyramids and other mathematical figures" (*Opere*, ed. naz., XVIII, p. 293).

This conferring of an independent nonsensible existence as real upon the abstracted common sensibles, making them primary and the proper sensibles secondary, is not borne out in reality. The grasp of the former presupposes the initial grasp of the latter. For the common sensibles the use of more than one sense can be required to avoid error. In keeping with this, perception by a single sense can be deceiving. Thus optical illusions, deceiving to the eye, require correction by a ruler (touch). The proper sensibles, one or more, are needed to certify the common sensibles, and not conversely.

What prompts science, from Galileo and Newton onward, to seek numerical explanations? Such a search represents the innate desire of the mind for unity—and number is multiplicity measured by unity. However, the unity which measures reality is not the quantitative unity of number, restricted to the material, but the all-encompassiing unity of being, actualized in its universal dependence upon God, himself One.

Chapter 5

Modern Science and Motion

As noted in a previous chapter, the first steps of modern physical science can be found in the works of Galileo and Newton in the seventeenth century. As will be seen, there is a continuity between these founders of modern physical science and their early Greek predecessors, the founders of natural philosophy.

What is the form or structure to be discerned in any art or science? This carefully laid-out form is to be a collection of general principles in which various properties are predicated of the subject of the art or science. The art or science will involve, therefore, a subject—in the case of physical science, material being—upon the analysis of which will depend one's understanding or definition of the subject. The decision as to what may be predicated of the subject in the general principles of the science will depend on that understanding. In the case of physical science, the subject can be taken first in terms of its most obvious property, namely, motion. All material being, in effect, is considered as being able to move, and does indeed reveal itself to us by the motion which our senses perceive. Not surprisingly, then, the basic principle or proposition from which Galileo, and after him Newton, begins, is the supposition of a body in motion. About such a subject it is predicated that, left to itself, it will continue uniformly (i.e., at a regular rate of speed, neither accelerating nor decelerating) in a straight line. On this principle the whole of modern physical science is based.

The supposition by Galileo of a body moving uniformly in a straight line as the basic fact of science involves, in the description of this motion, and later in the description of regularly or uniformly accelerating or decelerating motion, the concept of the moving body's being at a point in any stage of its motion. The body can not only start from a point and terminate at a point, but at any instant of its motion it is also at a certain point. It is not surprising that one should so conceive the case and draw one's diagrams accordingly—since this is how things seem to be. And it is here, right at the very beginning, that one should ask: *"Can* a moving body be at a point?"

A. Founders of Modern Science

But before examining this question, one should authenticate Galileo, and subsequently Newton, as the representative founders of modern physical science. This will be done by citing the authority who, in his turn, is considered as having further advanced, by the theory of relativity, Newtonian physics to its present farthest point, namely, Albert Einstein, in his book, *The Evolution of Physics* (Einstein and Infeld, New York: Touchstone Books, 1967). Einstein considers that the transition from physical science as formulated by Aristotle in the fourth century BC to modern physical science as inaugurated by Galileo, took place when, instead of considering that a body moved only so long as something was pulling or pushing it, one took the view that, if all friction were removed, a body in motion would tend to move indefinitely in a straight line. (One is not obligated to consider how and when the body began to move, since it would not be impossible for a body to have always been in motion.)

Writing first of all of Galileo's role in modern physics, Einstein states: "The discovery and use of scientific reasoning [as in his supposition of a body moving indefinitely in a straight line with no forces acting upon it] by Galileo was one of the most important achievements in the history of human thought, and marks the real beginning of physics" (ibid., 7). "The new clew [in solving the mysteries of nature] found by Galileo is: if a body is neither pushed, pulled, nor acted upon in any other way, or, more briefly, if no external forces act on a body, it moves uniformly, that is, always with the same velocity along a straight line. Thus, the velocity does not show whether or not external forces are acting on a body. Galileo's conclusion, the correct one, was formulated a generation later by Newton as the *law of inertia*. It is usually the first thing about physics which we learn by heart in school, and some of us may remember it:

> Every body perseveres in its state of rest, or uniform motion in a right line, unless it is compelled to change that state by forces impressed thereon.

We have seen [Einstein continues] that this law of inertia cannot be derived directly from experiment, but only by speculative thinking consistent with observation. The idealized experiment [of a body's continuing to move indefinitely in a straight line once friction and other forces are removed] can never be actually performed, although it leads to a profound understanding of real experiments" (ibid., 8-9).

Here we have a first example of the application of something learned in logic, namely, the possibility of the fallacy of consequence. In effect, what is being said is that *if* we suppose the basic motion of a body to be uniform motion in a straight line, *then* we can give an explanation of certain effects (e.g., a body's moving in a curve would be due to some added force, such as gravity). But we would be committing the fallacy of consequence if we were to say that, because the body is moving in a curve, therefore its natural motion must be in a straight line. This applies to all physical theories which explain the appearances. The theory explains the effect, but the effect does not demonstrate that the theory is the true explanation. When the ground is wet, the theory that it must have rained explains this effect—but this does not mean that the theory is what actually took place.

B. Physical Theories As Models

That physical theory in general is not proposed by the moderns as being a statement as to the true nature of things, but solely as a model which satisfies the appearances, may be derived from a further statement of Einstein. "Physical concepts are free creations of the human mind, and are not, however it may seem, uniquely determined by the external world. In our endeavor to understand reality we are somewhat like a man trying to understand the mechanism of a closed watch. He sees the face and the moving hands, even hears its ticking, but he has no way of opening the case. If he is ingenious he may form some picture of a mechanism which could be responsible for all the things he observes, but he may never be quite sure his picture is the only one which could explain his observations. He will never be able to compare his picture with the real mechanism and he cannot even imagine the possibility or the meaning of such a comparison. But he certainly believes that, as his knowledge increases, his picture of reality will become simpler and simpler and will explain a wider and wider range of his sensuous impressions. He may also believe in the existence of the ideal limit of knowledge and that it is approached by the human mind. He may call this ideal limit the objective truth" (ibid., 33).

From the above quotation one is able to gather what is the present-day educated view toward reality. One can never know it objectively; models or pictures are composed, not simply as temporary measures with practical utility, to be employed while the grasp of the objective facts is being pursued, but because that is all one can ever obtain under any circumstances. The actual facts of objective reality, if there even is such a thing, must remain a closed book (or, in Einstein's terms, "a closed watch") to us.

This represents a certain evolution in Western educated thought. At the time of Aristotle, in the fourth century BC, with whom the bulk of organized scientific thinking had its origin, it was normal to invent models or pictures to explain the appearances of the material world, but this was considered only a step toward an ultimate correct grasp of reality as it was. Such a view continued with the foremost thinkers of the Middle Ages, such as Aquinas, who, in his own philosophical thinking, endorsed that of Aristotle. Theories intended only to explain the appearances were called dialectical; explanations verified as being in exact conformity with the facts were alone called demonstrative.

C. Are the Senses Reliable?

With Galileo in the seventeenth century, however, there already begins a shift away from the conviction that our senses perceive reality as it is, and can aspire, therefore, to viewing and explaining reality as it is. Galileo is considered as being the first to shift away from the reliability of the individual senses (sight, touch, hearing, smell, taste) to accord reliability solely to our perception of the common sensibles, i.e., those properties perceived by more than one sense, and which are not the unique purview of any one. Such are motion and rest, number, shape, and size. This means that, for Galileo, one's judgment through the senses that an object was moving or not would be naturally infallible, but one's judgment as to the proper sensibles (the objects of the individual senses, such as that some object is hot or cold) tends to be fallible. For example, hot water at a constant temperature, when one is taking a shower, tends to be felt, on different areas of the body, as more or less hot.

This is a reversal of the view from Aristotle to Aquinas, namely, that the senses tended to be, and were, infallible as to the proper sensibles, but could err (not, however, without possibility of correction) concerning the common sensibles. For example, when one is on a train stopped in a station and there is another train stopped alongside, one is sometimes not immediately able to discern, in the case of subsequent motion, which train is moving.

With Descartes, slightly later in the same seventeenth century, one has the introduction of methodical doubt. Descartes, fearing that his senses might deceive him (though not holding this as a necessity), decided to employ a methodical doubt concerning *all* the data of the senses, whether proper or common. That is, he would suppose his senses to be fallible and try to arrive at certitude concerning reality by purely internal means. Hence his famous "I think, therefore I am," where he started out to prove first of all his own existence from the fact that he thought.

The doubt concerning the veracity of our knowledge originating from the senses became absolute, however, with Emmanuel Kant in the eighteenth century. Kant decreed that our knowledge of the external world, originating from the senses, was innately nonobjective. One saw only the surfaces of things, the phenomena, and any supposition that one actually knew the natures of things, the noumena, or could know them, was an illusion. (Our knowledge was presumed to be vitiated by our projection of certain categories, such as space and time, held by Kant to be within the mind, into things themselves.) Kant's view has been the prevailing view in educated Western thought ever since—and the previous quotation from Einstein may be seen as an expression of it.

It is clear from the preceding cursory examination of the varying approaches to the validity of sense knowledge—all of which are already found among the first Greek philosophers—that any belief in the possibility of true knowledge obtainable through the senses implies the accompanying belief in the veracity of those senses. To deny the veracity of the senses need not be intended to deny the possibility of all truth, since the Platonists, while feeling that the senses were not the avenue of truth, nevertheless believed in true knowledge acquired elsewhere, from immaterial ideas with which the mind had contact.

But the denial of the veracity of the senses excludes all possibility of truth through them. And historically, once the veracity of the senses is denied, the supposition of true and certain knowledge obtained elsewhere, such as obtained by direct divine enlightenment, does not receive firm and consistent support. Thus, for Descartes, the fact that an idea was so clear and precise that he could not deny it showed him that it was true—because God must have been the cause of it, and God could not be the cause of anyone's being deceived. But what if someone else does not have such an undeniably clear and precise idea on the same subject? Would this not make the clear and precise idea of the other an illusion?

The question of the veracity of the senses, since such a supposition is a prerequisite to all intellectual knowledge so obtained (and not only to knowledge of the material universe as formulated in a particular science such as physical science), is properly maintained and defended in a general science. This science, which treats of being in common is metaphysics. Meanwhile, the present study will continue to take the veracity of the senses for granted.

The defense of that veracity in metaphysics does not consist in appealing to some other, more certain, source of knowledge to verify sense knowledge, but rather in showing that, despite what one may *say*, and even try to *think*, one inevitably, by his very nature, takes sense knowledge as true; nor does experience ever contradict this. Thus one shows that he who says he doubts sense knowledge, really does not do so, and is deceiving himself. Thus those who say that the senses cannot give us the true picture of reality, nevertheless describe things in the physical sciences in the way they appear to us. For example, they conceive of a body as truly moving, and its motion as being able to be opposite a point in space (whether that point is instrumentally identifiable or not).

D. Is Motion in a Point?

Having scouted these preliminary notions on the freeness of physical theory which can usefully satisfy the appearances without necessarily having to be true (the dialectical approach), and on the fact that physical descriptions are nevertheless taken as referring to a real world, one can now proceed to ask the question, "Can there be motion in a point?" There is no doubt about the fact that we would initially assume this to be the case. A body which starts from a certain point, and which terminates its motion at a certain point, would certainly seem to be opposite point after point in the course of its motion. Why can this not be so? It cannot be so because of the fact that motion is essentially something continuous and extended, whereas a point is something indivisible and unextended.

When a point on a body is opposite a point on a background, this is the case where the body is at rest or stopped. If the body is in motion, this motion is detected by the senses only when the body covers a certain extended, continuous space. For this motion, a given point on the body, previously opposite a point in the background when the body was at rest, must now also cover with the body a continuous, extended space. There are indeed points in the background of the trajectory of the body's motion from some starting point to some finish point. But the body, or a point on the body, is never at these intermediary points, because motion of the body, or of a point on the body, only exists when an *extended* space, which cannot be referred to an unextended point, is being covered.

If one were to propose letting a given point in the background—let us say a point in the middle of a given space in the motion—be taken as the point where the body is while covering that space, then one would find oneself obliged to say that already, when the body was just starting through that space, it would be at the point corresponding to the middle of that space, since that space designates the whereabouts of the body while moving in that space. Thus, although we would neatly like to suppose that, just as bodies start at points, and finish at points, they are also always at a certain point in the course of their trajectories, a closer examination forbids us to do this.

Nor is this any denial of the senses. Rather it is by using both our senses and our intelligence in analyzing the sense data that we are compelled to arrive at the conclusion that our senses do not tell us that a moving body is at a point, despite our initial superficial impression. This is an example of the proposition that the common sensibles, such as motion, which are discerned by several senses—as against the proper sensibles discerned by one sense alone, as in the case of the visible being perceived by sight alone, the tastable by taste alone—require a greater care or discernment than the proper sensibles. One is more easily mistaken concerning the shape of an object (one of the common sensibles)—as in the case of optical illusions involving straight lines which nevertheless appear curved—than concerning its color (one of the proper sensibles).

E. The Achilles Paradox

Zeno, a fifth-century disciple of Parmenides, starting from the concept that a moving body is at a point, arrives in his paradoxes (outlined by Aristotle in *Physics* VI on the quantitative division of motion) at the conclusion that one must consider motion an illusion. This is in support of the view that Parmenides felt compelled to take when confronted with the inability to explain the coming-to-be of things, the first problem of the Greek natural philosophers. They were agreed—as are we—that "from nothing, nothing comes." Consequently, when new beings came to be, such as in each spring's production of new things, they could not come from nothing of themselves.

Those philosophers who did not want to deny their senses and who at the same time could not have new beings coming from nothing of themselves, compromised by considering coming-to-be as a kind of process of rarefaction or condensation, of separation or bringing together. That is, the new thing would simply be a rearrangement of elements already present. But this would face the same difficulty about something coming from nothing: if what appeared was any different from what existed previously (e.g., if the shape or form was new), where did it come from? If the answer was that there was not anything new, despite appearances, then one would be obliged to say that appearances of newness and change were only illusions.

Since no one had succeeded in explaining genuine newness under any form, Parmenides, at least, felt compelled to declare all newness—and therefore all motion and change—an illusion. Zeno's paradoxes sustained this, since they appeared to demonstrate ineluctably that, although one *thought* one saw motion, nevertheless reason would condemn one to deny it as an illusion.

1. The Paradox

This is illustrated in his most famous paradox, the Achilles, as follows. Achilles, the great runner, sets out to overtake the lowly Tortoise, who has a slight head start. Although Achilles runs much faster than the Tortoise, and *appears* to overtake the Tortoise easily, nevertheless it can be demonstrated by strict reason that he cannot, and therefore actually never does!

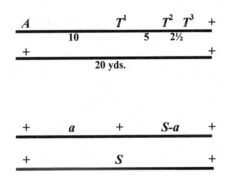

Let us suppose that the Tortoise has a 10-yard start on Achilles, and that the Tortoise runs half as fast as Achilles (which puts them in the ratio of 1 to 2, or ½). If the race began, Achilles would be seen to overtake the Tortoise in short order—at a point 20 yards from Achilles' start, in fact. Yet Zeno shows that Achilles can never run the 20 yards, nor ever overtake the Tortoise.

In effect, after the race begins and they both move off simultaneously, then by the time Achilles has advanced the 10 yards to the point T^1 where the Tortoise started from, the latter has in the meantime advanced 5 yards to the point T^2. By the time Achilles has covered the intervening 5 yards, the Tortoise has advanced 2½ yards to the point T^3. It is obvious that Achilles is never going to catch the Tortoise, since every time he advances, the Tortoise is simultaneously advancing a distance beyond the point which Achilles must first reach, equal to half the distance Achilles must first cover. The race becomes an infinite geometric series with a ratio of ½, where the successive steps taken by Achilles correspond to $10 + 5 + 2½ + 1¼ \ldots$ ad infinitum.

The series will never end, since each step will be half the preceding step and will have a positive value (it only being able to end if half of a preceding step could result in 0). Meanwhile Achilles can never overtake the Tortoise, since, while Achilles is covering one step, the Tortoise is covering the step beyond—and these steps never end. At the same time, they will never reach the total of 20 yards.

This may be easily seen from the fact that the successive steps taken by the Tortoise, and which represent the successive steps of the series, are each one a *half* of the distance remaining to the point of 20 yards. By always taking a half of the remaining distance, the remaining half will always separate the sum of the series from its never-reached limit. Thus, if one accepts the original description of the race—and no modern textbook questions its validity—one is logically obliged to arrive at the same conclusion as Zeno and Parmenides: Achilles *appears* to overtake the Tortoise indeed—at the point of 20 yards, in fact—but the elements of the race show that in reality he *cannot* do so. His motion and subsequent overtaking must therefore be an illusion. So concluded (logically) Zeno and Parmenides—but not the moderns.

How do the modern textbooks argue? They set up the Achilles as Zeno did, i.e., as the sum of an infinite geometric series with a ratio of less than 1 (such as ½). They then proceed to argue that, although by its very nature, such a series cannot be gone through to a term or cannot reach its limit; nevertheless, since one actually *sees* Achilles catch the Tortoise, then it must have been gone through. The reason is that, when Achilles catches the Tortoise, there are no more steps to the series. The Tortoise will somehow have had to make a zero-step while Achilles is covering the step behind him. One has stumbled on the great discovery that the impossible is sometimes possible. Needless to say, the reasoning employed here involves the fallacy of consequence. One is arguing as follows: If Achilles could go through the infinite series, then he would catch the Tortoise; but he does catch the Tortoise; therefore he must have gone through the infinite series.

2. Its Critique

The fact that, from something supposed, something follows, does not mean that, if one has the supposed effect, the supposed cause need be at work. Thus, from the supposition that a car is out of gas, it follows that it will not start; but from the effect that a car will not start, one cannot argue to the absence of gas being the cause at work. Further, if the supposed cause involves certain impossible suppositions—in this case the going-through of an infinite series which, by its very nature, must continue without end—then such a cause must be eliminated as a possibility. Starting, therefore, from one's knowledge through the senses that Achilles does catch the Tortoise, one would know in advance that any explanation of this fact that involved the necessary conclusion that he could not catch the Tortoise must be intrinsically erroneous. And this is the case of the presentation of the race as an infinite geometric series of ratio less than 1.

One would examine this seemingly plausible explanation to find the flaw. And the immediate flaw consists in the depicting of the race as a series of motions from point to point—since this implies a moving body to be at a series of points during its motion, which further examination shows to be untenable, motion being extended, points being unextended. The comparison of the two courses of Achilles and the Tortoise must therefore be in terms of two continuous motions not able to be divided up into segments marked by points.

The error of the moderns is further compounded by their application of the formula for the sum of an infinite geometric series of ratio less than 1 to explain what happens in the case of the Achilles. That formula is $S = a/1 - r$. If applied to the present problem, it gives the correct answer: the sum of Achilles' steps, the point where he reaches the Tortoise, is 20 yards (where $a = 10$, and $r = \frac{1}{2}$). But what does this formula stand for? Actually it stands for, as one may see by its origin, not the sum of the steps of an infinite series, but the *limit* which the series never reaches!

The sum of the steps of a geometric series of ratio less than 1 may be set down as follows: $S = a + ar + ar^2 \ldots + ar^{n-1}$. This can be worked into a formula by multiplying by r, and then subtracting the result from the original, as follows:

$$S = a + ar + ar^2 \ldots + ar^{n-1}$$
$$-rS = \quad - ar - ar^2 \ldots - ar^{n-1} - ar^n$$
$$S(1-r) = a - ar^n$$
$$S = \frac{a - ar^n}{1 - r}$$

In order to get the correct sum in a given case, one need only fill in a, the first term, r, the ratio, and n for the number of steps. Thus, using the values given here for the Achilles, the sum for the first 3 steps would be:

$$S = \frac{10 - 10(\frac{1}{2}^3)}{1 - \frac{1}{2}} = (10 - 10/8)2 = 17\frac{1}{2}$$

May one employ this formula to arrive at the sum of an *infinite* geometric series of ratio less than 1? Plainly such a series cannot have a sum, since, in the above formula, no matter what value one takes for the term n (the number of steps in the sum), it is necessary to take yet another beyond, and yet another beyond—ad infinitum. What can one do? One may assign the *limit* (so-called) of the sum, which it will never reach, but which it will be considered to be constantly approaching—if one may be said to be approaching that which one may never reach!

How may this be done? If one considers the formula, one will note that certain elements remain constant (the value of a and r, with only n constantly augmenting). But as n augments, the value of ar^n approaches closer and closer to 0, without, nevertheless, ever reaching 0. Consequently, since in the expression $a - ar^n/1 - r$, ar^n moves closer and closer to 0, one may consider the *remainder* of the expression as the value to which the sum moves closer and closer.

Hence the expression $a/1 - r$ may be viewed as the *limit* toward which the sum of an infinite geometric series of ratio less than 1 constantly moves, but never actually attains. The reason is that from this limit must always be deducted the value $ar^n/1 - r$, which, while growing smaller and smaller as n increases, nevertheless never becomes 0. Thus the expression $a/1 - r$, while roughly referred to as the "sum" of an infinite geometric series of ratio less than 1, actually represents the limit of that series, to which it approaches, but actually never reaches.

Consequently, if the race between Achilles and the Tortoise is the sum of an infinite geometric series, and one applies (to predict the point where Achilles and the Tortoise will be abreast) the formula for the "sum" of such a series, one is actually (while correctly predicting the point where Achilles and the Tortoise meet at 20 yards) really stating the point toward which the race tends but never reaches! This is exactly the point made by Zeno: you see Achilles catch the Tortoise, but your mathematical calculations show you that he does not do so. In effect, the true sum of the series thus presented, where ar^n will always have some actual value, will always be less than 20 (the point where Achilles and the Tortoise meet), always less than the limit.

What should one do at this point? First of all, since all our knowledge originates from the senses, one will not begin by denying the senses. Rather, one will take the considered sense data as the basic facts, to which all other subsequent explanations must conform. In the race of Achilles and the Tortoise, what are the basic, not-to-be-denied, sense facts? We see Achilles overtake the Tortoise. Therefore, we will accept no subsequent explanation of this fact—such as that the race may be viewed as an infinite series of steps from point to point. This latter explanation will entail, if one is consistent with one's premises (as the moderns are not, but the Greeks were), affirming that Achilles cannot actually catch the Tortoise. Rather, one will base oneself on the fact that, if Achilles and the Tortoise start off together and finish at the point where they are both abreast, they will have, in the same amount of time, covered distances proportionate to the difference in their rate of speed. One will therefore set down the distance covered by both as proportionate to their ratio of speed, as follows:

$$\frac{\text{Distance covered by T}}{\text{Distance covered by A}} = \frac{S - a}{S} = r, \text{ which becomes } S = \frac{a}{1 - r}$$

One has now the formula that corresponds to the experimental facts which the formula for the sum of an infinite series actually does not, since it entails stating that the answer given is the limit which the sum does not reach.

In conclusion, one may present the reasoning of Zeno and Parmenides, that of a critical approach, and a summary of algebraic computation.

a. Zeno's Argument

If the race between Achilles and the Tortoise is the sum of an infinite series of ratio less than 1, then Achilles can never catch the Tortoise.

But the race between A and T is indeed such an infinite series (as the accepted description of it shows).

Therefore, despite what one sees, one must deny that A catches T (and subsequently motion and change in general).

b. A Critical Approach

This approach starts with the fact that, since Achilles does catch the Tortoise, one must have a reduction to the absurd in Zeno's reasoning. One will see that the conditional syllogism is unassailable, namely, that if the race is considered an infinite series, Achilles cannot catch the Tortoise. Consequently, since he does catch the Tortoise (denial of the consequent), the antecedent, namely, that the race is an infinite series, must be false. An examination of this supposition now known to be false (since, if followed through, it will contradict the irrefragable data of the senses, the bedrock of our thinking) makes evident that it is totally dependent upon supposing, in order to consider the motion of Achilles as a series of discontinuous segments, that a moving body, when in motion, is at a point. If this is untenable, so is the description which depends upon it.

c. Summary of Algebraic Computation

The sum of a converging geometric series, i.e., of ratio, r, less than 1, of n terms, with the first term designated as a, is obtainable algebraically:

$$S = a + ar + ar^2 \ldots + ar^{n-1}$$
$$-rS = \quad -ar - ar^2 \ldots - ar^{n-1} - ar^n$$
$$S(1-r) = a - ar^n$$
$$S = \frac{a - ar^n}{1-r}$$

The limit of such a series is obtained by considering ar^n as 0 (which it never actually becomes, since it is by nature a fraction of a previous positive term). Hence one has:

$$\text{Limit} = \frac{a}{1-r}$$

Realistically, however, the true sum, no matter how many steps are taken, will be separated from the limit by $ar^n/1 - r$, a positive value:

$$S = \frac{a - ar^n}{1 - r}$$

Each additional term will cover, by its very nature, a fraction $(1-r)$ of the remainder—the distance to the limit.

The reason why the formula, Limit = $a/1 - r$, correctly indicates where, experientially, A will overtake T, is that the expression represents the continuous distance, S, covered by Achilles when the course is correctly viewed as a comparison between two continuous motions:

$$\frac{S}{S - a} = \frac{1}{r}$$
$$rS = S - a$$
$$S(1 - r) = a$$
$$S = \frac{a}{1 - r}$$

3. Its Destruction of Contradiction

As has been seen, a correct answer to the Achilles Paradox is forthcoming without any invoking of an infinite series. But is not even this answer subject to Zeno's critique that the race is in fact a geometric series of ratio less than 1, and that, this once admitted, the race can never be completed regardless of what one seems to see? Here one will take as the unshakable primary fact, even before any reasoning, that which the senses transmit, namely, A does overtake T. By virtue of the primacy of the sensible fact, any reasoned explanation which would lead to an answer contradicting that fact, would be excluded as having to be in error, and in its place an answer would be sought that would be in accord with the sense evidence.

It will be noted that the reasoned answer which contradicts the sense fact likewise bases itself on sense: the description of the race between A and T as a geometric series is based on supposed factual observation of their progress, taken as going from point to point. Consequently, if the subsequent answer is in contradiction with sense evidence, it must be because the original observation was in error, namely that of the race as a motion from point to point; i.e., A in his movement first reaches the point where T started from, goes through it and next reaches the point that T had reached while he was reaching T's starting point, and so on in ever-diminishing intervals.

If there is no such thing as motion in a point, then the race cannot be validly so described, and consequently cannot be depicted as a diminishing infinite series—leading to a paradox. The solution can then be given, with no intervention of infinite series, simply as the calculation of two continuous motions in proportion to respective velocities. It is very natural to assume, when a body moves from a starting point to a finish point, that, at any moment of its motion between the two, it is also at a point, which may be duly designated in a diagram. Thanks to this, Zeno can set up his paradoxes. But can a moving body be at a point? What would this suppose? Actually it would require supposing the self-contradictory, which cannot exist.

How does this come about? Let us suppose a body which is moving from **A** to **B** to be, in the middle of its motion at a midpoint **M**. But motion is continuous. Thus a body has not moved until it has covered a certain distance. But whatever is continuous is divisible. Thus the motion of the body at the point **M** is able to be divided. One may suppose it to be divided at the midpoint. It follows that during the first segment of the division, the body is already at the point **M**, since the whole motion occurs at **M**. Consequently, the body is already at **M** before completing its motion at **M**. It is at **M** before fully arriving at **M**, which is contradictory, implying being simultaneously at **M** and not at **M**. Similarly one can state that, while the body is already at **M** during the first segment, it then continues to move ahead during the second segment—without, however, leaving the point **M**, which is also contradictory.

From such consequences one is obliged to recognize that, despite one's inclination to believe that a moving body in the course of its motion must be, at any given moment, at a given point, this cannot be the case: a moving body can therefore never be at a point. One can see the basic reason for this in the fact that, while a point has no extension, a moving body's motion, no matter how minute, must always be extended, thereby not allowing it to be identified with an extensionless point. Because of this, the race between A and T cannot be described as though it were a going from point to point, with A first reaching one point, then another farther on, and so forth—suppositions which are indispensable to Zeno's paradox. Actually, as stated above, one has two continuous motions whose lengths, during an identical time, will be proportionate to the respective velocities. With these factors known, the answer follows without contradictory suppositions and is experimentally verified.

Meanwhile, however, if one illogically supposes that a correct answer by that very fact validates the reasoning which leads to it, and therefore, in this case, because the formula employed yields by accident (by virtue of the suppression of the term ar^n) the right answer, one has now justified the acceptance into one's thinking of the impossible (going through an infinite series by nature unending) as possible. Then one is now launched into a realm opening into serious error (canonized in the theory of limits). Such error will be extended into the whole realm of thought as the great discovery that a thing may by a gradual process evolve into its contradictory, meaning that everything is intrinsically just as much its contradictory as itself. The bad is just as truly good, the false is just as truly true.

It is to be noted that all initiations to quantum theory begin by enunciating the impossibility of simultaneously measuring the position and velocity of a moving body or particle, considered in its motion to be at a point. Since it is never at a point in the first place, this is merely a dialectical supposition and the supposed impossibility cannot be viewed as referring to a real situation.

Chapter 6

Aristotle and Causality

Linked to the first steps of the founders of modern physical science was the thinking of their early Greek predecessors. These philosophers, who came into being around the fifth century BC, were those who, because of the advance of the practical arts of civilization, found themselves with sufficient leisure to be able to look for a rational explanation of the physical universe as an advance over a purely mythological one. The Greeks who undertook such an explanation did not believe any less in the divine origin of things, but they were aware that the mythological stories, assigning certain functions to certain gods, were man-made. Such undertakings had been those of Homer and Hesiod.

A. The Four Causes
1. The Material Cause

The Greeks set out to find a material explanation of the universe, i.e., one in terms of that out of which the universe was made. (This is the definition of the material cause, namely, that which is posited as that out of which something is made.) Traditionally, the first of the philosophers is Thales, who posited that the basic—and divine—element from which everything came, and out of which everything was made, was water.

Aristotle, who flourished in the fourth century BC, divides up the work of the cosmologists who were his predecessors in terms of whether they posited one element as the material cause of all things (as in the case of Thales, with water), or more than one (as in the case of Empedocles, who posited what was to become for centuries the traditional complexus of four basic elements, namely, air, earth, fire, and water).

Among those who posited a plurality of elements, some posited a finite number, as did Empedocles. Some posited an infinite number, as did Anaxagoras, with his position that everything is contained in everything, and Democritus, the founder of the atomic theory, who posited that everything is composed of varying arrangements of an infinite number of invisible, indivisible (the meaning of *atom*) particles.

As we can see, current physical theory finds itself today at the level where the Greeks started. In effect, the theory of the four elements of Empedocles held sway for a long time to be extended, starting with Lavoisier in the eighteenth century, to the 109 known elements of today. These elements in turn have been reduced back to the atoms of Democritus, insofar as all the chemical elements are now considered as being composed of the same basic protons and electrons in varying arrangements. Forward steps are considered as being taken in the sense of finding still more material particles, starting with neutrons, neutrinos, mu-particles, and so forth.

Aristotle pointed out, therefore, how his predecessors, in looking for the cause of the physical universe, started out by looking only for the material cause, namely, for that out of which the universe could be considered to come. Some of them, indeed, such as Parmenides, found the problem of coming-to-be insoluble; that is, they were not able to explain how new beings could become without supposing them to come from nothing, which was inconceivable. Therefore they were constrained to deny becoming (a denial supported by Zeno's paradoxes), and with it the data of the senses, and to consider the totality of being as rigidly one, with all change and motion an illusion. Hence, there is, properly speaking, no question of a cause of everything, since cause implies the duality of cause and effect. And, if everything is absolutely one, there is no such duality.

2. The Efficient Cause

However, it soon became evident that a sole material cause, i.e., the positing of one or more elements out of which the universe might be assumed to be made, was not enough, since things did not become of themselves. Wood, for example, does not turn into a bed by itself. Consequently, the Greeks had also to look for a cause whence motion comes, i.e., an efficient cause. Such a cause is posited by Empedocles when, in addition to the four elements which constitute the material cause, he found himself also obliged to posit an efficient or agent or moving cause to account for things coming into being by, according to him, the gathering together or separating of the different elements. This cause he names Love and Strife, with Love gathering things together, Strife separating them.

Here, too, one notices a further characteristic that Aristotle points out as present in all explanations practically from the start, namely, the fact that they invoke contraries (such as Love and Strife). This is due to the need of explaining opposing traits in things, such as hot and cold, hard and soft, and the like (and is just as present in our modern-day explanations, as, for example, in positive and negative electricity). If only one element was posited (e.g., water), then the contraries took the form of condensation and rarefaction (thus water, by condensation becomes a solid, by rarefaction becomes a gas). If several elements were posited (e.g., air, earth, fire, and water), then the contraries took the form of congregation (gathering together) and segregation (separating), the function of Love and Strife.

At the same time one will notice that the first philosophers, even when they refused to let themselves be trapped into denying motion and their senses by difficulties such as those proposed by Zeno, and insisted on the reality of change and becoming, nevertheless did not satisfactorily solve the problem of becoming. In effect, since the things that came into being were to be considered simply as rarefactions or condensations of an original element, or congregations or segregations of some several basic elements, they were not actually new things but would have to be declared still substantially the same initial element or elements. In rigid logic they would have had to hold the same as Parmenides, namely, that things other than the basic element or elements only seemed to be new and different things. However they instinctively knew that they were new and simply failed in giving an adequate explanation—which Aristotle, benefiting from his predecessors' efforts, was ultimately to do.

So far, "constrained by the truth," as Aristotle says, the first philosophers had been obliged to move along from positing a sole material cause to positing also an efficient cause—and in addition to matter, also motion. Here one may perceive a certain infelicitous separating of physics and chemistry—with the former concentrating on motion without concern for the material composition of things, and the latter studying the material composition more or less without motion. It is not surprising, then, that the two are merging again. In effect, new chemical elements are studied as having been brought into being by physical collisions, i.e., motions in cloud chambers, accelerators, and the like.

3. The Formal Cause

A very important cause, however, was still being omitted. One could indeed posit something as that out of which something was made, and some motion as educing it out of the matter. One could say a desk was made out of wood by a carpenter. But in what way would this explain how a desk was different from a chair? There was something more upon which the existence of a desk depended as differing from the existence of a chair—namely its shape or form, i.e., the formal cause. Aristotle points out that there was little reference to an explicit formal cause until the Pythagoreans and one of their inheritors, his own master, Plato.

The Pythagoreans were followers of Pythagoras, whose philosophic school flourished in a Greek colony in southern Italy, and which is credited with initiating the decimal system, the multiplication table, the Pythagorean theorem, and so forth. Because of their discoveries of the possibility of representing physical realities in terms of mathematical ratios (e.g., in music), the Pythagoreans endeavored to consider numbers as the essence or form of all things, and consequently to express the essence or form of each thing by a number.

This tendency to try to express reality in terms of numbers is, needless to say, just as alive today—and quantitative realities are indeed expressible in terms of numbers. For example, one can measure a length in terms of a number of quantitative units such as inches, feet, and so forth. For practical purposes one even measures nonquantitative realities in terms of numbers—for example, one's intelligence in terms of the numbers of an IQ evaluation. So long as one does not consider numbers as really expressive of nonquantitative realities (which they denote only in a practical way), one will not fall into error. The Pythagoreans—and many since them—were so impressed by their mathematical discoveries that they not too surprisingly concluded that everything could be expressed in numbers.

Plato, while being inspired by the Pythagoreans, nevertheless did not make numbers the essences of things. Instead of numbers he chose Forms or Ideas, and made them, not the essences of all things, but the models or exemplars of them. This was Plato's answer to the recognition of law and form and constancy in nature. Since the individual, material objects of nature were themselves always changing, always varying, they themselves could not incorporate form and constancy, but were rather reflections of a separated form and constancy, the true reality. Every transient, earthly form would be the reflection and distant participation of a separated (i.e., separated from matter) single, unique Form or Idea, its exemplar.

When one perceived the existence of form and order, law and constancy, in nature, this would not be direct knowledge from nature itself, from sensible reality, but rather a reminiscence of a past spiritual existence when one knew the immaterial Forms. Sense knowledge, therefore, does not give the knowledge of the universal and permanent, upon which science is built, but rather simply triggers the recollection or reminiscence of that knowledge previously had. For example, one has the concept of a perfect circle. For Plato it does not come from sense reality; rather the various imperfect circles one sees reawaken in one the previous spiritual knowledge of a perfect circle, the Form of a perfect circle. St. Augustine, in his early, Manichaean days inclined to this outlook.

4. The Principles of Change or Becoming

Aristotle was a devoted and assiduous pupil of Plato's Academy, the name given to his group, originating perhaps from the property's having belonged to a man named Academos. Subsequently he became the tutor of the young Alexander (later to become Alexander the Great), son of Philip of Macedonia. When Alexander, shortly after, launched out on his military career (which included taking over Athens before starting out for the Near East), Aristotle began a school of his own in that city, which, for reasons equally as obscure as those explaining the name of Plato's Academy, became known as the Lyceum. Aristotle then proceeded to solve successfully the problem of becoming which had baffled his predecessors—profiting of course, though, from their efforts.

How did he do this? First of all, Aristotle refused to deny his senses, as did, for example, Parmenides, in keeping with the apparent results of Zeno's paradoxes. Rather, in keeping with sense knowledge's data, he had no doubts that new things truly came into being. At the same time, it was obvious that they were not coming from nothing. They were always, indeed, seen to come from something preexisting, for example, the plant from the seed. The problem, therefore, was to identify how they preexisted in that from which they came. Aristotle saw that a simple reshuffling of preexisting elements would not account for the existence of a genuinely new thing that was not there before. Thus, in the combining of the sperm and the ovum in human generation, one has the generation of a completely new being which clearly did not preexist in either of the components. The same is obviously true in the case of other animals.

Aristotle noted why his predecessors were always obliged to invoke contraries in their explanations of the coming-to-be of things—since things come to be from their contraries! That is, what is necessary, for example, for Bill to become a musician? Whatever conditions one may lay down, the one that is absolutely indispensable is that previously he be a nonmusician. That is, none but someone who is not a musician can become a musician. In this sense, things do indeed come into being from their contraries; that is, musician comes into being from nonmusician which has the potentiality of becoming musician, such as some man.

In this process Aristotle also draws attention to the fact that, although contraries come from each other, in the sense that one follows the other, they are nevertheless not made out of each other. Musician is not made out of nonmusician, any more than house is made out of nonhouse, or hot out of cold. Plainly there is a common substratum which is acted upon when a being, which was described previously in terms of one contrary, is now able to be described in terms of its opposite. Thus, when nonmusician becomes musician, the latter is not made out of the absence of being a musician, but is made out of the substratum out of which musician is capable of coming, namely, the man who has the capacity to become a musician. When musician is educed out of this subject or substratum, nonmusician (its contrary) ceases to be—but clearly the subject, which has remained throughout the change, does not.

With this insight Aristotle is able to enunciate the three principles of any change; namely, a common subject, a contrary which comes to be, and the opposite of that contrary which precedes it. In order for musician to come to be, one must have a subject, which, from being nonmusician, becomes musician. Aristotle is then able to cut these principles down to two, namely, the subject, and the new form (e.g., musician) in the subject. The third element (nonmusician) does not have to be anything real, it being sufficient to have simply the absence of that form which is to come to be.

Then where does the new form come from? It comes out of the potentiality of the subject, a potentiality which is discerned by the fact that a given subject is able to be the seat of first one contrary, then another. For example, water is able to be the subject, first of hot, then of cold. Plainly the cold did not come out of the hot. Rather, a same subject, previously susceptible of the form of hot, shows that it has the potentiality to cease to be hot and become cold. The subject is therefore the vehicle of these changes, with the new forms existing in it in potency. How do we know all this? Because we see it happen.

So far the changes, or comings-to-be, in the examples have been in the accidental order. That is, a new substance has not been produced, but only a new accidental situation in a substance which remains the same substance. Thus, when nonmusical man becomes musical man, there has indeed been a coming-to-be, something new has come into existence, namely, the quality of being musical in the man who previously was not musical. As in all changes, the substratum or subject remains the same. In the case above, the subject or substratum was the substance, man. But what if one has a change in which a whole new substance comes to be? This is clearly the case of the ovum and the sperm in human generation. Quite plainly, from the result, a whole new substance has come into being, a substance which is clearly neither the ovum nor the sperm, but the new cell. The change is therefore radical, and the substratum must be in such cases not something which retains a permanent form, as in the case of man in the transition from nonmusical man to musical man. Yet there is a substratum.

This substratum or subject which comes to light as having to exist when whole new substances emerge is designated by the term *prime matter*. The form which, allied to this prime matter, constitutes the substance is called the substantial form—for example, the form of man which is the term of the union of ovum and sperm, the form of neither of which is man. Plainly, since matter cannot exist without some form, the new form, in a substantial change, does not emerge out of matter without any form. Rather, in the matter which previously had other forms (e.g., the form of the ovum and the sperm), now, by the action of an agent, the matter ceases to become suited for those two forms and they cease to exist—while simultaneously out of the potentiality of that same matter there is educed the new substantial form here designated as man.

At this point one will note a remarkable similarity between the first philosophers and the moderns. As already stated, the first philosophers failed to identify immediately the most important cause of things, i.e., the formal cause, that by which something is what it is (as man in the case of the union of ovum and sperm). Rather they began by the sole material cause (i.e., that out of which something was made, such as one of the four elements), adding subsequently an efficient cause, or that from which motion comes, such as the Love and Strife of Empedocles, or the Mind of Anaxagoras. In the same way, the moderns have made no progress toward the formal cause.

Thus a present-day textbook on human generation will indicate the material cause (i.e., the ovum and the sperm) and the efficient cause (i.e., the bringing together of these elements)—and the diagrams will illustrate this. But there is no identifying of the new being that has come to be. Where did it come from, since it is not simply the addition or juxtaposition of ovum and sperm? The new being is treated as though it were simply an addition of the old being. Thus the analysis of a full-grown human being would treat him as though he were a certain total of individual cells of various sorts. And yet the most real thing in the person is the one self, the single form, which is in no way acknowledged or explained.

Consequently, in perusing modern-day textbooks, we should be aware of the fact that we are not getting a description of whole substances, such as whole human beings, but only, at best, of certain causes, such as the material (and this in an inadequate way, as with the early Greeks, who had the same elements—today, atoms, molecules—remaining as though multiple in new beings which are clearly one). Aristotle's analysis makes it clear, however, that in new substances we must acknowledge entirely new forms (whatever their external resemblance to the old), which have come, under the action of an agent cause, out of a prime matter which is endowed with the possibility of being the matrix for their production.

5. The Final Cause

This cause, that for the sake of which, the cause of causes, has yet to be treated. Aristotle points out that even his predecessors who had some explicit notion of formal cause, as did Plato, nevertheless did not explicitly treat of the final cause. This cause is the end or purpose which would set the efficient cause in motion, which in its turn would then educe the new form out of matter (following always the directives of the final cause or purpose, the process terminating when the final cause or purpose is fulfilled in the form produced or in a subsequent use of that form). The end or purpose, which is the final cause, which moves the efficient cause to act—and is, thereby, the cause of the actuality of all the other causes—is of course some good to be obtained or realized. Aristotle points out how Plato introduces the Good as a cause, but only as a moving or efficient cause, not as a final cause or that for the sake of which.

Therefore one has four causes involved in the being of material things, two of which are intrinsic to the thing, namely, the matter and the form; two of which are extrinsic to the thing, namely, the efficient cause which educes the new form out of the matter, and the final cause (the purpose or end) which sets the efficient cause in motion. This sequence of causality is brought out in both natural and artificial things, in both substantial and accidental changes.

In the realm of artificial things and merely accidental change, one has the case of the carpenter who, as an efficient cause, educes the form of a desk out of lumber as a material cause. The form of the desk is only an accidental form, since one has not a new substance (with therefore a new substantial form, such as water, as deriving from hydrogen and oxygen), but solely a change of shape in a substance which remains, namely, the wood. The carpenter, meanwhile, has been motivated by a final cause or purpose, such as the need to earn some money, which has set him in motion as an efficient cause.

All things put together by the human being, and which remain composed of a multiplicity of individual substances (such as a clock, a radio, a computer), are clearly not one substance with one substantial form, but a multiplicity of substances with an accidental shape or form of the whole. One will note the tendency to try to treat single substances (e.g., living substances such as man), as though they might ultimately be reduced to the notion of a kind of machine with various electrical circuits. Such treatment never accounts for that which makes a man, a man, namely, his single and unified form which is himself.

B. Chance and Randomness As Causes

Among the causes of things, chance and randomness are sometimes counted. Thus, if someone were to ask how Henry won the Irish Sweepstakes, the answer might well be luck or good fortune, under the general heading of chance or randomness. On a more universal scale, to chance or randomness is attributed the very order of the universe. Thus the theory of natural selection for living things implies that, by pure chance, in a given area certain organisms find themselves better adapted than others to the local situation. They survive (survival of the fittest) while the others do not. Chance, not any design, has naturally selected them.

This idea dates back to Empedocles, who explained how the various races, including the race of human beings, came to be by random combinations of parts—the best adapted to the given situation then surviving. "Wherever then all the parts came about just what they would have been if they had come to be for an end, such things survived, being organized spontaneously in a fitting way; whereas those which grew otherwise perished and continue to perish, as Empedocles says his 'man-faced ox-progeny' did" (Aristotle *Physics* 2.8.).

How can we identify those events we call chance events? They may be seen to be exceptions in those events which happen for the most part. Thus, some things happen always, such as the sun always comes up each morning. Other things do not happen quite always, but for the most part. For example, airline departures are on time for the most part; bank tellers are honest for the most part; people who buy lottery tickets lose for the most part.

Where does chance come in? It comes in as an exception in that which happens for the most part. Thus one rushes to the airport to catch a plane; one is late and the plane should have left; but one arrives and the plane has not yet taken off; so one gets on the plane and says,

"Am I lucky!" What has happened? In things which happen for the most part, i.e., punctual airline departures, an exception has taken place. If the exception is in my favor, it is good luck or good fortune. If it is against me, such as the airport cab getting a flat and my missing the plane, then it is bad luck or misfortune.

Here one will note a further characteristic in chance events; namely, that they are in the category of things that could have been desired or planned (either as happening or not happening). Thus, when one catches the plane through luck, it is something one would want to do, plan to do. If one meets one's future wife because one has gone on a blind date out of a purely superficial motive such as doing a favor for a friend, this is luck. The reason is that to meet such a person would have been something one would have planned if possible.

One will further note that the terms *good luck, bad luck, good fortune, bad fortune,* and the like, not only are restricted to things that could have been planned or intended, but also are restricted to beings which could plan and intend, i.e., rational beings. Thus, strictly speaking, if a horse should happen to walk out of a barn just before the barn accidentally collapsed, one would not normally say that the horse was lucky. However, one might well say it of the horse's master if he should have happened to have accidentally led the horse out at this time, similarly avoiding a sad fate. Insofar as children do not yet have the use of reason, one notices that one does not apply the terms of *luck* and *fortune* to them either. One would not say that a three-year-old child was lucky because it was not able to unscrew the cap on the aspirin bottle and swallow its contents. But one would say that its parents were lucky that it did not happen.

Why are such chance events unpredictable? They are unpredictable because we are only in a position to predict those events of which we know the cause. For example, we predict that the sun will rise tomorrow because we know the apparent motion of the sun and its regularity. We predict that the airplane will take off on time for the most part, because that is what we see happening. Why is it that we cannot predict (unless some sort of rule has been established by induction) when it will not take off on time? We cannot, because there can be a quasi-infinity of causes of such an event. And we cannot know such an infinity, such as mechanical defects, bomb scares, and so forth.

The determinists, such as Laplace, would hold that our inability to predict is simply due to the fact that we do not know all the circumstances involved, and that, if we did, we could in all cases predict exactly what would happen. It is true that we do not, but, even if we did, we must face the fact that material nature is naturally corruptible, has an innate tendency to disintegrate—in the lesser number of cases. And finally, there is human free will, which can, if it chooses, violate any rule that has been arrived at by observation, such as that a mother will not hate her child or that an honest man will never commit a dishonest act.

Does this mean that such events, which we surely see to exist, are innately unpredictable? They are certainly so for us—since we cannot know all the causes involved in events that escape our predictability. For example, we cannot know for sure how a person's free will is going to act. But one will notice, however, that all such events are called chance events because they depart from a rule or consistency that we have come to know by induction from the senses. Chance therefore presupposes a rule or order to which it is an exception. If there were no rule or order, there would be no chance.

We can see, therefore, that chance events are under the same power which is responsible for the rule and constancy in events. This power, unlike us, by virtue of that causality, could make events follow a rule inviolably (e.g., every child would be born with ten fingers), but chooses not to have such an inviolable regularity in material things. This can be a reminder that, if things are regular, they do not need to be, but are simply so maintained by the ruling First Cause of events, something we might not appreciate if all events always occurred with inviolable, predictable regularity.

C. Chance and Probability Theory

As has been seen, the area of chance, of good or bad fortune, of good or bad luck, is the area of the exceptions in things which happen for the most part. Thus, when one starts out on a trip, one does not normally expect a flat tire. For the most part, indeed, this does not happen. But it does happen sometimes, unpredictably. And this is the area of chance. Complementing this is the area of probability. Going over past experiences, one might say, for instance, "When you start out to take a fifty-mile trip in your car, the probability that you will make it without a flat tire is 98 percent." In other words, in things which happen for the most part (auto trips without flat tires), it is possible to estimate the degree in which this most part will be found. It may be 60 or 90 percent (it would have to be something over half). It is always something less than 100 percent, where one would no longer be in the category of things happening for the most part. In doing this, one is estimating varying degrees of probability.

One will notice that one can predict the rule that has been perceived inductively from experience (e.g., that a child will be born with both eyes the same color)—being in error in a relatively minor number of cases, namely, the exceptions. On the other hand, one cannot predict the exceptions, since they do not have a steady, uniform cause detectable by experience.

Probability, as understood by Aristotle, embraces the area of things which happen for the most part, and which are known to do so by observation. Such observations inductively formulate a general rule, such as that smallpox vaccinations will normally be effective. But Aristotle also envisaged an area of things which were always true—for example, that the sum of the angles of a plain triangle is two right angles, that the whole is greater than the part, and other propositions in which the predicate was of the nature of the subject, so that, given the subject, one could not fail to have the predicate. Thus the proposition *Every odd number is indivisible into even parts* would be always true because, given the nature of an odd number formed by adding an indivisible one to an even number, it necessarily follows that it cannot be divided evenly.

So long as one admits that there are areas of things which are always true, which cannot have exceptions, one is admitting the notion of absolute truth, and, by extension, absolute goodness. Such absolutes are able to appear as restrictions to the absolute of human freedom. Thus, supposing that it could be proved or established with absolute certitude that God exists, then one would no longer be free, if one were to live in keeping with reality, to entertain as a legitimate possibility the prospect of living as though there were no God.

But supposing that everything, absolutely everything, may be placed in the area of probability only, of that which happens for the most part; then it follows that there is no proposition the contradictory of which one may not legitimately entertain. Even if it should seem to have been proven that God exists, the wise human being, the person who knows that all propositions represent probability at best, will say to himself: "The existence of God is at best only highly probable, the characteristic of all our knowledge; hence I must entertain as possible that he does not exist." In general, then, nothing will be held absolutely. No matter how true a proposition may seem, no matter how well-founded a law of morality, the enlightened human being will understand that he must entertain the possibility of the contradictory—and can act on it when he so chooses, since it too is probable.

Just as the exceptions in that which happens for the most part have a certain probability—in that if it is 90 percent probable that one will not have a flat tire on a given trip, to this there is a 10 percent probability that one will have a flat tire—so, too, if nothing is considered as absolutely certain, unable to have exceptions, then of any proposition its contradictory enjoys probability. Realistically, however, one will note that, in the case of things happening for the most part, the probability of things happening for the most part is predictable, whereas the identification of the things happening for the lesser part, the exceptions, is not predictable.

This universalization of probability is found in modern probability theory, where all events are considered as enjoying simply greater or lesser degrees of probability. This means, since *probable* means that which is not necessarily so, that there is nothing held which one will not hold as being able to be contradicted, as able to be, in a given case, not true. Thus events which happen always are not considered in a separate category from those which happen for the most part, but simply as enjoying the extreme, or limit, of probability—with events which happen never occupying the other extreme.

In keeping with this, all events are ranged on a scale from 1.00 to 0, with events which happen always having a probability of 1.00, and then descending through varying degrees of probability (such as .75 or .66) to events which happen never, with a probability of 0. Under this concept, if something occurs always up to now, or seems necessarily true, this does not mean that the situation has to remain, since it is not necessary, but only probable.

Needless to say, with this concept, nothing is to be held henceforth as being absolutely true, or absolutely good, without any possibility of contradiction or reversal. Even the most certain things one will now hold as being able to be contradicted. And the contradiction of propositions hitherto held as certain (such as *The whole is greater than the part*) will be indicated as a fruitful avenue of investigation for the progress of science. Hence Cantor's theorem: *The whole is equivalent to a part of itself.*

The kind of thinking that lends itself to considering that all things, all truths, enjoy at best only a high degree of probability—and that consequently one may legitimately take the opposite, but also probable, viewpoint—is encouraged by the modern discoveries that come out of the contemporary solution of the Achilles Paradox, to the effect, for example, that the impossible is also possible. It is intrinsically impossible for Achilles to catch the Tortoise; yet he does it; so the impossible must also be possible. This conjoining of contradictories in a continuous sequence—whereby, for example, the probable (that which is able not to be) merges with the necessary (that which cannot not be), which will henceforth be considered simply as an extreme in probability—is incorporated in the theory of limits, considered to be one of the great milestones of modern mathematical advancement.

D. The Theory of Limits

What is the theory of limits? It is the theory according to which, if one entity is able to draw materially closer and closer to another entity—in such a way that one is able to come as close as one wishes, i.e., no matter how materially close one comes, one is able to come still closer by a succeeding step—then one assumes that eventually, by having gone through an infinity of steps, one reaches the limit. Thus, in the case of the Achilles, the entity that approaches the other, from which it is separated by shorter and shorter intervals, is the course of Achilles, constructed out of a successive addition of lengths (such as 10, 5, 2½, 1¼, ... ad infinitum). The entity to which it is considered to approach, the limit, is the point where Achilles is seen, in actual fact, to overtake the Tortoise (e.g., at 20 yards, in terms of the example given above). Nevertheless, in terms of his course as set down as an infinite series, this is seen to be intrinsically impossible, i.e., against the very essence of the course, in which, invariably, only half the distance remaining to the limit is ever added on in the succeeding steps.

The fact that Achilles, in reality, does catch the Tortoise at a predictable point, lends credence to the supposition that he has in fact gone through an infinite series, that the variable (the sum of his steps) not only approaches, but actually attains the limit. As seen above, this thinking employs the fallacy of consequence: if Achilles could go through an infinite series, he would catch the Tortoise; but he does catch the Tortoise; therefore he has gone through an infinite series. (In reality, the fact that he catches the Tortoise indicates, not that he has gone through an infinite series, but rather that the explanation which supposes his course to be an infinite series must be set aside, since in such a way he could not catch the Tortoise.) Nevertheless, such an explanation lends credence to the discovery that the impossible is also possible.

What is involved here is set forth by Aristotle when he shows that the infinite which we know is actually contained within the finite! Thus, if we take a given length (e.g., 20 yards), and begin dividing it by 2, always putting one half aside and then dividing the remaining half by 2 (which will give one a series of steps corresponding to those in the example of the Achilles), one will notice that the number of the segments will grow ad infinitum, as will likewise the length of the sum of the segments—and yet the sum will never reach the finite limit (in this case 20 yards)! The reason why one does not reach the limit is clear: one always goes only half the remaining distance to the limit. Here one will notice the cause of this impossibility: it has nothing to do with the number of steps but lies, rather, in the *form* of the procedure which invariably always takes one-half of the remaining distance, thereby intrinsically preventing the limit from being reached.

But the limit itself is a misnomer—a verbal snare creating the illusion that the unattainable is attainable. In effect, what does one mean by limit? What would one call the limit of the water in a swimming pool? Would one call the fence around the swimming pool (which the water of the swimming pool does not reach) the limit of the water in the swimming pool? No, one would normally call the limit of the water in the swimming pool the farthest point reached by the water, which would coincide with the surface of the wall enclosing the water. Thus, in our normal use of the word *limit*, we are implying that that which limits is in contact with that which it limits, that there is no intermediary, that they touch. If there is an intermediary, such as a concrete wall and walk around the water of the pool, itself surrounded by a fence, it is the surface of the intermediary (the surface of the wall touching the water) that one would call the limit of the water, not the fence, even though it encloses. Thus, while every limit encloses, whatever encloses is not necessarily a limit.

In the theory of limits, then, one has begged the question in denominating as the limit that toward which a variable is considered to approach without being able to attain it. The reason is that such a denomination implies a touching or contact between that which is being limited and the limit itself—the very thing that has to be proved!

A supposedly classical example of the theory of limits is the procedure for squaring the circle. Squaring the circle is nothing other than the endeavor to measure the circumference of the circle in straight lines (or the surface of the circle in squares), the only procedure of measurement available to us, i.e., rectilinear measurement. It is easy to see that an inscribed polygon will to some extent approximate the area or shape of a circle, such as an inscribed hexagon. If one continues to double the sides of such a polygon, its shape and area approximate more and more that of the circle. Its perimeter approaches the circumference of the circle; its apothem approaches the radius of the circle. But the inscribed polygon, while approaching the circle as its limit, nevertheless can never reach it, since the straight lines of the polygon's sides will never be able to coincide with the curvature of the circle's circumference. One has another infinite series where the limit could be reached only if the extended sides of the polygon, by continuous subdivision, could reach the status of a point, which would then coincide with the circumference of the circle. No one pretends to show how this might be done, i.e., how the extended might become the unextended.

But spurred on by the example where Achilles does the impossible and reaches the limit, one will close one's eyes and assume that by a similar number of infinite steps successfully gone through, the inscribed polygon could be made to coincide with the circle, to reach its limit. Thus the theory of limits consists in supposing, without grounds, that somehow infinite series can be gone through and limits reached. These suppositions are held even though, by their very nature, the limits in question always have an uncrossable barrier, comparable to the cement between the water of the swimming pool and the fence, between them and that which they are said to limit. Where, for example, is the real limit of the inscribed polygon whose sides are being constantly doubled? Is it the circumference of the circle with which, by the very nature of an extended straight line, it can never coincide, never touch? No, its real limit is the form of the polygon. It is the form or nature of the polygon, composed out of straight lines which cannot be able to be equated with curves, except in a point to which neither can be reduced, which prevents its reaching the circle even though its sides should be multiplied forever.

E. The Demonstrative and the Dialectical

What, then, is a truly intelligent and critical attitude toward the assumptions of the theory of limits? Since it is clear that the inscribed polygon, for example, never can reach its limit (the circumference of the circle), must one reject all calculations of the circumference of the circle in terms of the perimeter of a polygon (which is the basis for all values attributed to π)? Obviously not, since such calculations have great practical value, and are the only way open to us to make calculations of curved objects in terms of straight lines for practical purposes.

What a critical approach requires is a distinction between the demonstrative and the dialectical, i.e., between what is proved and what simply satisfies the appearances. Thus, the proposition that an inscribed polygon, if one continues to multiply its sides, eventually coincides with the circumference of the circumscribed circle, is not proved or demonstrated (in fact it may be shown to be indemonstrable). It is, therefore, not demonstrative or known to be true. Consequently, one will not hold it.

But to hold the same proposition, i.e., that an inscribed polygon of a great number of sides may be equated with a circle for practical purposes of calculation of curved entities in terms of straight lines, is perfectly legitimate. That is, one does not hold it as a demonstrative proposition, i.e., as a true proposition (namely, that a polygon may be, in fact, equated with a circle), but as a dialectical proposition; namely, a proposition which has practical value, without necessarily being true.

Here one will note that to hold a proposition as merely dialectical, i.e., as not being necessarily true, but simply as saving the appearances, as having a certain practical value, does not of itself exclude the possibility of its also being true and demonstrative. In effect, many propositions, which later turn out to be provable and true, initially begin simply as intuitions or hunches which satisfy the appearances. The squaring of the circle, however, is able to be demonstrated as not able to be true.

In holding unshakably to the veracity of the senses, and in maintaining the distinction between the demonstrative and the dialectical, between what one holds as true and what one holds for practical purposes, a thinker enjoys a true of liberty of thought. He can, for example, in all his practical activity and computations, consider all physical and mathematical science as purely dialectical, leaving to a later investigation whether, in the speculative order, he will consider any of the various formulas from which he derives practical benefit as being demonstrative or true.

F. Universal Randomness

It is clear that, if one does not make a critical distinction between the demonstrative and the dialectical, the true and the useful, and considers the merely dialectical as true (e.g., considers that, by multiplying its sides, a polygon somehow ultimately does become a circle), one finds oneself brought to the eventual denying of all objective truth. In other words, is a straight line different from a curved line? Not really, because they eventually merge in the squaring of the circle. Thus a straight line is also not a straight line, because it is able to become, by a continuous process, a curve. Thus any thing may be rightfully considered not only as what it is, but also as what it is not, i.e., its contradictory. Consequently, one cannot say absolutely that anything *is*, because it also *is not*. This is incorporated into the theory of probability, where, on the basis of supposedly successful contradictions of what was considered uncontradictable (e.g., the possibility of going through an infinite series), even what is considered certain is now considered as able to be contradicted, i.e., merely probable.

Since nothing is certain in reality, then one will not look for any laws, any structure, in reality. Rather it will be left up to the human mind to construct models or pictures of its own to satisfy the appearances. Thus all knowledge becomes dialectical, tentative, provisional, reversible—and one does not commit oneself to anything. Thus, on Monday one may find it convenient to hold the proposition *A man should be honest*; on Tuesday one may find it convenient to hold the contradictory *A man need not be honest*. Since one dare not maintain that there is any objective order in the universe and that the senses and the mind are able to discern it, then, even if one does think of the universe as being really there, one will not attribute the order one also sees there to any determinate cause. Rather, one will attribute that order to randomness, to the random congregation of molecules. Thus the evolution in the animal kingdom will be held as the result of randomness, just as Empedocles had proposed in his primordial statement of a survival of the fittest which brings about a natural (i.e., nonordered) selection.

Here again one will see, if one considers critically, the unreasonableness of inventing a hypothesis of randomness to account for the order one perceives in the universe, when, insofar as any experience tells us in the case of those things we do know, order is always the result of some plan and intent except for a few chance cases in a very minor degree. Thus a man could select all fifty-two playing cards in a deck at random and have them come out in perfect order. But one knows that the chances of this are utterly minute. Also one knows that it need never happen, no matter how many times the man tries; since, if one were to say that it must eventually happen, one would be introducing a determining factor which would follow a fixed pattern, which would contradict the indeterminism of chance.

This brings out the profound, but overlooked, fact that chance is conceivable only against a background of law. It is conceivable only as an exception to something regular and determined. If there is no determination (and this must be ultimately by a mind which has the power to conceive and make the determination), then there is no chance—since chance is an exception in something determined.

Needless to say, that which is chance to us—because it is an exception to a rule which we have come to know inductively, such as that children will be born with ten fingers—is not chance absolutely. That is, it must ultimately have a cause which controls it. This power will be the same First Cause that also causes the rule.

Chapter 7

The Moving and Measured Universe

Following a treatment of causality, Aristotle analyzes motion, the basic property of all material things. In addition to this analysis, he treats the extrinsic measures of motion, namely, place and time.

A. What Is Motion?

Since all our knowledge of the physical universe—and it is with sense knowledge of this universe that our thinking originates—is connected with motion, to the point that without motion one would know nothing about it, it is important to try to grasp a definition of motion. As has already been noted, all physical systems are constructed upon a certain concept of motion. Thus modern physics, considered as originating with Galileo and Newton, takes as its basic postulate that a body at rest or in motion in a straight line will of itself continue in that state of rest or uniform motion in a straight line. All subsequent conclusions are deduced from this initial postulate.

First, there is no doubt about the existence of motion: we see things moving from place to place, which is the basic and most obvious sort of motion, local motion. We see things moving from one quality to another, as when the color of an apple moves from green to red, the temperature of water moves from cold to hot, a motion in quality sometimes called alteration. We see living things go from one quantity to another, as when a plant grows, or an animal in old age declines, a motion in quantity, called growth (or decline).

These are the three fundamental types of motion: motion from place to place, motion in quality, motion in quantity. One will notice how the two subsequent ones depend upon the first. For example, the water does not become hot until the source of heat is moved close to it; the apple does not become red until it is moved into the sun; the plant does not grow until nourishment is moved toward it.

At the same time there is that radical change whereby a whole new thing comes into being. Here motion precedes the change, and also follows it, but the change itself is not properly motion, since it is instantaneous. Thus when sperm and ovum meet to constitute a new cell, the change from being two substances to becoming a single new substance is indeed a change, but not a motion—although there is motion preceding the change (a substantial change, i.e., a change resulting in a new substance), namely the local motion bringing the two cells together; and motion subsequent to the change, such as the motion of growth on the part of the new cell.

The reason why one does not call a substantial change a motion is because a motion is something observable by the senses; for example, the motion of a man from one place to another, the motion of an apple from green to red, the motion in quantity of a flower from bud to full bloom. But in a substantial change—such as when a new, previously nonexisting life comes into being, as in the generation of an animal, where one does not have simply a change in a preexisting substance, as in the growth of a man, but the production of a new substance (with the accompanying cessation of the previous substance or substances, such as the ovum and sperm)—one will note that one observes what precedes the change, and what follows the change, but one does not perceive the change itself, since it is instantaneous.

Thus, in generation, there is no intermediate time when one has neither the ovum nor the sperm on the one hand, nor the new cell on the other: the ceasing-to-be of the ovum and sperm coincides with the coming-to-be of the new cell. Similarly, in a change from life to death, the body is either living or dead: there is no possible in-between state. One perceives the two terms of the change with the senses, i.e., life, then death. But one does not, because of its instantaneity, perceive the change itself. Therefore, in conclusion one will say : while all motion is a change, i.e., a going from one term to another, not every change is a motion, specifically in the case of substantial change, called either generation (coming-to-be) or corruption (ceasing-to-be).

As may be seen, motion is an in-between thing. Thus the motion of a man going from Chicago to New York does not exist before he starts out from Chicago, has ceased to exist when he arrives at New York. It exists only so long as he is between Chicago and New York! Hence its tenuousness, since it exists only so long as one is in movement; when one has arrived, it has ceased to be. Plainly it will not stand still to give one a chance to study it. One will also notice how motion requires continuousness or extension in space and time. A man cannot move from Chicago to New York, unless there is a certain continuous space separating them. Otherwise nothing we call motion can be observed.

Likewise, if it is to be observed, the motion must take time. This will appear even more obvious when time is seen to be nothing more than the measure of motion, i.e., the measure of one motion in terms of another (e.g., the sun) with whose motion the motion of the hands of a watch is synchronized—which motion of the hands of the watch is in turn used to measure other motions, such as the motion of a man going from Chicago to New York.

Since motion is one of the basic, obvious things we see, we cannot find anything more obvious in the sensible world in terms of which we can describe it. Aristotle therefore has recourse to the most universal concepts we have, i.e., concepts which are even broader than the sensible world and apply to any kind of being, such as the being of our thoughts. These concepts are the concepts of act and potency—already touched upon in arriving at the concept of primary matter as that cause in which the forms of material things which newly come to be, exist in potency before coming into act. Aristotle therefore defines motion very adequately and distinctively as the act of a being in potency as such.

What does this mean? First of all, motion is an actuality, something that exists (and is, in this case, discernible to the senses). Thus, when one moves one's hand, one knows that there is, during that time, in addition to the being of the hand itself, an additional being, the being of the motion (which ceases to be when the hand stops—but whose reality is undoubted, such as should it terminate in a slap).

But what kind of an actuality is this? The actuality of something that remains, such as the actuality of a house after it has been built?

Clearly not. The actuality of motion is instead like that of the building of the house. As long as the house is being built, as long as it is not completed, as long as the finished house is still in potency, then one has the motion of building. But when the house is completed, then the motion of building has ceased to be. Hence motion is seen to be the actuality of something in potency as such, i.e., precisely as being in potency. The motion of the building of the house is an actuality which indeed exists, but only so long as the house is in potency, i.e., incomplete, not yet finished, not actualized. When the house is now an actuality, the motion of building no longer exists. Motion is therefore the act of a being in potency as such.

A further consideration is worth investigating. When one body is moving another, such as a hand moving a hammer, where the hand moves and the hammer is moved, does one have one motion or two (i.e., a motion of the hand and one of the hammer)? One will notice that it is really one and the same motion, i.e., the motion by which the hand moves the hammer is the same as the motion by which the hammer is moved. One may see a similar analogy in the case of the teacher teaching and the student learning: that which the teacher teaches is also that which the student learns.

Should one say that a teacher could teach a lot more than the student actually learned or assimilated, one would specify the meaning of *teach* as signifying the actual communicating of knowledge to the student, in such a way that the teacher would be said to have taught that which the student learned. Here, too, such as in geometry, what the teacher would be said to have taught the student as one acting (as agent) would be exactly that which the student would be said to have learned as one receiving (as patient, from the Latin word meaning 'to undergo').

Consequently one will say that, in the case of one body moving another, the acting and the receiving are the same motion. One must note, however, that, in the founding of modern physics by Galileo and Newton as mentioned above, the basic postulate (i.e., of a body at rest or in uniform motion in a straight line) does not suppose that a body in motion needs to be moved by another body. If it is supposed as being in motion, no outside source is considered as having to be invoked to account for its supposed uniform motion in a straight line. An outside force would only be supposed in the case of an acceleration or deceleration of its motion.

Finally, one will note the relationship of motion to the concept of nature. What is meant by *nature*? When we speak of the nature of something, such as a cat, we are referring to that in the cat which makes the cat behave like a cat. And since the cat's behavior as a cat takes the form of motion (its motion of growth, its local motion, and so forth), one can designate or define its nature as the principle of motion within the cat. Since this principle of motion within the cat accounts for the cat's acting like a cat, one will note that the nature of a thing is often identified with the form, or formal cause, of the thing. It is, however, a form in matter, and this too is implied in the notion of nature.

In general, then, the nature of a thing will be that principle within a thing whence emanates the motion and change of a thing, a nature expressed in the form, a form which is in matter. Thus nature in general, as referring to the totality of the material universe, will indicate the acknowledgment of a principle or principles within things causing the motions and changes that we see externally manifested.

One will recall that the term *nature*, from the Latin *natura*, meaning 'things to be brought forth, to be born', is derived from the intrinsic principle seen at work in the coming-into-being of animals, and is then extended to the coming-into-being process seen in the whole material universe. The corresponding Greek word is *phusis*, with its adjective *physika*, i.e., 'physical, natural things'.

It is also appropriate to note here the difference between natural and artificial. That is, what is natural is that which proceeds from the nature of a thing, i.e., from an interior principle. If a thing has a motion and a being which is not from within, but from without, one has an artificial thing, an artifact. Thus the being of a clock is really from without, and its motion is communicated from without; it is an artifact—and actually a composite of many distinct substances. The motion of a flower is a motion from within; such a motion is a natural motion. If one planted a bed, it would grow—if it did—not according to its externally imprinted, artificial shape, but according to the internal nature of the wood composing it.

B. Infinity

Infinity soon enters into one's consideration of the physical universe. In effect, Zeno's Achilles Paradox, which caused Parmenides to deny motion, has its effect because it implies that Achilles must go through an infinite series of steps in order to overtake the Tortoise—and the infinite is untraversable, cannot be gone through. This may be further seen in the fact that the material world from which our knowledge starts appears to us as continuous. Motion is continuous—and one of the definitions of *continuous* is that which is divisible to infinity. All the early philosophers tended to invoke the infinite in one way or the other in their explanation of the causes of the universe, as a kind of reservoir out of which everything could be brought and produced. Also it would be natural enough to consider the universe either as extending infinitely in all directions, or, if not, at least to be surrounded by a kind of infinite space.

More precisely, what do we mean by the infinite? (And the question is just as apposite today as it was at the time of the first western philosophers, since today's first-graders are promptly introduced to finite and infinite sets—the former being, for example, the set of fingers on one's hand; the latter, the set of the natural numbers, or the set of the points on a line.) Certainly the basic notion of the infinite is of that which cannot be gone through. Thus, no matter how far one counts with the natural numbers, 1, 2, 3, ... , one never comes to a last number such that there cannot be one more beyond. So one says, "The set of the natural numbers is infinite." The same may be said of Newtonian space, i.e., the space conceived of in Newtonian physics: it proceeds indefinitely in every direction, i.e., to infinity.

Can there be an infinite body? If there were, then that would have to be the only body, since the coexistence of any other body would imply a limit to the infinite body, somewhere where that body was not. The only chance would be for many finite bodies, bodies such as we see around us, to add up to something infinite. But plainly the finite added to the finite can give only the finite, no matter how long one continues—just as, in the natural numbers, starting from 1 or 0, one always has a finite number, no matter how long one keeps on adding. The universe, therefore, composed as it is of finite bodies (which renders impossible any single infinite body), must be finite in extent and mass at any given moment.

The infinite space one might conceive of beyond the ultimate rim of the finite universe is seen to have to be either absolute nothingness from a material viewpoint, i.e., complete absence of matter, or else simply a finite projection by the imagination of a space surrounding the rim of the material universe. This space, having been created by the imagination, exists only so far as the imagination imagines it—comparable to the mathematical line continued to infinity, which, since it exists only in the imagination, extends only so far as one imagines it, i.e., a finite amount. Here one will see the rightness of Aristotle's observation that geometry, while using the term *to infinity*, does not actually use the infinite, but simply prolongs a finite line so far as is needed.

Where, then, does one encounter an infinite known to us? Ultimately, the only infinite we have contact with is the infinite in the sense of the unfinished or incomplete within the finite! It is nothing more than the potentiality of something always actually finite, to become, at least theoretically, always something else, but still within the finite. Thus one might say that a ball of putty has an infinity of shapes, in that, whatever shape it may have at a given moment, it is susceptible of yet another shape, and yet another, and so forth. Thus the ball of putty has always, if one shape succeeds another, a finite number of shapes, starting from the first one at its origin; and its infinite potentiality for further shapes will be realized, not in an infinite number, but in a finite one. Thus one sees that the infinite we know is associated with imperfection, since it presumes, in the succeeding possibility of shapes in the putty, that it never arrives at a definitive, terminal shape which would fully actualize its possibility. Thus one would like a human being's knowledge to grow and grow, but eventually to reach a completeness—and not to be perpetually condemned to be always incomplete, always unfinished within a certain finite limit, which is the characteristic of the infinite we know.

Where is this infinite able to be investigated most thoroughly? It is in the division of the continuum. For this one may take any finite length. (It may be given a numerical value if one wishes, such as 20 inches.) One will then begin to divide this length in two, removing one portion and then repeating the process with the remainder. First of all, one will quickly see how this process can go on to infinity, i.e., not be able to be gone through or traversed no matter how long it is continued—since in taking each succeeding portion, it will be, by definition, only one-half the remainder. Thus the process can go on forever, to infinity, and yet one will never exhaust the initial finite length. Hence one has the statement that the infinite known and talked about is nothing other than a potentiality in material things, such as in a line to be divided indefinitely, which denotes an incompleteness or an unformedness within the finite.

This division of the finite continuum is also able to account for the genesis of the natural numbers and their supposed infinity. In effect, one can label the first half-portion divided off from the initial finite length as 1, the succeeding half-portions as 2, and so on. Keeping time with the continuing division of the continuum, one will have the continuing augmentation of the natural numbers. How far will the process go? It will go, in a clearly finite way, just so far as one carries it. How many actual divisions are there? There is just that finite number, starting from 1, that one chooses to make. But what of the further infinite possibilities of dividing the ever-present remainder of the continuum? These possibilities are just that, purely potential and not actually existing. Thus, if one were dividing a ruler, one would have only as many divisions as one had actually made; other, still potential, divisions would be clearly nonexistent in actuality, and need never exist. And since they do not yet exist, they are clearly unknowable—as would be some future shape in the ball of putty.

Applying this to numbers so generated, one notices that the numbers come into being as the numbers of something, such as of the divided-off segments of the finite length and will correspond to the finite number of segments produced. The addition process will clearly always be the addition of the finite; i.e., one more to the finite, i.e., the first one. Since the total number of objects in the universe is necessarily finite (the universe being finite added to the finite), this number is attained, and if necessary exceeded, by purely finite counting. Consequently, what one thinks of in the infinity of the natural numbers is really nothing other than the possibility of augmenting any finite number in a purely finite way, to whatever extent one wishes.

Therefore one will say of number that, although it may be increased indefinitely—matching the possibility of proceeding on indefinitely in the division of the continuum—it, corresponding to a finite number of objects (real or imagined), remains finite. There is no actual infinite series of natural numbers. The potential infinity of natural number, i.e., its possibility of indefinite increase, is realized only in the finite. This corresponds to the infinite we know, which is merely the unfinished or uncompleted within the finite. It is natural that, when it becomes actual, it should become finite, finished, terminated.

In keeping with the generation of number from the division of the continuum (although this is not indispensable to the knowledge of number, which is simply plurality measured by unity, i.e., a certain plurality of things measured off in terms of one, plus one, plus one, and so on), one will notice two facts. There is a certain smallest number one cannot go below, namely, 1; there is no greatest number, i.e., every number can be exceeded, by the addition of 1. The first fact is due to the reality that, divide as one may, one cannot divide anything except into two ones. (Even something denoted one-half or one-quarter is still a one, with a further addition, such as half or quarter, denoting its relation to another one.)

The converse is seen to be true in continuous quantity or magnitude. (Number, being the measure of a certain plurality, i.e., of discontinuous units in terms of unity, is referred to as discrete quantity, the subject of arithmetic. Magnitude, or extension, where one has quantity as undivided, is referred to as continuous quantity, the subject of geometry.) In continuous quantity, such as the line that is divided in the generation of number, it is plain that there is no smallest quantity, at least theoretically, since, no matter how many times one has divided a line in half, one can still continue to divide it into ever smaller quantities. But there is a greatest quantity, in that, since no body, or continuous quantity, may be infinite in actuality, then there is no body which has such a potentiality, i.e., to be infinite. There is then some greatest finite continuous quantity which will not be indefinitely exceeded, since the bodies in the universe, and consequently the universe itself, have a definite and ordered shape and form.

Aristotle draws attention to the fact that some think of the infinite as all-inclusive, in the sense of that beyond which there is nothing. But he points out that this is really the finite; since, if one could come to the end of something (beyond which there would be no more of that thing), this would signify that the thing was limited, finite. In order for something to be infinite, it is necessary that beyond it there always be something of itself, i.e., no matter how far one goes, there is yet more beyond.

As one sees, this applies to the infinite-within-the-finite that we know, in that, in the division of the finite continuum, there is always something beyond—in that, no matter how many divisions one may have made, there still remains the possibility of further division (which division, if made, will still remain within the finite). This always-something-beyond in the division of the continuum is something possible, not actual. The actual number of divisions, no matter how far one goes, always remains finite.

Paralleling the division of the continuum is the generation of number. The series of numbers at which one arrives, starting from 1, and proceeding by the addition of one, plus one, plus one ... , remains always finite. The possibility of something-always-beyond derives from the possibility of further division of the continuum; but plainly the number of divisions, no matter how far one goes, will remain always finite.

Thus the only infinite we know—the only "that which beyond which there is always something of itself" we know—is nothing other than the basic indetermination of matter. That is, there is always a further (at least theoretical) possible division of something material precisely because things in matter do not have rigid, permanent forms. (Thus, if something has a very definite and permanent form, it resists division. If it has little or no form, it is indifferent to division—as are certain lower, but not higher, forms of life.)

As has also been seen, the something-always-beyond in the realm of the infinite we know is a something which remains permanently potential, never actual. Thus number is potentially infinite, in that, to every number, one can add a still higher number; but that number does not exist until one does so—and when one does so, it becomes a finite number. Thus, for us, the potential, not actual, infinite (always contained within the finite) never becomes an actual infinite, but always an actual finite. It is simply the indefiniteness of matter always taking some definite or finite form.

The only true, actual infinite is the divine infinite. In the divine infinite, that which is always beyond is fully actual. As one can see, this is a necessary property of the divinity, in that, should any characteristic of the divinity come to an end in any way, then the divinity would be limited in that respect. But since nothing limits itself, there would then be something else limiting it. The first being, therefore, must be the cause of limitation in all others, but itself unlimited—which means that, in every sense, in every direction, there must always be something-actual-beyond.

Needless to say, our finite minds cannot conceive this, this going on and on, with always something actual, something fully existing. We can conceive of it only in the negative way, by saying that in the divinity there is complete actuality, with no bounds.

As will be noted, the infinity with which we are familiar, the infinity which is the always-something-beyond of the divisibility of matter, and which is due to the imperfection or formlessness of matter, does have a bound; namely, the finite, the definite form, into which it is always actualized. Thus, the infinity we know is a potential infinity, consisting solely in the formlessness of matter insofar as it is able to be ceaselessly divided, and exists actually only as the finite; whereas the divine infinity is an infinity which is completely, boundlessly actual, and is the absolute fullness of form.

C. Place and the Void

Since local motion, the fundamental motion which the other two (motion in quality and quantity) presuppose, is motion from place to place, it is vital to analyze what place is. We think of place as containing the body which is in it. It is a kind of immobile container, since when the body moves, the place where it was remains.

In the course of his investigation of place (*Physics* 4.3.), Aristotle gives a very helpful examination of the different senses in which one thing may be said to be *in* another:

1. as the finger is in the hand, and generally the part in the whole.
2. as the whole is in the parts: for there is no whole over and above the parts.
3. as man is in animal, and generally species in genus.
4. as the genus is in the species, and generally the part of the specific form in the definition of the specific form, such as animal is in rational animal, the definition of the specific form of man.
5. as health is in the hot and the cold, and generally the form in the matter.
6. as the affairs of Greece center in the king, and generally events center in their primary motive agent (or efficient cause).
7. as the existence of a thing centers in its good, and generally in its end, i.e., in that for the sake of which it exists—as one speaks of someone's heart being in or not in his work.
8. in the strictest sense of all, as a thing is in a vessel, and generally in place.

In the succeeding chapter, Aristotle sums up the essential characteristics of place:

1. Place is what contains that of which it is the place.
2. Place is no part of the thing.

3. The immediate place of a thing is neither less nor greater than the thing.
4. Place can be left behind by the thing and is separable.
5. All place admits of the distinction of up and down, and each of the bodies is naturally carried to its appropriate place and rests there, and this makes the place either up or down.

Aristotle adds the above fifth characteristic, in keeping with his view that the reason a heavy body falls to earth and a light (i.e., lighter than air) body, such as some gas, rises, is not because of gravitational attraction or differences of pressure. Rather it is from the fact that every element has its own proper place in the universe (starting with earth at the center, then, in succeeding layers, water, air, and fire), and that each element is given by nature an impetus toward its proper place. Consequently, if earth is above its normal region, it will tend, by its very nature or form, to return to that region. There will be, therefore, an absolute up, i.e., toward the extremities of the cosmos, in the direction of fire; an absolute down, i.e., toward earth at the center.

Abstracting from the cause of a given body's moving to or from a certain place, one can nevertheless identify place itself as the innermost motionless boundary of that which contains. Thus the place of the water in a glass would be the inside surface of the glass, as well as the surface of the air on top of the water. The place of the glass would be that which surrounded the glass, inside and out.

This may seem to lead to certain difficulties, if every body is to be considered to be in place as being surrounded by the surface of one or more surrounding bodies. The reason is that one would then ask about the place of the whole finite cosmos, which, by definition, would have simply nothing beyond, once one reached its finite corporeal confines. In this sense one would have to say that the universe as such is not in any place, but that everything in the universe finds its place in it.

One might ask what would be the place of a ship anchored in a moving river, since that which surrounds it is not motionless, but moving. Since actually the place of the river would be determined by the confines or banks of the river, and not by the moving water, the moored ship would have a definite position in the river as a whole, despite the moving water around its hull. In the case of a growing or declining thing, the place of that thing would of course grow or decline with it.

What of the position of a place itself? How could one define it with immobility unless the coordinates to the confines of the universe itself were nonvarying? At least one will consider the place of a thing immobile, whether one is able to determine with certainty its immobility. Meanwhile, one can always determine relative immobility. Thus a deck chair can be in an immobile place with respect to the coordinates of a ship—while both chair and ship are actually in motion down a river.

What of the void? What do we mean by it? It is a place without a body. That is, considering place as the first immobile surface of the surrounding body, and then removing the body so surrounded, what would remain would be a void or vacuum. Is a void necessary for motion? Some have thought so, in the sense that one body could not enter a place unless a preceding body left it empty or void. But this is not necessary. For example, a body immersed in water in a glass could move with circular motion within that glass without any void being necessary.

With modern technical advances, one endeavors to create a void or vacuum within a given container, but this would be only in a limited way, in that one does not pretend to eliminate the passage of light through such a container—which passage, to the extent that light is a wave, requires a medium.

In effect, because of the wave motion of light, scientists found it necessary to posit a medium (the ether) in the heavens. The name was derived from the fifth element of the ancients, out of which the heavenly bodies were thought to be composed. Although scientific experiments, such as the Michelson-Morley experiment, destined to detect the ether drift (an effect that one would expect to derive from the movement of the earth through the ether), have never detected anything; nevertheless one continues to postulate such a medium—possibly of an exceedingly subtle nature.

Meanwhile, one will notice that the reference to a void in ordinary physical literature, such as the void presumed to exist between the nucleus of an atom and the orbiting electrons, is only to a limited void, which nevertheless requires some kind of medium for waves, fields of force, and so forth.

D. Time

Just as events take place in a certain place, they also take place in time. One speaks of some task taking a long time, of some period being a happy time, and so forth. What then is time? We are familiar with time as a measure. Thus one might say, "The trip took three hours." Here the trip is measured, as to its length, by a certain time. One notes that time measures the length of things—and not immobile lengths—but rather the motion of things against a background of length or extension. Thus a trip which is said to take three hours is a certain motion against an extended background. This motion is measured by comparing it to another similar motion. During the time that the object of the trip is moving, the hands of a watch have made three complete circuits. These circuits in turn are each regulated by matching them with the apparent daily circuit of the sun through the heavens—twenty-four circuits of the hands of the watch for one circuit of the sun.

The motion, then, that time measures, is a motion according to before and after in space. That is, a body must be able to be perceived as going through one extended space, the before, and then a succeeding space, the after. The space the body goes through may be divided up into before and after units by comparing them with other such units. Thus one such unit will correspond to the motion of a minute hand around a watch. The space covered while the minute hand was making its circuit will be referred to as having been covered in one hour of time. Plainly, as the motion progresses, succeeding units on the watch—each one an after with relation to a preceding before in space—may be counted or numbered: one hour, two hours, and so forth.

One will note that the before and after of time is derived from the before and after of space. Thus, when one says, "John arrived an hour after Henry," this after in time corresponds to an after in space that was being traversed by, for example, the hand of a clock. With these notions, one is able to envision Aristotle's definition of time: the measure of motion according to before and after (*Physics* 4.11.).

As may be seen, the notion of time involves the notion of motion, and, in that motion, succession. Thus, even in our own consciousness, without reference to external sensible succeeding motions, we are able to have a sensation of time passing by the consciousness of the succession of our thoughts. In the external forum, we note that, if the succession is slow in coming (e.g., the succession between the nonpresence of a called taxi and its arrival), we say the time is long. When the succession is rapid (e.g., when days of a vacation appear to succeed each other rapidly), we say the time is short. This all implies that if there is not succession or change of some sort, there is no time.

Thus in the case of the divinity, where all is completely actual, and there is nothing new to come about that does not at present exist, there is no time, but rather a perpetual now. Thus, events which are future to us, since they are already totally in the power of the divinity (i.e., their complete realization already resides within the power of the divinity), are therefore present to the divinity. This is nothing else than the total actuality of being—an infinite that knows no bounds, not in potentiality, but in actuality.

There remains the question of the now in time, the instant. What is it? The now is plainly the division between past and future. How long is it? Although we consider time as extended, being the number of a continuous motion, the now has no extension: it cannot be a minute long, or a second long, since by the time one arrives at the end, or even the middle, of these time periods, the beginning has already ceased to exist—and the future does not yet exist. The now is therefore comparable to a point dividing a line into two segments. There is a length before it, and a length after it—but it itself has no length, and is simply a division (but not a part). The now of time is like such a point, but a point in motion, which constantly moves along, matching the motion of that which is the measure of the time, or of that which is being measured.

The now has existence inasmuch as that of which it is the now, the existing thing, has existence. It is in a sense synonymous with the existence of the thing; and, in a general way, one can equate the time of a thing with the existence of that thing. Thus the time of a man who lived seventy-five years would simply be his existence for seventy-five years. Thus the time of something is not different from the existence of that thing—long or short, temporary or perpetual.

Insofar as the thing exists in a milieu where there is sensible change, then the continuing existence of that thing may be measured in uniform units of that change, such as apparent circuits of the sun in the heavens. Although the existence of the thing as time does not add any new reality, nor do the continuing units of movement that are counted in time; that which is added in the notion of time is the note of counting or numbering, when time is taken as an actual number of motions paralleling the existence of the thing being timed.

In order to have number, at least to have it expressed, there would have to be a mind numbering or counting. Thus the special aspect of time, over and above the existence of the thing, and continuous motion susceptible of being divided (at least mentally) into units, is the fact of the numbering or counting of that motion by a mind. Otherwise, the time of a thing and the existence of a thing are identical. The fact that the existence of material things takes place against the background of successive sensible changes, which succession can be counted as a measure of the existence of the thing, gives us time.

E. Designations Accompanying Motion

Certain designations accompany motion, especially local motion. These terms are as follows:

1. Together and Apart

Things are said to be together in place when they are in one place (in the strictest sense of the word *place*) and to be apart when they are in different places. Thus two books would be said to be together when their surfaces were touching and a single place would encompass them. If another book was between them, each would then have its separate place and they would be apart.

2. In Contact

Things are said to be in contact when their extremities are together. Hence two books touching each other on a bookshelf would be in contact. *Touch* and *contact* have the same Latin root: *tangere* (to touch).

3. Between

Between is that which a changing thing (if it changes continuously in a natural manner) naturally reaches before it reaches that to which it changes. Thus, if someone going from Chicago to New York would pass through Pittsburgh, Pittsburgh would be between Chicago and New York.

4. In Succession

A thing is in succession when it is after the beginning in position or in form or in some other respect, and when further there is nothing of the same kind as itself between it and that to which it is in succession. In this respect, one house can be in succession to another, even though there may be something between, provided it is not a house. Similarly, one day can succeed another as touching. That which is in succession, is in succession to a particular thing, and is something posterior. Thus Tuesday is in succession to Monday, but not Monday to Tuesday.

5. Contiguous

A thing that is in succession and touching (in contact) is contiguous. Two books side by side on a bookshelf would be contiguous—but not two houses with a driveway separating them.

6. Continuous

The continuous is a subdivision of the contiguous. Things are called continuous when the touching limits of each become one and the same, and are, as the word implies, contained in each other. Continuity is impossible if these extremities are two. This definition makes it plain that continuity belongs to things that naturally, in virtue of their mutual contact, form a unity. And in whatever way that which holds them together is one, so too will the whole be one, for example, by glue or organic union. Given a piece of wood which one then saws in two at a certain point, if one then brings the two pieces together again, they will now be in contact. Hitherto, at that same point, they were continuous. To the extent that two pieces of metal rod welded together now make one, they are continuous. The same would be true if two pieces of wood were glued together so as to make one, with intervening glue.

When one compares the six above terms, it is obvious that *in succession* is first in the order of analysis. The reason is that whatever touches, which is *in contact*, is necessarily in succession, but not everything that is in succession touches. Thus numbers are in succession but not in contact—things being counted need not touch. Further, if there is *continuity*, there is necessarily contact. But if there is contact, that alone does not imply continuity. The reason is that the extremities of things may be together without necessarily being one, but they cannot be one without necessarily being together. So natural junction of the continuous is last in coming to be; for the extremities must necessarily come into contact if they are to be naturally joined—as, for example, in a skin graft.

F. Motion and Its Contrary

In things that have no contrary, i.e., where there is no intermediate state between two extremes, there is no motion. Examples would be going from life to death, and in general, going from being to nonbeing, or from nonbeing to being. This is so because motion represents the process between the two extremes.

We note that motion is denominated more from the term-to-which than from the term-from-which; more from the goal than from the starting point. Motion to health we call convalescence; motion to disease, sickening. One notices that contrary motions are motions to contrary goals: the motion from sickness to health is the contrary of the motion from health to sickness.

Motion may likewise be considered as contrary to its corresponding state of rest, i.e., leaving a place as contrary to staying there. In keeping with this, just as motion to opposite goals will be contrary, such as that from sickness to health and from health to sickness; so too will be rest in those states, such as rest in the state of health will be contrary to rest in the state of sickness. Insofar as motion or rest may be violent or unnatural (as, for example, when a heavy body is moved upward against its natural downward motion, and is retained against its nature in a position above), one will consider the unnatural rest of such a body in a position above as contrary to its natural motion downward away from that position.

G. Division of the Continuous

Today it is customary in textbooks to present a line as composed of points. One will assume that every line, long or short, is composed of an infinity of points. These points are further assumed to correspond to the natural numbers (1, 2, 3, ...), which are therefore considered to be existing in actual infinity on the number line. Finally, one will further assume that all types of real numbers (numbers not involving intrinsic contradictions, such as the imaginary number √-1), both irrational and rational, will find their place on this number line composed of an infinity of points.

Thus the irrational number √2, standing for the diagonal of a square of side 1, is considered, because it is greater than 1 and less than 2, to have a place on the number line somewhere between 1 and 2. This is assumed even though no one pretends to be able to establish its value. Actually no proof, or reason, exists that *any* two straight lines should be commensurable. Hence the incommensurability of side and diagonal of a square, i.e., the inability of representation as the ratio between two whole numbers, should not be surprising.

In light of the notions of the terms *continuous, in contact,* and *in succession* as defined above—things being continuous if their extremities are one, in contact if their extremities are together, and in succession if there is nothing of their own kind intermediate between them—nothing that is continuous can be composed of indivisibles. For example, a line cannot be composed of points, the line being continuous and the point indivisible. For the extremities of two points cannot be one, since of an indivisible there can be no extremity as distinct from some other part. Neither can these extremities be together, since that which has no parts can have no extremity, the extremity and thing of which it is the extremity being distinct (Aristotle *Physics* 6.1.).

Moreover, since indivisibles have no parts, they must be in contact with one another as whole with whole. And if they are in contact with one another as whole with whole, they will not be continuous; for that which is continuous has distinct parts, and these parts into which it is divisible are different as being spatially separate.

It is plain that everything continuous is divisible into divisibles that are infinitely (i.e., indefinitely) divisible. The reason is that if it were divisible into indivisibles, we should have an indivisible in contact with an indivisible, since the extremities of things that are continuous with one another are one and are in contact.

The same reasoning applies equally to magnitude, to time, and to motion: either all or none of these is composed of indivisibles. In effect, if the magnitude **ABC** is composed of the indivisibles **A,B,C,** each corresponding part of the motion **DEF** of **Z** over **ABC** is indivisible. So **Z** traversed **A** when its motion was **D, B** when its motion was **E,** and **C** similarly when its motion was **F.** Now a thing that is in motion from one place to another cannot at the moment when it was in motion both be in motion and at the same time have completed its motion at the place to which it was in motion. For example, if a man is walking to Thebes, he cannot be walking to Thebes and at the same time have completed his walk to Thebes.

But when **Z** passes through **A** with the motion **D**, then, since **A** is indivisible, there is not a question of **Z** being in an intermediate state before having passed over **A**. Since the distance and the time are indivisible, then, for the part of the motion that is **D**, **Z** has passed through it without passing through it: that which is walking will, at the moment when it is walking, have completed its walk. Therefore **Z** will have gone over the whole of **ABC** by the motion **DEF** without ever having moved, i.e., without having gone through any intermediate state antecedent to a conclusive state. The reason is that an intermediate state antecedent to a terminal state would imply a divisibility of motion, but we have supposed it as composed of indivisible motions.

It is obvious that time must also be continuous. For, given two things, the quicker of the two traverses a greater magnitude in an equal time. It will likewise traverse an equal magnitude (i.e., equal to that covered by the slower) in a less time. Further still, it will cover a greater magnitude in less time (since it can go still farther, without using up all the remaining time). Because of this, the quicker will divide the time—going an equal or greater length in less time. During this less time, the slower will have gone a lesser length (the slower will therefore divide the length)—which the faster will once again have traversed in a less time than that of the slower. Hence time and length are infinitely divisible. Hence both must be continuous, since that is the characteristic of the continuous, namely, to be infinitely divisible.

Here one should note that while neither magnitude, nor a corresponding time occupied in covering that magnitude, can be quantitatively infinite as to their extremities, in the sense of going on and on in extension; nevertheless, both can be infinite in the sense of divisibility, i.e., no matter how many finite divisions can be made, more finite divisions are possible.

One may also easily see that a passage over finite distance could not occupy infinite time—since the finite distance would be exhausted by a finite time—nor an infinite distance in finite time. (One can envisage, however, a circular finite motion, requiring a finite time for each revolution, which could continue on indefinitely.)

Nothing can be at motion in a present or instant in the sense of the instant dividing past and future. For if it were possible, there could be both faster and slower motions in this present. But the faster could cover the distance covered by the slower in less time than the slower. And therefore the present, or instant now, in which these two motions took place, would be divisible. But we have supposed it to be indivisible.

In the same manner, nothing can be at rest in a present. For if it could, then the same present would serve both for a thing's being at rest and its starting to move. The reason is that if the starting point of motion were another instant separated from the instant in which the thing was at rest, there would necessarily be an intervening time of rest between the two—two instants not being able to be in succession as touching. But a thing could not be simultaneously at rest and not at rest, i.e., in motion. "Again, when we say that a thing is at rest, we imply that its condition in whole and in part is at the time of speaking uniform with what it was previously: but the present contains no 'previously'—consequently, there can be no rest in it" (Aristotle *Physics* 6.3.).

While motion reaches completion in an instant, there is nevertheless not an instant marking the beginning of motion. In effect, when a body in motion comes to a state of rest, there is a division between the motion and the rest. And this division cannot be extended, since the body must be either in motion or in rest. There is thus a last instant of motion, which corresponds to, and is identical with, the first instant of rest.

Yet the moving thing is not both in motion and at rest in that instant, since neither of these takes place in an instant; but rather the termination or extremity of the motion, itself not motion (comparable to the point which is at the extremity of a line, which is itself not a line), coincides with the instant which is at the beginning of the rest. This latter is, in the same vein, the extremity of the rest (and comparable to a point at the beginning of a line). Just as two points touch at a point which is actually the extremity of each (and therefore, while materially one point, is formally two—an end of one line and a beginning of another), so too a motion and the subsequent rest succeed each other in a common instant.

But while there is an ultimate instant of motion, coinciding with the beginning of the rest, there is not, however, a first instant in motion (nor a first point where motion begins). This has to be so, since, when a body starts to move, one cannot say that it is already moving at the instant when it starts, since this instant cannot be separated from the ultimate instant of rest (there not being able to be an intervening space which is neither motion nor rest).

So a body moves *from* some certain instant (the ultimate instant of rest), and *from* some certain point, but, nevertheless, one cannot mark off some first instant, or some first point, when it is moving. One cannot place it *beside* the starting point, since two instants of time, two points of space, cannot be contiguous or touching. When one discerns the motion, a certain space will already have been covered, a certain time will already have elapsed. One can take smaller and smaller segments of time and space in the direction of the starting point, but one will never be able, by this process, to eliminate this space. (One will also say, therefore, that whatever is in motion at a given time must have been already previously in motion.)

It should be noted in passing that, while it is possible to divide up local motion, and also quantitative motion (i.e., growth or decline in living things, measuring, for example, successive largening or successive shrinking), it is not possible to do this directly to qualitative change, such as in the change of an apple's color from green to red. The reason is that there is no continuity in qualitative change which may be divided up into segments, with, for example, a half-way mark.

Just as starting-up must occupy time and cannot occur in an instant (as seen from the consideration above to the effect that there cannot be any first instant or point in motion), so too coming-to-a-stop must occupy time, one not being able to juxtapose side by side some last instant when a thing is in motion and some first instant when it is at rest. There is thus no last instant when a thing is in motion itself. In the same sense, there is no final point on the extended part of a line before one comes to the unextended end-point. The final point is thus the end of the line, but it is not part of the extension of the line.

Zeno maintained, in one of his paradoxes, that a flying arrow went from start to finish without ever moving. His argument was that, at any moment of its flight, the arrow would be at a certain point—and whatever is at a certain point must be at rest (since what is at rest is indeed at a certain point). This, however, supposes that the arrow's flight may be considered as a succession of moments, i.e., of indivisibles. But we have already seen that motion can take place neither in indivisibles of space (i.e., points) nor of time (i.e., instants or moments). Consequently the supposition of Zeno, i.e., of a moving body being at a moment opposite a point, cannot be accepted as an explanation of what one sees, and is rejected.

Finally, no process of change is infinite: for every change, whether between contradictories (e.g., life and death) or between contraries (e.g., hot and cold), is a change from something to something. Thus in contradictory changes, the positive or negative, as the case may be, is the limit. For example, being is the limit of coming-to-be and nonbeing is the limit of ceasing-to-be. And in contrary changes the particular contraries are the limits, since these are the extreme points of any such process of change, and consequently of every process of alteration. Similarly, contraries are the extreme points of processes of increase and decrease: the limit of increase is to be found in the complete magnitude proper to the peculiar nature of the thing that is increasing (e.g., a bear grows only to a certain size), while the limit of decrease is the complete loss of such a magnitude.

Locomotion, however, is not always between contraries; yet it too must be finite. For, since it is inconceivable that that which is in a process of change should be simultaneously unable to complete the change—similar to a thing which cannot come to be, being in a process of coming to be—then it must be assumed that, if that which is in locomotion is in a process of changing, it must be capable of completing the change. Consequently its motion is not infinite; and it will not be in locomotion over an infinite distance, for it cannot traverse such a distance.

One finite process of change could, however, be followed by another finite process. For example, a process of locomotion could be followed by a process of alteration, and that by a process of increase. And this could continue indefinitely so far as the time is concerned. "If it is to be one process, no motion can be infinite in respect of the time that it occupies, with the single exception of rotary locomotion." (Aristotle *Physics* 6.10.). Yet, while this is possible—for example, perpetual rotation of heavenly bodies—it is not thereby necessary.

Current physics textbooks, such as Giancoli, in dealing with relativity, suppose that the impossibility of determining absolute rest (and consequently of absolute motion with respect to such rest) makes all motion relative. Thus, if a man pedals his bicycle at a speed approaching the speed of light past a building, this is considered equivalent to the building's passing him at equal velocity in the opposite direction while he pedals in place. But such an equivalence is not true in reality.

When a finger nail on a nail file goes from **A** to **B**, the motions of the nail down the file, and the file down the nail, while mathematically equivalent (there being no motion in mathematics), are realistically two different motions, as can be perceived experientially. This is the case whether the coordinate system is moving or not. Therefore the absolute perception of motion is not dependent upon the ascertainment of any state of absolute rest.

Chapter 8

Existence of First Mover

A. Proof for external mover
B. Proofs for God's existence
C. God's attributes
D. God in revealed truth

Aristotle terminates his general inquiry into the nature of the physical universe, wherein motion and change as discernible by the senses furnish the starting point, by arriving at the existence of a first mover, itself unmoved. On what is this based? It is based on what Aristotle considers to be a necessary consequent of the analysis of motion in physical bodies; namely, that motion, whether perpetual or having started at some certain time, by its very nature requires a mover from without. This mover from without will itself be moved by another, or be moving while itself unmoved. The chain of movers which are in turn moved by another must necessarily terminate at a first mover unmoved, since one cannot have a regress to infinity in such a chain. Otherwise, if this termination is not reached, the motion we sensibly perceive here and now, having to go through an *infinite* sequence before reaching the present situation, could never reach the here-and-now situation we perceive.

A. Proof for External Mover

Aristotle's argument for the necessity of positing an external mover for every physical body in perceivable motion is not based upon establishing visually some external physical contact as the cause of motion.

The reason is that such contact certainly does not appear; for example, in the case of a projectile such as a ball thrown by the hand, where there is indeed a visible external mover (namely, the moving hand) up to the moment the ball leaves the hand, but no visible mover henceforth as the ball moves onward in its flight.

Rather Aristotle's argument is based on the analysis of the requirements of physical motion considered in itself. This analysis leads to the conclusion that, if a body in motion could be considered as able to be in motion without an external mover being required, this would be equivalent to the body's being simultaneously both in potency and in act under the same aspect, i.e., being both moved passively, and actively moving, under the same aspect. Such would be contradictory, and therefore impossible.

It is this impossibility which prevents a person, capable of lifting a weight equivalent to his own weight, from lifting himself. What would be occurring if one could lift oneself? The hands on the bootstraps which would be doing the lifting would be simultaneously, and under exactly the same aspect, both lifting the body and being lifted by that body. They would be simultaneously, and under exactly the same aspect, both in potency and in act; they would both be and not be under the same aspect, which is impossible.

Since it is impossible to both be and not be something at the same time and under the same aspect, it is clear that, if the concept of a body in motion without requiring an external mover necessarily involves postulating that the body would be simultaneously in potency and act under the same aspect (which is impossible), then a moving body cannot be in motion of itself.

If one accepts Aristotle's analysis, then the very nature of things, specifically the impossibility of something's both being and not being at the same time and under the same aspect, will prevent a body's being in motion without an external mover. Subsequently it will be one's task to try to give a satisfactory account of how such a mover is present in various cases. But the proof will not depend upon such an account, since it is antecedent to, and independent of, such explanations.

Therefore the explanations could be of a purely dialectical nature, i.e., not claim to do any more than satisfy the appearances. There is no difficulty, of course, in accounting for an external mover in the case, for example, where a hand moves a stick, with which it remains in contact. But what of the case, mentioned above, where a thrown ball leaves the hand and continues by itself? An explanation for this may be given in terms of a continuing impression by the mover even when clear-cut physical contact has ceased.

This explanation would be in keeping with the Aristotelian notion that the natural motion of bodies to various regions (e.g., the motion of a liquid toward earth, the motion of a gas upward) is assignable, not to some external force drawing those bodies (e.g., the force of gravity drawing a body downward), but rather to the very form of the body, which includes an impulsion toward the proper place of that body.

Since such bodies are generated, the natural motion of a body subsequent to generation would be a continuation of the motion induced by the generator along with the form. An example of this would be the reversal of direction by water, first rising as a vapor and then falling, upon condensation, as a liquid. The cold that would cause the condensation of the vapor as an agent acting from without would be the cause of the generation of liquid from the vapor. And along with this new form would go a new motion, namely, one downward toward the earth.

In this context, the case of a projectile could be considered as a case of a violent or nonnatural form and consequent motion induced by a generator. Such form and motion lasts a certain time but eventually dissipates and the natural form and motion, derived from the generator in nature, again assert themselves. Thus the natural motion of a ball, consequent upon the natural form induced in it by its generator, would be downward; but a thrower, as a kind of generator by violence, could temporarily induce a violent or nonnatural form in the ball by impelling it upward. The upward motion concomitant with this nonnatural form would gradually wane as the nonnatural form imprinted on the ball gave way once more to the natural form. Then the ball would begin to fall downward by its natural motion in keeping with its natural form imprinted upon it by its generators.

B. Proofs for God's Existence

But what of the first mover? If the impossibility of a recession to infinity necessitates that the first mover must move without being moved by another, how does it escape being both in potency and act? Obviously such a mover must be itself the source and possessor of all actuality, must be itself pure act, in such a way that it communicates its actuality to others, being itself the infinity of actuality. Plainly such a mover cannot be material, since the very notion of matter is that of potency which must be actualized by another, as is likewise the notion of physical motion, namely, that of an act whose nature is to be in potency to a term.

From this analysis one sees that the first mover unmoved at which Aristotle arrives in his *Physics* (bks. 7-8) is indeed God. The reason is that the requirements of such a mover can be satisfied only by a being whose characteristics—pure act and other comparable attributes—are those we attribute to the creator and ruler of the universe.

In keeping with this, Aquinas, employing the reasoning of Aristotle, envisages five possible ways for the human being to know of God's existence. These proofs—starting respectively from the analysis of motion, efficient causality, necessary and contingent being, the degrees of perfection in things, and final causality—are set out together in the *Summa Theologiae*. Each proof reflects the work of Aristotle, evaluated and assimilated by Aquinas.

Thus, in the first way, through the analysis of motion in the sensible world, one arrives at the existence of a first mover unmoved, whom all understand to be God. From the notion of the unmoved mover one arrives at the notion that God must be pure act, without composition of potency and act. Consequently, there is in God no coming-to-be, no new thought, no new willing. All is in act, always.

This immediately introduces the note of how we conceive such things as pure act, pure actuality, arrived at by proceeding from effects to cause. It is clear that this involves negation. In other words, we are very conscious of the transition from potency to act, as when a body begins to move, but are unable to conceive of absolute, unlimited actuality, even when our reasoning tells us it must exist—if only for the reason that our powers of conception are limited to the finite, limited world we see around us. So our concept of pure act, which we cannot know in our present state, consists in a negation of potentiality, which we do know.

But is there nothing positive? Obviously there must be something, some being, that is pure act. This is brought out in the fourth of the five independent proofs, which argues from the varying degrees of being in things (of goodness, of life, of being itself) that there must be one first—one that is itself being par excellence and the cause of all other degrees of being, goodness, life.

Therefore we conceive of God from the effects of nature as being in pure act, and the cause of all other being, infinite, unchanging, eternal. As shown in the second proof from efficient causality, the causality denoted in the beginning of action which shapes things, God is necessarily the beginning of all such action, not only when the being already exists, but of the action that produces the whole being to start with and which maintains it in being. All of this is calculated to cause us to realize that we are, so to speak, completely surrounded and engulfed by God; since our every move, our every action, our very being—and this applies to all the being in the universe—depend absolutely on him.

And since part of our being involves intelligence and will, and it is an individual substance of intellectual nature that is denoted a person, we are aware that God, the individual substance which is the cause of all, is himself supremely intelligent and willing, and person par excellence.

Yet we perceive that the divine power is not exercised in a rigid, unvarying way. The material being around us, all bodies as such including our own, come into being and pass away again, making place for other beings. In the third proof it is argued from a universe of contingent beings (i.e., beings that are able not to be) to the existence of a necessary being, one that cannot not be.

Why is this? Because in an indefinite span of time (since each being we know is by its material nature destined eventually to cease to exist) then such a being by now would already have become nothing. The continuing existence of contingent being, therefore, demands the existence of a necessary being which both produces it in being and maintains it in being.

Yet, since this universe must necessarily show forth the hand of its maker, and since no one created being can do this adequately, the universe does this by varying types of being that, in their diversity, represent the single divine perfection. Hence the presence of both contingent and necessary being in the universe (the latter still, however, dependent upon the divine will), with, under contingent being, the action of free will. This faculty is not determined to one single act, but by choice may act or not act, and act in one way or in an opposing way. Yet it is clear that this operation of free will (since all being, including the free will, depends totally upon the divine will both as to existence and activity) does not have an existence and operation that is outside the divine control, or that may, absolutely speaking, withstand the divine control.

Finally, as is apparent from the awesome overall consistency and order of the universe (an order which is maintained without any possession of intelligence on the part of the elements other than those which are rational beings), there must be a supreme or divine intelligence ordering all things to the end preconceived by that intelligence, ordering being for the sake of some purpose or intent, and the order being measured by that purpose or intent. This is the conclusion of the fifth proof, from the consistency and order in the universe.

From this one is aware that all things are ordered infallibly by God—their total being and action depending upon him who has produced them from nothing, and to which they would return should the divine will be withdrawn—to the end that he has determined. They are moved to that end according to the natures that God has created. On the one hand, nonrational nature, ultimately ordained to the rational nature, moves to the end ordained with necessity; while the rational nature moves toward it freely, with a freedom (image of the divine freedom) which nevertheless does not step outside the divine power, but remains subject to it. There is no difficulty in conceiving that God should move our wills freely toward himself, since they belong to him more than to us. The mystery lies in how the will can turn away from God, even supposing the divine permission. Yet such is the case—always reversible, however, by the divine will.

What is the end to which God has ordered the universe? Since God is himself infinitely all-good, all-perfect, and the fullness of being, he himself is the end of all things which he wills to be. Thus every being that is brought into being is given thereby a share of the divine being; and since goodness is seen to consist in being, the good it receives in the form of being is an act of the divine love—love in its most perfect sense being the wishing of good to another. For the rational beings created by God, human beings and (as stated by revelation) angels, this sharing of the divine good takes the special form of actually knowing, loving, and enjoying the divine good on the divine level, with the love of friends sharing in the same one infinite good.

Needless to say, while the love of God to the best of one's ability is the highest and most divine occupation of the human being, to be able to see God as he is in himself and to love and enjoy him as a friend, can only be by a special act of God's love elevating the human being above all the demands of his nature to the divine plane. This goal is knowable to the human being only by God's revelation—although one can argue that God's divine intent is already discernible in the fact that he has deliberately implanted in the human being's nature the intellectual appetite to seek the cause of any effect, and that God himself, as he is in himself, as the cause of all things, is the only answer to that divinely implanted appetite which he has not implanted in order then to thwart.

Knowledge of God through reason is, then, knowledge through the external world perceived as an effect of God. From effects one arrives at a knowledge of God as the cause reflected in these effects, a cause infinitely excelling these effects which cannot do full justice to the divinity. This knowledge, as already stated, is to a great extent negative, as when one realizes that God is infinite, meaning nonfinite; that he is eternal, meaning not in time.

The positive aspects of the knowledge of God consist in perceiving that those aspects of reality known to us which do not contain in their concept any note of limitation or imperfection, such as being, goodness, intelligence, love, are true of God in a much higher way, reflected in, but not equated by, the effects in the universe.

This knowledge in which something seen in an effect is predicated of the cause, but necessarily in a way that connotes a whole new degree of perfection we cannot fully grasp, is called analogical knowledge. The classic example is that of the term *healthy* as applied both to the living animal and to medicine. The living animal is healthy essentially, the medicine is healthy insofar as it causes health; thus, in a related, but not equal, sense. So too are terms such as *being* and *good* as true essentially of God, and true only in a lesser and analogical way of the being of the universe.

C. God's Attributes

In considering knowledge of God, one first realizes he cannot be a body, since this latter is by nature limited to its form—and nothing limits itself. Furthermore, not only is the composition of matter and form, essential to bodies, necessarily excluded from God, but likewise all composition—that of potency and act (as already mentioned), essence and existence (true of contingent being, able not to exist), genus and specific difference (concomitant to matter), substance and accident (the latter implying being by addition to the former).

The simplicity or noncomposition of God is a simplicity of perfection, since in God there can be no restrictive aspects—as composition would entail, one element of the composite naturally limiting the other, by being another being than it. Since perfection implies fullness of being and it is this desired fullness of being which is denoted goodness, God, the supreme being, is necessarily the supreme good.

God is also the supreme beauty. What is beauty? Beauty, like good, is based on form as expressing full actuality of being, but they differ in notion in that good is the object of appetite; whereas beauty regards the cognoscitive powers, being defined as that which pleases when seen. Obviously all the beauty of the universe is some reflection of the divine beauty.

Consequent upon the divine fullness of being is the divine infinity. What is meant by infinity? At first one might define it as that beyond which there is nothing. But a closer inspection reveals that this is actually what the finite is; namely, that beyond which there is nothing of itself. Therefore it is that which is finished (as the word *finite*, from *finis*, denotes), terminated, has come to an end; whereas the infinite cannot come to an end and must be that beyond which there is always something of itself.

Do we know any such infinite? Paradoxically, the infinite we know is contained within the finite, and has the note of unfinished, to be completed—if ever—by the finished or finite. Thus, given a one-foot ruler length, it may be divided in two, and the first half set aside; the remaining half may then be divided in two and the same process repeated. As the pieces are set aside and counted, one will have an ever-increasing number. How long can this go on? Theoretically, there is no end, since each time a remainder is cut in half, a half remains. The one-foot ruler can never be exhausted, while the process goes on to infinity, and number constantly increases.

What is the characteristic of this infinite within the finite? In making the division there is indeed always something beyond, a subsequent segment to be cut, a subsequent unit to be added. However, this beyond is not actual, but purely potential. The next segment to be counted does not exist until it is cut. Meanwhile the number of added segments remains always finite, infinite only in possibility, in a possibility which can never be realized except into a further finite and always confined within the finite.

From the viewpoint of its being unfinished, this infinity is an infinity of imperfection, becoming actual in the finite. Such an infinity is due to a certain formlessness of matter; the more perfect the being, the more indivisible it is.

But we are aware that, as applied to God, we are speaking of an infinity of perfection. In God the beyond is actual; no matter how far one might progress, one does not exhaust the unbounded actuality of God. Because of this, God not only encompasses all things, but is in all things, present to all things, giving them being.

Consequently God is also immutable; that is, there is nothing new to be actualized in God since, by virtue of his being pure act, all possibility is already actualized to infinity. To imply something new in God would be to imply that he was not infinite, that there remained, beyond a present limit of actuality, something yet to be actualized.

In keeping with God's pure actuality, infinity, immutability, he is also necessarily eternal—above time in an everlasting present. In effect, time is marked off by a succession of events measured against some kind of continuous motion, such as that of the earth around the sun or the moon around the earth, enabling one to say that something happened three moons ago. But in God all is actual to infinity; there is nothing new to come. Hence, no time; hence eternity, denoting the changeless present of a being that is pure act, infinite, eternal.

Finally, God is necessarily one, since any divisibility would imply noninfinity—one part excluding the infinity of another part.

D. God in Revealed Truth

Although the names given to God are intended to designate him, nevertheless they are not based on a direct knowledge of his nature, but of that nature as seen through effects. Hence the name *God*, meaning the very divine nature, nevertheless has its content from what is known of God in creatures as the universal provider of all things. Of all the names of God, *He who is* most properly designates him, by acknowledging in him the infinity of being and by its lack of any particular note; since any specific predicate, while stressing one aspect of the infinite divinity (which actually is absolutely one), must necessarily neglect another.

God, the cause of knowledge, knows himself and knows other beings. He knows the latter because it is he who conceives them in the divine mind and wills them to be. And since every aspect of the being of every being is from him, he necessarily knows every being, even the least, in the very core of its being. He knows the future of all being, contingent or necessary, because it is he alone who plans that being and causes it to be in the mode that he wills. And, since God is life, all things coming from God are life in God.

How do things come into being? By an act of the divine will executing what the divine intellect has conceived. (The distinction of faculties is, of course, based on our grasp of God through effects which display these different characteristics, while the divine being itself is absolutely one. Thus we attribute realization to the divine will.) Clearly this will shall be always fulfilled, since all being in the universe, created from nothing by God, remains completely subject to the divine power. Yet that power is such that it can allow free will to turn, if it wishes, away from the divine will. This is no absolute power to turn away. Yet God has given the human being the consciousness that, within the divine power, he has nevertheless sufficient freedom to be accountable for his acts.

What then of evil in the world? The great cataclysms (earthquakes, tidal waves, floods) and the individual suffering, how is God related to these? Clearly, if he has created a universe in which such physical evils can come about from the normal functioning of the laws of nature, he is the cause of those evils; but not for their own sake, since the physical universe exists for the rational creature, who in turn exists for God. Consequently, all events, whether physically good or bad, are part of a steady intended progress of the rational creature turned toward God to his ultimate happiness. This is stated succinctly by St. Paul: "All things work to good for those who love God" (Rom. 8:28).

What God does not intend, of course, what it is impossible for him to intend, is a turning away from the divine will, which, as identical with the divine essence and the divine goodness, is the end of all things. Nevertheless, since all things are in the divine power, sin, this turning away, need not be permitted by God, who yet is no way responsible for it. Once permitted, the divine mercy can still, if it wishes, turn the sinner back. Such is an eternally generous and loving intervention of the divine power.

This brings one to the divine love. Love desires the good that it does not yet possess, and enjoys it when possessed. For God there is the eternal enjoyment of the divine good possessed, identical with the divine being. But from the existence of the universe it is evident that God loves others also. The reason is that the being of everything is its good; and the universe has this good which God wishes it to have and which is thereby, as a free giving of good to another for the other's good, an expression of love. This is true especially if it entails, as in the case of the rational creature, a wishing of good to another considered as oneself, which is the good of friendship.

The measure and spontaneity of the divine love may be seen from the fact that, in a creature's love for the good, the good in the one to be loved must already exist if it is to arouse love; whereas with God the divine love not only loves the good, but itself graciously first creates in the creature the very good that makes him lovable. Does God love some things more than others? Plainly, since the degree of love is proportional to the degree of good, for whatever being God freely gives more good, there is an accompanying greater love.

An aspect of the divine love is the divine mercy, mercy especially referring to having pity on the defect of the one loved, and relieving that defect as though it were one's own. Such an attribute belongs most of all to God who is alone without need or defect himself, and who can restore all the defects of others. This he does most specially in giving his pardon and love to the sinner who in no way merits it.

The divine plan in the divine mind whereby God lovingly wishes to share his goodness and creates the rational creature in his own image to share with him the divine happiness is called divine providence. In executing it, God chooses to use secondary causes, which thereby are given a share in his causality. Yet the divine being remains still that which is absolutely in direct sustaining contact with every being. This infallible contact and guidance toward himself of the rational creature is called predestination, which, while moving the rational creature toward himself freely, is nevertheless infallibly fulfilled as in everything which God wills.

It is plain from human consciousness that it is possible to resist and turn away from the divine call, a call given to all. "God wishes all human beings to be saved" (1 Tim. 2:4). For someone to turn away and separate himself eternally from God, he must do so seriously and freely, and against the expressed will of God, thereby himself determining his destiny. One can only be lost by one's own decision, which, as freely taken, God need not reverse.

But the power of the divine love is not thereby condemned to unfulfillment, since the sharing of his love which God wills to be, will inevitably be; and those who are called to it will freely and infallibly embrace it, turning, if God wills, even from determined sin. In this fulfillment it is evident also that God has determined that, at various times, his grace will be granted as an answer to prayer for oneself or others.

In conclusion one bows before the divine power, a power exercised to communicate divine love to human beings and angels, and wherein it is always love and mercy which predominate. Total submission to the will of God is intended only that the rational creature may move unerringly to the intended joy of the eternal sharing of the divine happiness.

As noted elsewhere (p.91), the proof of the existence of God through motion depends on the truth of the axiom *Whatever is moved, i.e., is in motion, is moved by another.* This axiom is contradicted by Galileo's successful supposition implied in the first law of motion that a body in motion, to continue in motion, does not require a mover. Such suppositions, as with subsequent suppositions of relativity, are held, not as proved, but because, once made, they reliably lead to predictable desired results. Such a supposition does not of itself refute the axiom *Whatever is moved, i.e. in motion, is moved by another.*

Meanwhile, an analysis of the conception of motion without a mover is confronted by the contradiction inherent in the concept of "lifting oneself by one's bootstraps." If one supposes one part as moving and another as moved, then, since they are joined, the moving part is necessarily moved by the moved part, is both moving and moved—an intrinsic contradiction. Hence one is obliged to say that, whether successfully explainable or not, a body in motion requires an outside mover. Motion is a new transient being over and above that which is moved, as in the case of a movement of the hand.

Recognizing the difficulty, science proposes an imaginary, undiscovered and unproved and self-contradictory entity called inertia to account for why a body keeps moving when it is moving, and does not move when it is immobile. One need only ask: "What is it?" This imagining is a recognition that motion is a transient being over and above the being of the thing. Like all being it must ultimately be produced and transiently maintained by God, however explained ("in whom we live and move and have our being" Acts 17: 28).

Chapter 9

Transition to Modern Science

A. Laws of accelerated motion
B. Universal gravitation
C. Light as waves in ether
D. Is the ether there?
    1. Theories about the ether
    2. Einstein's special relativity
E. General relativity
    1. Gravitational and inertial force
    2. Light has mass
    3. Curvature of space

After the realistic or physical view of the universe arrived at by Aristotle, Galileo inaugurated a transition to a dialectical approach, in which an abstract mathematical view is substituted for a physical one. This approach consists in taking as the basic motion of the universe the supposition that a body in motion will continue of itself in uniform rectilinear motion indefinitely, if unaffected by any other force.

This new view is a dialectical one, since it is aimed at a theory which will supply principles from which the appearances of things may be deduced or explained, without regard to whether this theory corresponds in every detail to demonstrable reality. Thus, in the supposition of a body in motion continuing to move of itself without requiring the action of any external mover, Galileo is omitting an aspect of motion which, in any realistic interpretation, Aristotle considered unable to be omitted. Aristotle himself is responsible for the distinction between demonstrative and dialectical propositions, the former conforming strictly to reality and the latter merely satisfying the appearances.

This approach is also mathematical in that it abstracts from sensible reality to conceive of a body moving uniformly in a straight line in a mathematical, placeless space—a situation nowhere realized, or realizable, in sensible reality.

It should be noted here that the transition from a realistic and demonstrable view of the universe to a purely dialectical one under Galileo is not to be identified with the transition from the Ptolemaic (geocentric) system to the Copernican (heliocentric) system. This shift occurred nearly a century earlier, with the publication in 1543 of Copernicus's work, *On the Revolutions of the Heavenly Spheres*. These two systems represented simply two successive views of a same physical universe, understood in the same realistic or Aristotelian terms, with the Copernican being substituted for the Ptolemaic on the basis of its being better able to account for the various aspects of the heavenly motions. Such motions are rendered complicated when the earth, in keeping with one's first impression, is taken as the center; but are rendered simple and harmonious when the sun is taken as the center.

In this new view of the universe brought about by substituting the sun for the earth as the center, everything else, however, remained the same. Motion, for example, would continue to require a mover from without. The basic motion of the universe would continue to be, not rectilinear motion, existing only between the center and periphery of the spherical universe, but the continuous circular motion of the heavenly bodies.

Galileo's shift, however, consisted in a whole new outlook. It was a shift from the physical to the mathematical sphere, which necessarily entailed that all subsequent explanation of the universe would be, not in terms demonstrable to the senses, but in dialectical terms with abstract mathematics supplying formulas. Such formulas, while not explaining the physical reality, would nevertheless permit one to deduce answers for various practical situations. Thus the dialectical consideration of a circle as a polygon of a certain number of sides allows one to compute a numerical ratio between a rectilinear diameter and a rectilinear polygon taken as a substitute for a nonrectilinear circle.

A. Laws of Accelerated Motion

Galileo, in his epoch-making work, *Dialogue on Two New Sciences*, expresses his discovery of a mathematical expression for the regularly increasing velocity of a uniformly accelerating body, and likewise for the distance covered by the body during a given period of acceleration. Galileo derived these laws from visual experiments, set up with the simplicity of genius. He was able to work out these laws by using an inclined plane with regular space intervals marked off on it, along which a ball would roll, with a water clock (i.e., a clock which would mark off uniform time segments by uniform quantities of water flowing into a receptacle) to measure the times.

Employing such a plane and letting the ball roll down a graduated track while the water clock marked off regular time intervals, Galileo noted that, if the ball covered 1 space interval in the first measured time interval, it would cover 3 more space intervals during the second time interval, 5 more during the third time interval. This could be stated as follows: in 1 time interval, 1 space covered; in 2 time intervals, 4 spaces (i.e., $1 + 3$) covered; in 3 time intervals, 9 spaces (i.e., $1 + 3 + 5$) covered.

It is clear from this that the spaces covered are proportional to the squares of the times; and that the distance covered after a certain number of time units will be equal to the distance of the original space unit (corresponding to the first time unit) multiplied by the square of the times. Thus, supposing that a ball rolling down an inclined plane is seen to cover 10 feet in the first second; then, taking 10 feet as the space unit and 1 second as the time unit, the distance the ball will roll down the plane in 3 seconds will be 10×3^2, namely 90 feet.

Once this formula is achieved, one can then go on and take the case of a body in perpendicular free fall simply as the extreme case of an inclined plane (i.e., a plane inclined to 90 degrees). Experimentally one will discover that such a body falls 16 feet (approximately) in 1 second (i.e., the first second). Such a body would then fall 16×3^2 (144) feet in 3 seconds. This formula for the distance covered by a free-falling body in a certain time, is usually expressed as follows: s(distance) $= \frac{1}{2}gt^2$. Here g equals 32 feet, t is expressed in seconds, and $\frac{1}{2}g$ represents the original space unit (16 feet) corresponding to the distance the body falls in the first second.

From this same experiment on the inclined plane it is also possible to derive the formula for the increase of velocity (or instantaneous velocity). In effect, Galileo points out that a regularly increasing velocity will be one which will acquire equal increments of velocity in equal times.

If one turns back to the original experiment, where the accelerating ball covers first 1 space, then 3 additional spaces, then 5 additional spaces (in three successive equal time units), one will notice that the regular increase of velocity per time unit takes the form of 2 more space units covered than the number covered in the previous time unit (i.e., 1, 1 + 2, 1 + 2 + 2).

Consequently, if after every time unit, there is an increase of velocity of 2 space units per time unit; the velocity after 1 time unit, where the body has started from zero velocity, will be 2 space units per time unit. After 2 time units it will be 2 more (the regular increment), i.e., 4 space units per time unit. After 3 time units it will be 6 space units per time unit.

One sees therefore that the velocity after any given number of time units (such as 3) will be equal to the number of time units multiplied by twice the original space unit (such as 16 feet, corresponding to a time unit of 1 second, in the case of a free-falling body). This means that the formula for the velocity of a regularly accelerating free-falling body after t seconds will be that amount of seconds multiplied by twice the unit distance (namely, 2 x 16, or 32, the value denoted by g). Hence the formula will be as follows: $v = gt$.

The dialectical nature of such formulas, which work so admirably, may be seen from the fact that they are derived from considering the motion of the ball down the inclined plane, not as a single continuous motion (which it actually is), but as a series of segments of motion from point to point, i.e., the regularly spaced measuring points on the inclined plane. If the body were actually to be at these points in the course of its motion, it would have to stop at each one of them and then start again; since, while a body is in motion, it cannot be at a point. Nevertheless, by considering a moving body as though it were at a succession of points, i.e., by taking a dialectical approach, one arrives at extremely useful formulas. These formulas are dialectical in that, while incorporating postulates from which one can deduce answers that accord with the appearances, they are nevertheless not based on a demonstrated conformity with reality, with the real situation.

B. Universal Gravitation

What did Newton add to Galileo's basic concept of a body continuing of itself in uniform motion in a straight line? He added the concept of universal gravitation. Previously all elements were considered as moving toward the earth's center in a superimposed order of earth, water, air, and fire, with the heavenly bodies, starting with the moon, having no gravitational effect at all. The reason was that all gravitational motion was that of an element toward its proper graduated place, whereas the place of the heavenly bodies was that of the spheres in which they revolved. With the advent of Newton's concept of universal gravitation, every body was considered as attracting every other body, the attraction of the bodies for one another being proportional to the product of their masses: $m_1 \times m_2$.

By combining this concept with Galileo's concept of the basic motion of bodies as that of motion in a straight line, Newton was able to add to Galileo's laws of accelerated motion. His new added law was that the gravitational attraction of masses for one another was inversely proportional to the square of their distances: $m_1 \times m_2/d^2$.

Galileo had already conceived of interpreting the curve traced by a falling body which has been given a motion along a line parallel to the horizon as the component of two motions. These two motions would be the rectilinear motion of the body in the direction in which it had been projected (e.g., parallel to the horizon or tangential to the earth) and the perpendicular downward motion of the body caused by gravitation.

He was thus able to plot out the curve on a graph. Each successive point represented, at regular time intervals, the component of a certain distance traveled horizontally at the uniform projected velocity, with an accelerating distance traveled vertically in keeping with the formula for distances covered by free-falling bodies in regular time intervals. Thus, while the coordinates of the horizontal axis would be proceeding at regular intervals (e.g., 1, 2, 3, and so on), the coordinates of the vertical axis would be proceeding according to squares (e.g., 1, 4, 9, and so on). These successive rectilinearly attained coordinates, if connected, represent a parabola, the actual curved reality.

In line with this same thinking, Newton conceived that, if the body in question, elevated above the earth (e.g., on top of a high mountain), were each time given a greater horizontal impetus, the curve of its fall to earth would extend farther. Finally one could theoretically reach the point where, because of a greater and greater horizontal impetus, the body would eventually fall in a curve which, instead of meeting the earth, would run parallel to the curvature of the earth. The body would be in orbit around the earth!

Newton conceived of the motion of the moon around the earth, of the planets around the sun, as just such a case. That is, the moon's rectilinear motion, at right angles to the perpendicular motion of gravity toward the earth, was of a sufficient impetus that, even though by the motion of gravity it kept falling toward the earth; nevertheless the curve of its fall caused it, not to strike the earth, but to perpetually curve around the earth. This is precisely the principle, anticipated by Newton, later applied to orbiting spaceships.

Conceiving the motion of the moon around the earth as a component of a rectilinear motion perpendicular to the force of gravity, and that force itself, Newton set out to calculate the distance which the moon (while moving rectilinearly by its own motion) was also falling perpendicularly toward the earth—compared to the distance covered by a body closer to the earth in the same interval. Having detected that the moon appeared less strongly attracted to the earth than bodies closer to the earth (e.g., a stone dropped from a certain height), he set out to compare the two.

Knowing how far a body close to earth fell in a certain interval, he set out to calculate how far the moon fell toward earth from its rectilinear course during the same interval. In doing this he was able to disregard the mass of the moon since, in the Galilean notion, all bodies fell toward earth at an equal velocity regardless of their mass.

The distance Newton had to calculate was the difference between what would have been the position of the moon in a rectilinear course after a certain interval from a certain point of its orbit, and the actual position of the moon after such an interval. The difference would represent how far the moon had fallen. Newton calculated this using the Pythagorean theorem on rectilinear coordinates.

What he found was that the comparative distances of a body falling to earth during a certain interval and the fall of the moon during that same interval were in the inverse ratio of the square of the radius of the earth (i.e., the distance from the center of the earth to its surface) to the square of the distance from the center of the earth to the center of the moon.

Thus Newton was able to enunciate his mathematical contribution to the dialectical interpretation of physical reality, namely, that the attraction of two masses for one another, expressed by the velocity of their accelerating motion toward each other, is inversely proportional to the square of their distances: $m_1 \times m_2/d^2$. This, of course, also explains why the same body accelerates as it approaches the earth, since there is a gravitational force of attraction between the two bodies.

C. Light As Waves in Ether

Simultaneous with Newton's formula for universal gravitation was his theory on light. This theory resulted in the concept of white light as composed of light rays representing all the colors of the spectrum. Light as conceived of by Newton remained, however, a rectilinear, corpuscular motion, traveling through empty space when it traveled from the sun to the earth.

Newton's Dutch contemporary, Huygens, however, adequately demonstrated the wave nature of light, detected, for example, by the interference lines when light waves flowed around small objects. Since a wave could not be transmitted without a medium, it was therefore necessary to fill up the presumed empty space between the light-emitting sun and planets, such as earth, so that the wave motion of light could be transmitted. The medium was called ether by Huygens, the same name as that given by the ancients to the fifth element, out of which the heavenly bodies were assumed to be composed.

An analogy denoting the impossibility of a wave without a medium is easily found in *Alice in Wonderland* by Lewis Carroll. When his famous Alice encounters the grinning Cheshire Cat perched on the branch of a tree, this cat then proceeds to vanish gradually, starting from the tip of its tail, until only the grin remains—an accident existing without a substance.

One will note, however, that this filling up of empty space would not occur from an Aristotelian viewpoint, since in his *Physics*, Aristotle, from his analysis of place and space in the cosmos, concludes that there is no void within the universe. Hence the space between the sun and the planets, even if no medium were physically detected, could not be void.

D. Is the Ether There?
1. Theories about the Ether

Although the positing of a medium, the ether, was necessary to account for the wave motion of light through the space of the solar system—and, in fact, throughout the universe with its light-emitting stars—no physical effects of this ether could be detected. The most famous attempts to do so were those of the Michelson-Morley experiment, originating at the Case Institute in Cleveland in 1877.

These experiments were conducted on the supposition that the universe was now filled with an immobile ether, the vehicle of light. In that case, the earth could, in its course around the sun, be considered in the manner of a ship moving through an immobile sea. Given such a situation, one could then conceive of it as though the earth were a vessel moored in stream with the stream running by it. In other words, the same effect would be present whether the earth were moving through an immobile ether; or the earth was moored, and the ether was moving by it.

Since, from such a moored position, if a vessel then proceeded to move a certain distance up the stream and return, it would take a longer time than for the same vessel to go an equal distance sidewise to the bank and return; it was conceived that if a light ray went a certain distance and returned in the direction of the ether flow, this would take a longer time than if a light ray went a same distance sidewise and back. This difference of time would show up in interference lines when the two light rays met on their return.

Despite the refinement of these experiments, no time lag could be detected. No sign of the ether was forthcoming. An Irish physicist, Fitzgerald, suggested that the reason for no time lag was that the length of a moving body contracted in the direction of its motion—the Fitzgerald contraction. Hence the arm along which the light traveled when it was moving into the ether contracted with the earth's motion. This contraction shortened the length of the trip forward and back, and thereby shortened the time necessary and made it equal to that of the light which would go to the end of the sidewise arm and return.

The Fitzgerald contraction explained the fact that light appeared to show no time lag as it moved against the ether, by the supposition that the length of bodies contracted in the direction of the motion, as that motion increased in velocity. The longer time that light would be expected to take in going back and forth, on the arm of the Michelson-Morley apparatus directed into the ether, would therefore be eliminated by the arm's simultaneous shortening in the direction of the motion.

This supposition, however, presupposed an immobile ether, through which the earth, and light on the earth, would be moving as the earth moved around the sun. The earth's motion around the sun being calculated at 30 kilometers a second (approximately 20 miles a second), then, when a beam of light was sent along an arm of the Michelson-Morley device in the direction of the earth's motion; this would be comparable to a boat (the light) moving upstream in a current (the ether) which was going by at a rate of 20 miles a second.

This would be expected to retard the up-and-back motion of the light traveling at a rate of 186,000 miles a second. But, according to the experiment, as has already been noted, it did not appear to do so. This failure to detect any time lag between light's going in the direction of the earth's supposed motion through ether and back, as compared to a motion along an equal length sidewise and back, received a suggested explanation by the Fitzgerald contraction, presupposing a proportional contraction in the direction of motion.

But could one not suppose that, instead of the earth's plowing through the ether (and, with it, light rays directed in the direction of the earth's motion), the ether in the region of the earth was carried along by the earth, thereby eliminating the going-against-the-current effect? This supposition would be comparable to considering the ether moving along with the earth as similar to the medium of air being carried along by a moving railway car.

Inside such a car (the moving earth, carrying its ether or medium along with it) everything (specifically, the time taken by light to go in the direction of motion and return) would take place in the same way as though the car were standing still. For example, a fly could fly back and forth with the same ease as though the car were standing still—even though the car might be moving with a velocity in excess of the fly's ordinary maximum speed.

This would then explain why light would be found to be moving with the same velocity in any direction on a moving earth, just as though the earth were standing still. But certain other findings appeared to eliminate this supposition. In effect, if light was moving with its usual speed of 186,000 miles per second in the direction of the earth's motion, while at the same time the earth was also moving forward with a velocity of 20 miles per second; then an observer in space would note that light was moving with an absolute velocity of 186,000 plus 20 miles per second. This is the same as if a fly, winging down a railway car at a velocity of 15 miles per hour in the motionless air of the car (while the car itself was moving ahead at the rate of 30 miles per hour), would be attaining an absolute velocity, measured by an observer outside the car, of 15 plus 30 (45) miles per hour.

But all measurements indicated that light moved through space always with the same constant velocity regardless of whether the source of the light was moving or not. These measurements were made on the light emanating from pairs of revolving stars. As one star turned toward the earth, while another turned away from it, the light from the star turning toward the earth could be expected to receive an added impetus from the star's forward motion. This is the same as if a ball would be moving faster with absolute motion if it left the hand of a thrower who was at the same time moving forward, than if thrown with the same force by a thrower who was standing still. Despite this prediction, light was never found to be exceeding its velocity of 186,000 miles per second.

Therefore it was concluded that light must always be held as moving with a constant velocity, regardless of whether its source, such as a source on the moving earth, was in motion or not. The calculation of this velocity was first ascertained by the Danish astronomer, Roemer, at Paris in the eighteenth century. Perceiving a time lag in the eclipsing of the moons of Jupiter and comparing this to the difference of distance between Jupiter and Earth as they both orbited around the sun (being sometimes on the same side of the sun, sometimes on opposite sides), Roemer attributed this to the fact that light, traveling at a finite speed, was taking a longer time (hence the appearance of a time lag in the perception of the eclipses) to cover the greater distance. Hence he was able to arrive at the first calculation of c. Previously light had been considered as propagating instantaneously.

While light is taken as always moving with a constant velocity (denoted by the symbol c for the velocity of light in a vacuum), this does not mean that it always moves with an identical velocity regardless of the medium. Thus the constant velocity of light is slower in the medium of air or water, as against its velocity in a vacuum by a coefficient proportional to the refraction index of the medium.

The supposition of this constant velocity, however, presents a dilemma to the mythical observer in space. The reason is that, while an observer on earth would see light on earth in a vacuum moving in the direction of the earth's motion with a velocity c, the observer in space would have to add to that velocity the velocity of the earth's motion. He would thus arrive at an absolute velocity which would be the sum of the two. But light cannot exceed its velocity c.

Plainly it is here that the Fitzgerald contraction will have to be used. The mythical observer in space will have to say that the reason why the observer on earth considers that light on earth is moving with the velocity c (even though the earth itself is also moving) is that, in the latter's particular coordinate system (to use a term employed by Einstein), lengths contract proportionally in the direction of the motion. As a result, even though light appears to be moving with a velocity c to the observer on earth, it is actually moving with a velocity less than c to the observer in space who knows that the lengths on the earth against which the speed of light is measured have actually contracted in proportion to the earth's forward motion.

In 1904, a Dutch physicist, Lorentz, elaborated the transformation (subsequently called the Lorentz transformation) required for the following puzzling events. With this transformation an immobile observer in the immobile ether, with light moving at the constant velocity c, could relate to himself the apparently discordant events of another observer on a moving earth, also seeing light moving with the velocity c. The Lorentz transformation consists not only in shortening the lengths in the other system, as supposed in the Fitzgerald contraction, but also in slowing down the clocks (i.e., the time) proportionally.

Thus, with relation to this latter supposition, even though a beam of light on earth traveling in the direction of the earth's motion, from one point to another, would take a longer time than if the earth were at rest (since, during the time the light beam took to go from the first point to the other point, this latter would have advanced a certain amount in absolute space); nevertheless the time increase would not appear, since the clock would be running proportionally slower.

2. Einstein's Special Relativity

The stage is now set for the appearance, in an article published by Einstein in 1905, of the special theory of relativity. It was special, as against a later, more generalized theory appearing in 1914. It treated relativity, since it will do away with absolute immobile ether and absolute motion, and consider all determinations of motion or nonmotion as simply relative to the observer. Einstein, born in Ulm, Germany, and a graduate of the Zurich Polytechnical Institute, was then a twenty-six-year-old employee of the Swiss Patent Office in Bern.

In effect, when the mythical observer in outer space considers the earth as moving through space at 20 miles per second in its course around the sun, how does he know that he himself is immobile? That is, how does one establish a fixed point in the immobile ether, against which absolute motion or rest may then be judged? In the Aristotelian system, the earth was taken as immobile and at rest, and motion could then be judged in reference to the immobile earth. With the substitution of the sun for the earth in the Copernican system, one could then assign the same value to the sun and make it the immobile standard of reference. But on what grounds could one be sure that the sun—and the solar system with it—was not itself moving through space? Really none.

Newton simply made the assumption of absolute space and absolute time, as a kind of rigid three-dimensional structure extending indefinitely in all directions with an equal regular and absolute time accompanying it. Thus he says: "Absolute space, in its own nature, without relation to anything external, remains always similar and immovable. Absolute, true, and mathematical time, in itself, and from its own nature, flows equably without relation to anything external." (Isaac Newton, *The Principia*, Translated by Andrew Motte, Great Minds Series [Amherst, NY: Prometheus Books, 1995] 8). With the positing of an immobile, corporeal ether as the vehicle for light waves, immobile empty space now became filled with the ether.

The ether once posited, one could then possibly identify absolute motion and absolute rest by being able to detect a certain resistance in a presumably moving coordinate system from its motion through the immobile ether. But the Michelson-Morley experiment, set up to reveal any such resistance encountered by a body moving through the ether (where light rays moving in the direction of the earth's motion would play the role of a ship moving upstream against a current), revealed no such resistance. The experiment's data would not even give any reason to postulate an ether. If there is no way of even detecting the ether, then there is no way of detecting absolute motion.

It was at this point that Einstein simply chose to forget about the nondetectable ether, and with it absolute motion. Before him, the concepts about motion underwent a transition from Aristotle to Galileo-Newton. For Aristotle, the downward fall of a stone from the top of the Tower of Pisa would be its natural motion, with an initial horizontal shove off the edge giving that motion a certain deformation. For Galileo, on the other hand, the initial horizontal shove off the ledge would communicate to the body its fundamental uniform motion in a straight line, with the downward curve of the body being explained by a deflection of the original rectilinear motion (horizontal to the earth) by a gravitational force acting upon it.

Whereas Aristotle's concept corresponds to a picture of a real nature, where bodies seek their proper place (e.g., a stone falls downward toward its place, earth, by a natural motion, as fire rises upward); Galileo's concept, the law of inertia, phrased by Newton in the first law of motion, starts from a purely theoretical, dialectical concept. This is a concept of a mythical body moving uniformly and eternally (to no place in particular) in a straight line. Nevertheless, the concepts of absolute motion and rest, of absolute time, were retained.

These were now to be done away with (along with the subsequent ether). In their place would be substituted the notion of the constant velocity of light as the framework against which events would be measured.

The situation of an observer in immobile space, relating to his frame of reference (or coordinate system) events as seen by an observer in another coordinate system, now becomes convertible and relative. In other words, since there is no way of knowing who is in absolute motion and who is in absolute rest, the observer on earth has just as much right to consider that his coordinate system is at rest while that of the observer in space is moving away from him, as the observer in space has to hold the converse. Just as the observer in space (e.g., on the sun which he takes as at rest) is able, by the Lorentz transformations applied to the distances and times of the earth's coordinate system, to relate those events to his frame of reference; so, in an exactly reverse way, an observer on earth, taking the earth as at rest, can relate to his system events in the sun's coordinate system.

That is, in both cases the observer will consider his system as at rest with relation to the other system whose distance from him continues to widen. In his system, light in a vacuum will be moving with the constant velocity c. In another system, light moves with the same velocity. Why is this so? It is because the clocks move slower and the lengths grow shorter with respect to those of the first system, allowing light to cover the greater distance brought about by the moving system in the same apparent time that it would take to cover the shorter distance when the system was at rest.

The suppositions of the Lorentz transformations, namely, that of the time growing slower and the lengths growing shorter proportional to the motion of the system, are truly dialectical. This may be seen from the fact that there is no way of knowing what system is actually at rest.

The reason is that light moves with the same constant velocity in all systems, and the laws of nature are the same in all systems just as they are the same, from the viewpoint of Newton's laws, inside a railway car whether that car is at rest or moving with uniform, nonaccelerating motion. ·Therefore the slowing down of time and the shortening of length in proportion to motion are simply suppositions made relative to another time taken as a norm and other lengths taken as a norm, namely, those of a system taken as at rest.

But if one should choose to consider the first system as at rest, which one is equally entitled to do, then it is the clocks of the second system which slow down with respect to the first, and the lengths of that system which shorten with respect to the first. So the matter of slowing down and shortening is not a matter of experimental perception, but rather a dialectical supposition relative to an arbitrarily chosen point of reference. This supposition is for the purpose of explaining the appearances as seen from that point of reference, the appearance being the apparent constant velocity of light in any system.

This does not prevent one, of course, after having deduced such suppositions from a dialectical picture created to explain appearances, from seeing whether such a supposition might not have some corroboration in reality. For example, one might check the reality of whether astronauts grow older more slowly from having moved at high velocities. Here one must remember that a top velocity for a spaceship of 36,000 miles per hour represents an increase in velocity only up to 10 miles per second as against 186,000 miles per second for light—the limit velocity in relation to which the various transformations are made. Thus one reads in articles that the astronauts have returned to earth some fraction of a second younger than the rest of us (because their time was temporarily slowed down during their high velocity period).

But what this really means is that, if an increase in velocity was really accompanied by a slowing down of time, then one would grow older more slowly at higher velocities. But the supposition that such a thing takes place is not derived inductively from observation, but is, rather, deduced theoretically from a purely imaginary premise, invented solely to explain appearances. It need not therefore follow in the real order. Whether it might or not would have to depend on actual experiential verification. Even then the satisfactory dialectical reason would still not have to be the true reason. In the same way the experiential verification of the supposition *If it rains, the ground will be wet*, by the fact of wet ground does not necessarily mean that it has rained.

E. General Relativity

What leads Einstein to the theory of general relativity? By the theory of special relativity, one will now abandon any knowledge of absolute motion or absolute rest, as being impossible to attain. One will then bring about a unifying view of the cosmos solely by choosing any frame of reference one wishes. For example, one may choose the earth as hypothetically immobile and then relate all other frames of reference to it by means of the Lorentz transformations. This will involve considering the clocks in other relatively moving systems as running slower, and the lengths as shorter.

But this system, whereby one could consider any system as at rest just as validly as any other (e.g., a system taking the earth as at rest just as validly as one taking the sun as at rest) and then proceed to relate all other systems to it through the Lorentz transformations, holds good only so long as the system is either at rest or in uniform (i.e., nonaccelerated) motion in a straight line. In such a system, all the Newtonian gravitational laws hold good whether the system is in motion or at rest—as they do, for example, in a train car moving in such a manner, or an elevator whose upward or downward motion is absolutely uniform. If all contact with the outside were removed, one could not tell, from the speed of light and from the fulfillment of the Newtonian laws, whether the system was in motion or at rest.

1. Gravitational and Inertial Force

But suppose that the train were to go suddenly around a curve. Now to the inside observer who, while the train was moving at a uniform rectilinear rate, may have considered himself at rest, there is a new phenomenon in his apparently stationary coordinate system, an inertial system obeying Newton's laws. There is a kind of reverse, or repulsive, gravity which pushes him away from one side of the train and up against the other side.

Likewise, for the observer in the elevator, should it begin a regular acceleration downward in free fall, the force of gravitation would disappear. In effect, if someone dropped an apple in the falling elevator, then, since the elevator and the apple would be falling with the same acceleration due to gravity, the apple would not move toward the floor and the laws of gravity would appear to be suspended.

Here one sees what was a clue for Einstein. This insight was that a change from uniform rectilinear motion could produce the same effect as (reverse) gravitation in the case of the train; also that an accelerated rectilinear motion could make gravity disappear in the case of the elevator. He formulated this as the equivalence of gravitational and inertial force. That is, the force of a body whose motion was constantly changing direction (e.g., the centripetal force or reverse gravity in a train rounding a curve) was equivalent to the force of a regularly accelerating body (e.g., the falling elevator) eliminating gravity by its downward motion.

The equivalence of gravitational force and accelerated motion was proposed by Einstein in a thought experiment in a paper in 1914, in which Einstein imagined the equivalent of a spaceship moving through nongravitational space. The ship and all the objects in it would be considered as moving along at a regular, uniform velocity—in an upward direction, let us say. To an inside observer with no view of the outside there would be no sensation of motion or of gravity. But suppose that the spaceship then began to accelerate, without this acceleration being communicated to the objects within it. Then the feet of the inside observer would be pressed against the deck with what would seem like the force of gravity, and an apple released from the hand would fall toward the deck with what would appear to be gravity.

Would there be a crucial experiment to discern whether indeed the spaceship was simply accelerating, or rather was motionless in a gravitational field? One might have recourse to a beam of light allowed to shine transversally across the spaceship, parallel to the floor. If the forces of gravity were at work, and the ship was at rest, then the light beam would go straight across, being an energy wave, immune to gravity. If the ship were accelerating, then the light beam would be seen to bend downward, since, due to the ship's upward motion during its transit, it would strike the opposite wall at a point lower than its starting point on the other side.

2. Light Has Mass.

But here is where Einstein introduced another epoch-making concept. This concept was that light had mass, and would therefore also deviate in a gravitational field. This would produce the same effect when the ship was at rest in a gravitational field, as predicted when the ship would be in accelerated motion upward. How could this be put to the test? The only way one could have light rays coming under the influence of a very strong gravitational field would be to watch the behavior of light rays passing close to the gravitational mass of the sun. This could only be checked out at a time when the sun would be sufficiently obscured for one to be able to watch the behavior of light rays passing near it—that is, during a total eclipse. This occurred in 1919 and confirmed Einstein's prediction, not to his surprise.

Why should light have mass in the first place, as it was not a substance, but rather a wave motion in a substance, namely, the ether? But, since Einstein had done away with the ether, it was necessary to give light itself a certain corpulence or mass for its voyage through empty space, a mass surrounded by a field of energy.

Further still, with the concept of the identification of gravitational mass and accelerated motion (embodying kinetic energy) under the aspect of similar effects being able to be produced by either one interchangeably, Einstein was moving toward the basic concept of the identification of mass and energy. In this concept mass would not be something wholly distinct from energy, but rather highly concentrated energy. He even arrived at a formula stating the equivalence of mass and energy, the famous $E = mc^2$.

How was this obtained? Light was known to exert a certain impact of energy on a surface. A Russian physicist, Lebedev, subsequently confirmed in the laboratory that the light momentum was equal to twice the amount of reflected energy divided by the velocity of light: light momentum $= 2E/c$. At the same time this light momentum would be equal to the mass of the light multiplied by the change of velocity caused by the impact—a change from a forward velocity to an equal velocity in reverse, a change therefore equal to twice the velocity: light momentum $= 2mc$.

Putting these two expressions together, one has $E = mc^2$. This means, of course, that a very small amount of mass equals, if transformed, a formidable amount of energy. The energy released by a 20-kiloton atomic bomb would be equivalent to one gram of mass.

Instead of ether-filled space, one would now have the mass of light traveling through space, surrounded by a periphery of energy. Light itself would be considered an electromagnetic wave, occupying those wavelengths perceptible by the eye. Similar electromagnetic fields of different wavelengths would be caused by electric currents and magnets. Here again one would have the concept of the energy's being concentrated in the actual mass of the electrons constituting the current, or the mass of the magnet—with the surrounding fields representing that energy in a diluted form.

Needless to say, from a realistic viewpoint, it would be better to consider energy as diluted mass, than mass as concentrated energy; since energy is expressed in the form of a motion and there has to be something to move, i.e., mass understood as a substance. Thus wind, by its motion, delivers a certain energy, such as to windmills. But there could be no such energy motion if there was not a certain mass of air to be moved. Hence the impact of an atomic explosion must depend on mass to convey the motion.

What was Einstein's goal in the theory of general relativity? His goal was to come up with a unifying picture which would embrace not only all systems either at rest or moving with uniform rectilinear motion—systems in which the Newtonian laws would be true and which could be related to one another by the Lorentz transformations—but also systems not moving in relation to one another with uniform rectilinear motion, systems in which the laws of Newton did not seem to hold good. Examples of the latter would include the train sharply rounding a curve, the falling elevator, the accelerating spaceship with its synthetic gravity.

3. Curvature of Space

In keeping with such a search, and in keeping with the supposition of mass as simply highly concentrated energy with lesser energy fields radiating out from it, Einstein, encouraged by the apparent bending of light rays in the sun's gravitational field, arrived at the conviction of the curvature of space. That is, space is signified for us by light rays, and, since those rays have mass, the rays (and with them space) are curved by nearby gravitational fields centering around concentrations of mass. The light-ray space of the universe as a whole is curved around the central mass of the universe.

The curvature of space could therefore tend to reunite, in a single general relativity theory, both uniform rectilinear motion and nonuniform, nonrectilinear motion. What would appear to be rectilinear motion to one observer, assuming light to be coming to him rectilinearly, would really be, on the assumption of the curvature of space, nonrectilinear. Newtonian laws of gravitation might not be present in one state and absent in another, but might simply represent different states, accelerated or nonaccelerated, of the same system.

One of the deductions from Einstein's general theory of relativity, involving curvature of space around large gravitational masses (e.g., the sun) led to a satisfactory explanation of a 43-second lag in the precession of the perihelion of Mercury around the sun, unexplainable by pure Newtonian theory.

A further conclusion of the general theory is that we live in a non-Euclidean world, where the geometry is Riemannian geometry, with triangles of more than 180 degrees. Thus, if astronomers on Earth, Venus, and Mars sighted along lines between those three planets around the sun, the lines (because of their curvature due to the sun's gravitational field) would come in at the angles as arcs, not as straight lines. And the resulting triangles would have more than 180 degrees. This would be likened to a triangle traced on the surface of a terrestrial globe. Such a triangle, with the equator for its base and two meridians (meeting at the North Pole) for its sides, would already have 180 degrees just with the two base angles. This triangle traced on a globe does indeed represent curved space—what one would have if one took two-dimensional flat space, such as that of plane geometry, and then bent it onto the surface of a sphere.

Would we be living in such a space if light rays curved because of massive gravitational fields, producing a veritable curvature of space? Would we be in the dark about this, thinking light was coming to us rectilinearly, until the measurement of interplanetary triangles (whose angles would add up to more than 180 degrees) would convince us that we are really in a curved space, comparable to the surface of a globe? Not really. The reason is that the very supposition about light, which at first was supposed as rectilinear and later turned out to be curved, presumes our simultaneous grasp of both rectilinear and curved in order to make such corrections. In other words, these corrections are based on our discerning that what seemed to be rectilinear, is not really.

And in effect, the initial discerning of the bending of light rays, when coming from the stars and passing through the sun's gravitational field, depended upon being able to discern between the real position of the star (situated by rectilinear coordinates) and the apparent position of the star due to the bent rays being considered as rectilinear. As with all common sensibles, one of which is shape (e.g., the shape of a light ray), a final decision may depend upon several approaches. Thus a pencil half submerged in a glass of water looks broken to the eye, but another sense, touch, shows definitively that it is not. In the same vein we could state that a curving of light rays might make a given space look curved, while other investigation might show it to be rectilinear, or conversely.

In the theory of relativity, there are transformations relating not only to the space-separating systems moving with respect to one another, but also to the times in the different systems. Therefore space and time will vary proportionally as the system approaches the speed of light, taken as the constant against which all else is measured. Because of these transformations, necessarily the relativity world-picture will include both space and time in the space-time continuum. In such a continuum the three dimensions of space, for diagram purposes, are reduced to two with the time dimension then occupying the third.

Needless to say, all these transformations (e.g., the slowing down of time, the shortening of lengths) could be noticeable only when one is dealing with velocities approaching the speed of light. But the everyday world, with its far slower velocities, operates without them. However, Einstein's general relativity theory comprehends Newtonian principles, and also takes in cases exceeding the Newtonian framework (where high velocities require Lorentz transformations), and comprehends the rectilinear universe as a curved universe that only looks rectilinear. It is this general relativity which is now considered as the overall theory. Its purely dialectical nature—which does not exclude practical applications—may be seen from the fact that its bedrock is the constant velocity of light. Yet this constancy is taken only as a supposition, insofar as the clocks and lengths which measure it may with perfect validity be taken by an observer from another system as inaccurate.

Current physics textbooks, such as Giancoli, present relativity's time dilation (slowing down of time proportionate to velocity) by the dialectical expedient of considering one light beam as two. In a moving car a dropped coin appears to the driver to drop vertically but is actually moving in a longer parabola, as perceivable by an outside observer. Similarly in a spaceship a reflected beam to the roof appears vertical, but is actually moving and returning diagonally as truly perceived by an earth observer. A shorter beam means shorter time in terms of measurement by the speed of light—but the shortness here, and hence the slowness, is fictitious.

Chapter 10

The Theory of Everything

A. Dreams of a final theory
B. Christian belief not like scientific theory
C. Christian theory of everything
   1. A certain, comprehensive creed
   2. Belief in a loving God

The theory of everything. TOE. What does this mean? Just what it says. Science is now willing to explain everything. Even God? Yes, even God. Current theoretical physicists such as Stephen Hawking tell us that if science succeeds in giving us a coherent theory of the universe, we will know "the mind of God." Does this mean the God whom Christians believe to exist? Not exactly, because, from the viewpoint of theoretical physics, we do not know whether this God exists or not. Hence theoretical science's goal of knowing the mind of God represents the formulation of a theory (TOE) which encompasses the single unified grasp of the universe which God would have had in creating the universe—if he exists which, to say the least, we do not know.

There is one problem that TOE immediately and refreshingly solves; namely, the problem of allotting separate, nonconfrontational areas to religion and science, or philosophy and science. The area question is now solved because theoretical science proposes to answer everything. There is no further confrontation with religion or philosophy because the problems the latter try to solve have been taken over by theoretical physics. Insofar as religion is concerned, it is seen as a kind of confirmation of science: the beliefs of the former with regard to the ultimate are now being precisely spelled out by the latter in mathematical formulations. Insofar as philosophy is concerned, it is dismissed in its present state as mere verbalizing.

A. Dreams of a Final Theory

Today science has the feeling that it is coming down the home-stretch toward a theory of everything, the TOE. It is such a theory that inspires the title of Steven Weinberg's recent book, *Dreams of a Final Theory*, reviewed in the *New York Times* Book Review section (March 7, 1993) by Paul Davies, a fellow mathematical physicist, and author of *The Mind of God*. The two titles are more or less synonymous, since the astrophysicist Stephen Hawking is on record as saying that when one achieves the former, one will also have the latter. (Shirley Mac-Laine has already journeyed to Cambridge to ask Stephen Hawking if he believes in a creating God. The answer is: No.)

What is meant by the theory of everything? It would be a formulation, in the terms of mathematical physics, of the ultimate meaning of the universe. The final steps to accomplish this involve uniting in a single formulation the forces ruling the universe, which science has now reduced to four: the strong and weak nuclear forces, electromagnetism and gravitation. Steven Weinberg, a Nobel Laureate, is considered to have united two of these, the weak nuclear force and electromagnetism.

Combined with the unification of the four forces must be the integration therein of the ultimate particles, below leptons and quarks, and which are to be discovered by massive particle accelerators—such as the superconducting supercollider under Waxahatchie, Texas. (Its construction, 2 billion or so dollars along, has been recently suspended by Congress.) The former director of the Fermilab Accelerator outside Chicago, Leon Lederman, another Nobel Laureate, supports with Weinberg the superconducting supercollider in order to arrive at an ultimate particle, the Higgs boson.

This particle suggested the title of his book, *The God Particle*, reviewed along with Weinberg's, the review itself being titled: "The Holy Grail of Physics." His original title, unfortunately, was *The Goddamn Particle*—because of the difficulty of finding it. The publisher said no. Meanwhile *God* is retained in the title. Why? One need only cite the title of the article by Kim McDonald, where the answer is revealed: "When It Comes to Books about Astrophysics and Cosmology, God Sells."

From all the above, the question naturally arises: Will God be included in the theory of everything? Needless to say, the notion of God cannot be omitted from a concept of everything. The position of spokesmen such as Weinberg is that, while a God (if God was known to exist) would be himself the theory of everything, science itself, despite complete openmindedness, cannot arrive at the affirmation of a creating and ruling God. Weinberg expresses nostalgia for such a God who, in addition to existing, would be a caring God (unlike Einstein's "God of Spinoza," who manifests himself in the order of the universe but has no care for the aims and actions of human beings).

Meanwhile, for Weinberg, an existing God would appear to be ruled out by the fact of the Holocaust. "For those who see no conflict between science and religion, the retreat of religion from the ground occupied by science is nearly complete.... I would guess that, though we shall find beauty in the final laws of nature, we will find no special status for life or intelligence. A fortiori, we will find no standards of value or morality. And so we shall find no hint of any God who cares about such things. We may find these things elsewhere, but not in the laws of nature.... Religious people have grappled for millennia with the theodicy, the problem posed by the existence of suffering in a world that is supposed to be ruled by a good God.... Remembrance of the Holocaust leaves me unsympathetic to attempts to justify the ways of God to man" (Steven Weinberg, *Dreams of a Final Theory* [New York: Pantheon Books, 1992] chap. 11).

In sum, for Weinberg, the concept of life as beginning spontaneously at a certain point from a felicitous, but unplanned, juxtaposition of physical elements, and subsequently evolving to its present intelligent state by Darwinian natural selection (subsequent to random mutation of genes), affords an "overwhelmingly successful theory.... It does not seem to me to be helpful to identify the laws of nature as Einstein did with some sort of remote and disinterested God. The more we refine our understanding of God to make the concept plausible, the more it seems pointless.... It would be wonderful to find in the laws of nature a plan prepared by a concerned creator in which human beings played some special role. I find sadness in doubting that we will" (ibid.).

There are, however, scientists who consider that the unproved assumption of a spontaneous origin of life from inert molecules requires an unwarranted act of faith. They point to the astronomical odds against the fine-tuned circumstances required to set the stage for life having come about in the universe fortuitously. On the contrary all the evidence would appear to point in the direction of a universe deliberately set up to evolve to produce the required conditions for life, and ultimately human life. This viewpoint is couched in the anthropic principle (from the Greek *anthropos* 'man').

Nevertheless its proponents in one form or another (such as the astrophysicist John Barrow of the University of Sussex, England) are careful to note that, while the anthropic principle of a universe designed to produce thinking man subsequent to the big bang would indeed account for our present state; nevertheless, this felicitous hypothesis does not of itself eliminate chance as the explanation of all.

Here one notes the strength of the act of faith given by science to the not yet scientifically established all-by-chance hypothesis. This gives rise to a certain irony: whereas in human experience order produced by chance is exceptional, the present state of scientific hypothesis would require an all-by-chance a priori mode of thought unless some kind of antecedent design (as supposed in the anthropic principle) could be proved as an exception.

Finally there remains the Gaia hypothesis (from the Greek *gaia* 'earth'), which takes the reasonable anthropic principle—reasonable because it furnishes evidence that the odds of a human-ordered universe evolving by chance are overwhelming—a step farther toward the solution to be avoided at all costs, while still keeping a nonthreatening stance. The hypothesis: we are indeed living in an ordered and intelligent universe (as science presupposes in order to function), but it is to be looked upon as a single living being, Gaia, of which, unless and until we hear otherwise from outer space, we are that intelligence's current highest expression.

As one can see, from the viewpoint of hypotheses, it would be even more intellectually satisfying to go a final step beyond the person-world of Gaia (with its necessary absorption and suppression of the transcendent identity of the human person) to the concept of a separated God, creator and ruler of the universe, ultimately understood as having made the human being in his own image and likeness. Science, however, will not go this far, but resolutely shuts down its horizon within the material domain, mathematically understood. Consciousness and sentiment are not excluded, but their explanation, if and when forthcoming, must be derived from the material and mathematical.

Therefore we are to consider ourselves as enclosed in this eternal, uncaused physical universe—to be understood by, but not transcended by, the highest evolved intelligence. Hence one finds Stephen Hawking responding, on the basis of a universe considered eternal and uncaused, that if the universe were created in time, a creator would possibly be called for, but in a universe considered eternal no such need would appear to arise.

Not surprisingly, Aquinas has anticipated Hawking. In two successive questions (1.44,46.) in the *Summa Theologiae*, Aquinas demonstrates, first, that everything must be created by God; secondly, that this truth is unaffected by whether or not the universe exists from eternity.

From the above, one has the general outline of the agreed-upon confines by science of the anticipated theory of everything ("The Holy Grail of Physics"): the physical universe, mathematically understood. Within these confines there is no limit to permissible hypotheses, from the somber outlook of a Weinberg with his universe impersonal and unfeeling to the more cheery anthropic principle, and the more feeling, in a pantheistic way, Gaia hypothesis. Needless to say, God is not omitted since today, while theologians are consulted less and less about God, scientists are consulted increasingly so. The notion of God is not discarded but is to be understood in a more enlightened way: the concept of a single unifying mathematical formulation will gradually replace the uncritical projection of the explanation of cosmic order and unity onto an imaginary, separated person.

Thus Davies, author of the book review above, sees religion, not as a threat to science, but as a confirmation of it: what you sought unknowingly, science now explains. Eventually the concept, God, will be properly understood. Carl Sagan tells us: "The idea that God is an oversized white male with a flowing beard who sits in the sky and tallies the fall of every sparrow is ludicrous. But if by 'God' one means the set of physical laws that govern the universe, then clearly there is such a God. This God is emotionally unsatisfying.... It does not make much sense to pray to the law of gravity" (*U.S. News and World Report*, December 23, 1991).

This has already been said by Ludwig Feuerbach who, in his work, *The Essence of Christianity*, stated that the notion of God was simply the projection of a suffering humanity's hopes and desires, whereas the only ultimate reality was the race, multiplying by generation (*das Geschlecht*). Marx and Engels declared their system, dialectical materialism, a.k.a. communism, as being the dialectics of Hegel combined with the materialism of Feuerbach.

B. Christian Belief Not like Scientific Theory

Meanwhile is the Christian waiting for this possibly approaching theory of everything on which science is working? No, he already has one, and it is expressed in the first article of the Apostles' Creed: "I believe in God, the Father almighty, creator of heaven and earth." This states the theory of everything, always and everywhere. Furthermore, it is not stated as theory, i.e., as a scientific concept by definition revisable, but as fact. A scientific theory, while constructed to provide an explanation of some aspect of reality (as the Ptolemaic theory was constructed to explain the apparent motions of the heavenly bodies around the earth), is not by that very fact considered by its formulators as true, i.e., as representing an existent state of affairs in reality. Its continuing retention will depend upon its ability to predict desired practical consequences. Thus the Ptolemaic theory, of the heavens moving around an immobile earth, continues to be preferred over the Copernican theory for celestial navigation, while its users need not in any way consider the theory as true.

At the same time a theory does not of its very nature exclude truth, i.e., representation of a factual state in reality. Thus the Ptolemaic theory, starting from the apparent immobility of the earth and constructing suppositions of the apparent motions of the heavenly bodies, was sufficiently well elaborated in its practical results and predictions as to be eventually taken as true. The heavens were indeed moving around an immobile earth, the central position of the latter being associated with the supposed property of earth, lowest of the four elements (earth, water, air, fire, in ascending order), to be thereby at the center.

What had been overlooked here? The fact that the Ptolemaic, or earth-centered, theory was not the only possible theory. If it had been, it would necessarily have represented the truth, been a factual representation. In other words, something real was causing the appearances; consequently, if only one explanation was possible, that explanation must be a reality. The argument might appear to have been clinched by the supposition that the earth, resting place of the heaviest element, was the universe's natural center of gravity.

Reasons such as this may have made an earth-centered universe certain and a fact for Aristotle and Aquinas, although they were aware that the appearances could also be explained by the earth's rotation. The heavenly bodies were considered as revolving around the earth in concentric orbs. Aquinas, while conceding the ability of the Ptolemaic eccentrics and epicycles to explain the appearances (*Summa Theologiae* 1.32.1.ad 2.), excluded them, because of clashes with reality, from any factual explanation of the heavenly motions, as undertaken in the *Metaphysics* (bk. 12).

As noted above, the notion of theory, as such, does not carry with it the note of right or wrong, true or false. The reason is that it is presented simply as an explanation of appearances, susceptible of being supplanted by a subsequent explanation that could explain the appearances more satisfyingly. Thus the Copernican theory, with the planets going around the sun rather than the earth, satisfied the appearances more gracefully and in a less complicated way than did the Ptolemaic theory with its epicycles and eccentrics. Nevertheless the earth-centered approach continues to retain greater practicality for celestial navigation.

Insofar as today's theoretical science is concerned, not only was the Ptolemaic theory not proved, but neither is the Copernican. Both are simply hypotheses that work, without claim of truth. Not that truth is to be disdained, but since Kant was "awakened from his dogmatic slumber" by Hume, his view that truth about reality is unattainable by the human mind has been incorporated into theoretical science, such as that of Einstein. Objective truth, while an ideal, is unattainable.

In contrast to theory, with its non-truth-claiming stance, there is belief, which, whether substantiated or not, does claim truth, i.e., objective reality. Thus, when one says to someone, "I believe you are lying," this is not being proposed as a theory to explain the appearances (as it well might), but is an affirmation of fact, to the effect that lying is actually going on, an affirmation of which true or false is rightly predictable (whether it can be determined or not).

This is the case with the Christian's theory of everything, as affirmed in the first article of the Apostles' Creed, "I believe in God, the Father almighty, creator of heaven and earth." This article states the existence of God, and that he is the creator of the universe—science's universe—as a fact, not as a supplantable theory. Nevertheless it is clear that what is expressed here as a statement of fact, simultaneously explains the appearances—and even more successfully and coherently than the anthropic principle (when held without God) or the Gaia hypothesis.

Science itself admits the hypothesis of a creating, all-powerful God, separate from the universe, as most comprehensive (see John Barrow, *The World within the World*), yet it is not considered as thereby in place. Why not? The answer: Only if randomness can be disproved as the cause of the order in the universe will the hypothesis of God come center stage. This will not be soon, as randomness as the cause of all, including the origin of life and a presumed evolution thereof by natural selection to the present human species, is not the object of scientific establishment, but of an act of faith. Like any act of faith (including the Christian faith) the holding of it is independent of proof. Belief is held by an act of the will, whereas proof is a demonstration to the intellect, dispensing with an act of the will.

Why is the holding by science of randomness as the cause of the origin of life and of subsequent evolution to rationality by natural selection, an act of faith? It is so because scientists themselves do not consider that such a scenario has been established by any cogent evidence—notwithstanding that it is presented to high school and college students in textbooks as a fact which had actually occurred. Why not call it just another theory—the theory of everything from randomness—capable, like any other theory, of being supplanted? Readers of the literature will note that the theory of everything from randomness is not held as provisional, like other theories (relativity, quantum theory), but as an established fact. It is necessarily held by an act of faith since, by science's own admission, no scientific evidence thereof is for the moment forthcoming.

What is the difference between the act of faith that science makes in the spontaneous origin of life, and subsequent evolution thereof from randomness, and the act of faith a Christian makes in the first article of the Apostles' Creed, "I believe in God, the Father almighty, creator of heaven and earth"? Both save the appearances of life in the universe, although the latter more reasonably than the former, in that there is neither experiential nor theoretic grounds for considering randomness as the ultimate explanation of the awesome complexity of life in general and human physical life in particular. The supposition of a creating, all-powerful God, source of all order and complexity, with all things ordained to himself, is perfectly coherent. Why then is it not the preferred hypothesis, since science is perfectly well aware of it?

Science's answer is that until randomness can be proved to be intrinsically void as the ultimate explanation of life, it will not feel compelled to search for an explanation outside the universe, i.e., in an immaterial God. Meanwhile the universe itself, serenely taken as eternal, requires no explanation. Insofar as the randomness explanation is concerned, while starting with the admission that for the living to arise from the nonliving is impossible, one then goes on to say that, given enough time, the impossible becomes possible, and then probable! This is science's answer (see Joseph S. Levine and Kenneth R. Miller, *Biology: Discovering Life*, 2d ed. [Lexington, MA: D.C. Heath and Company, 1994] 490-99). The ultimate scientific justification for a universe of ever-more-perceived harmony and complexity, surpassing human comprehension, as one of randomness, is simply a case of, in unscientific terms, wishful thinking.

C. Christian Theory of Everything
1. A Certain, Comprehensive Creed

What of the belief in God as creator and ruler? This belief is coherent, satisfying, and holds no intrinsic contradictions (such as that of making chance the source of order). Since as a belief it does not claim proof, what distinguishes it from other scientific hypotheses? First of all, as a belief, it affirms its object as fact, not simply as a concept. Since demonstration is not involved, authority is sought. Thus when one makes an act of faith in the effectiveness of a remedy prescribed by one's physician, one is doing it with one eye on the diploma framed on the wall bearing a medical school's testimony of competence.

In believing the Creed, expressing one's belief in God as there proclaimed, one is doing so because one believes that God himself has revealed this in the preaching of the word. Such a belief in God revealing as the foundation for belief in the articles of the Creed is likewise maintained, as in all belief, by an act of the will. A Christian likewise considers that this act of belief is a gift of God and not something for which one can oneself draw credit. Since this assent is held as deriving from God's goodness, from a God who can neither deceive nor be deceived, it is held with certitude, i.e., with the will's adhering to it without fear of contradiction. This characteristic does not belong to belief in general which, while holding its object as a fact, does not do so with certitude, since the object in question has neither been proved nor immediately perceived.

At this point one will note that the content of faith (such as what one believes in the first article of the Apostles' Creed; namely, that God exists, and exists as Father, and is the creator of heaven and earth) is not necessarily restricted to facts unknowable by reason and which must be revealed in order to be known, such as the Three Divine Persons and the Incarnation. Since human nature in its present fallen state does not necessarily perceive everything knowable about God by reason (starting with his existence and his attributes, such as omnipotence, infinity, eternity), God also reveals these knowable facts to the human being. This scope of God's revelation is stated in Vatican I, where a reference is made to the first article of the *Summa Theologiae* for the same teaching.

Interestingly, spokesmen for science such as Wiener and Whitehead are at one in agreeing that science operates on a belief in the objectivity of the discovered order of the universe. Why is this called an indispensable belief—indispensable since one would not dare to launch a space shuttle if one did not think the order of the universe to be factually valid? It is called a belief simply because science agrees with Kant that one cannot know the natures of things. Hence one cannot know that the laws of physics exist, but one must believe that they exist factually, once discovered, as a precondition for their utilization in human calculations.

If one does not feel bound by the Kantian strictures, as a Christian should not be, one is free to view such discovered laws as part of objective reality, with the process of their discovery (through observation, memory, experience, and the grasping of the universal) as set down by Aristotle on the first page of the *Metaphysics* in describing the origin of art and science.

As is defined in advance, the theory of everything of Weinberg, Barrow, Hawking, and others, is circumscribed by a universe which is material and which is to be evaluated numerically. The theory of everything of a Christian goes beyond this by holding, as a certain fact, the existence of an immaterial God from whom the physical universe proceeds and who is the total explanation of that universe. Part of that explanation consists in holding that the universe began in time, i.e., does not exist from eternity. This has been defined as revealed, by the Catholic Church, in interpretation of the scriptural words of Genesis: "In the beginning...."

Such a fact needs to be revealed since from a purely rational consideration of the universe there is no way of determining whether it began in time or existed from eternity. Even the big bang theory does not intrinsically require an origin of the universe in time. Science visualizes the possibility that the universe could have been opening and closing indefinitely like an accordion.

How does the Christian theory of everything square with the current scientific concept, shared by theoretical physics with biology, of a universe in which life began spontaneously and randomly? Is it necessary to exclude randomness? By randomness one understands the exclusion of any antecedent planning. The Christian faith could concede this insofar as the physical universe is concerned. In effect, Aristotle and Aquinas held for the possibility of such spontaneous generation, laughed at not so recently, and which science now holds.

The Christian faith, however, is more coherent than science, since the latter wishes to get something from nothing, order being produced by nonorder, on an ever-ascending scale, with no scientific basis for this act of wishful thinking. The Christian faith, however, by holding to a God who is the cause of all being, whether foreseeable in the laws of nature or not, reduces randomness to a higher cause, namely, God, who prescribes in his own ordering both events intrinsically predictable by known laws, and events unpredictable in this wise as having no per se cause in nature.

In keeping with this, the spontaneous generation of Aristotle and Aquinas, while having no proper cause in nature, did have a cause above the physical universe, namely, God, acting through the heavenly bodies, with or without spiritual intermediaries, angels. Thus one has the famous statement of Aristotle, "Man generates man, with the sun" (*Physics* 2.2.). So randomness need not be excluded as a cause in physics and biology, provided that randomness is not given as the final explanation, as it currently is in textbooks and theory, with no intellectual cogency. Why stop there? Because to go beyond means God.

2. Belief in a Loving God

But the Christian theory of everything has more: not only an explanation of the physical universe in which unplanned randomness can be made intellectually acceptable (though not thereby proved) by its reduction to the divine planning of an immaterial and all-powerful God, but also to a God who cares, as missed by Weinberg. Thus the Christian faith not only believes in God as a fact and as the creator of all, but in God as Father: "I believe in God, the Father almighty...." Proclaimed as Father, his relationship to creatures made in his own image is not only one of power, but of love. Faith requires one, therefore, not only to look on God as creator and ruler, but also as Father, as one who loves, with love meaning to see the other—in this case each man and woman—as one's own self.

Does the Christian faith believe in, as fact, the concrete manifestation of this love? It does so in the belief in the Incarnation of the Son of God: "God loved the world so much that he gave his only Son, so that everyone who believes in him may not be lost but may have eternal life" (John 3:16). Jesus manifests his own love when he says: "I give you a new commandment: love one another; just as I have loved you, you also must love one another" (John 13:34). That this love was the meaning of his existence he expresses in the words: "A man can have no greater love than to lay down his life for his friends" (John 15:13).

Jesus also makes clear that it is through him in his humanity that we are to arrive at the divinity of the Father in which, with the Son and the Holy Spirit, lies the happiness of the sons and daughters God has created in his own image for that end. Hence one says, at the end of the Apostles' Creed, "I believe in the resurrection of the body and life everlasting." This is to come about through the Son: "I am the Way, the Truth, and the Life. No one can come to the Father except through me" (John 14:6).

The central role of Jesus, the Son of Man, in the destiny of the physical universe, the universe studied by science, is stated by the article in the Apostles' Creed subsequent to the statement of the suffering, death, and resurrection of Jesus and his ascension into heaven: "He is seated at the right hand of God the Father almighty. From thence he shall come to judge the living and the dead."

Jesus set forth this fact, which will be the culmination of the physical universe, in his last words to the Sanhedrin, in which he finally reveals that he is indeed the long-awaited and longed-for Messiah foretold in their history, and the Son of God, in answer to the adjuration of the high priest that he state whether he was the Christ (i.e., Messiah), the Son of God. Jesus answers affirmatively and continues: "Moreover, I tell you that from this time onward you will see the Son of Man seated at the right hand of the Power and coming on the clouds of heaven" (Matt. 26:64).

It is against the background of the articles of faith that the Christian needs to place the physical universe in perspective. In the light of the articles of faith one views the physical universe as something passing and transitory, subordinated to God's plan of bringing all those he has chosen to eternal happiness with himself. When this has been accomplished on the Judgment Day of Christ (Matt. 25:31 ff.), the physical universe will have served its purpose as being the place where those created by God in his own image and likeness will have had the opportunity freely to declare themselves for him as their God, Savior, and ultimate happiness. The physical universe of the cosmologists would then have to be considered somewhat as a passenger ship which no longer has any purpose since all the passengers have permanently disembarked at their final destination, life with God.

However, the blessed will be living with Christ in their glorified bodies, accompanying, but not constituting, their divine happiness in God. Therefore it is understood that the meaning of the words, "new heavens and a new earth" (2 Pet. 3:13)—in the context of Our Lord's words, "Heaven and earth will pass away, but my words will never pass away" (Matt. 24:35)—is that, after the Last Judgment the physical universe will be present, now devoid of corruptible elements, accompanying the glorified bodies of the blessed: "Together the world will be renewed and man glorified" (*Summa Theologiae* 3.suppl.101.1.).

Such a view of the physical universe as transitory, and a means to an end, is more vast than that of contemporary cosmologists who see it as self-contained, with the human race simply as one small evolved part thereof. The Christian sees it as a temporal stepping-stone to eternal happiness with God, whose being, meanwhile, encompasses, penetrates, and enlivens all other being on an infinite scale, as Paul set forth to the Athenians (Acts 17:28).

In the *New York Times* Science section of November 9, 1993, the latest suggested defense was proposed against a detected wandering meteorite capable of bringing life to an end on earth if it crashed. Previously an orbiting atom bomb was proposed which by its impact would cause the meteorite to change course. In this case it would be an unfolded several-miles-wide mirror whose reflected ray would cause a gas reaction in the meteorite, propelling it in a different direction.

What is the Christian's reaction to this possible fateful collision, for which the odds are once every 500,000 years? He should recall that with the certitude of his faith he knows that the inevitable termination of this physical universe as we know it is essentially unpredictable, and inescapable: "But as for that day and hour, nobody knows it.... So stay awake.... You...must stand ready, for the Son of Man is coming at an hour you do not expect" (Matt. 24:35,42,44). Elsewhere Jesus tells us that the coming of the kingdom of God does not admit of observation (Luke 17:20).

How then does one prepare? One endeavors to be, by God's mercy, in the state of grace. Then one can go back to scanning the orbiting meteorites and comets, with the proviso: "Unless God comes to judge the world first, for which I hope I am ready." How totally different this is from a concept of a physical universe going on and evolving indefinitely—in fantasy ways thought up by cosmologists and astrophysicists.

When the Day comes, one knows with the certitude of faith that all the dead will rise again in complete maturity (which would apply to discarded embryos cultivated in vitro, if God has infused in them immortal souls from conception, as, for judgmental purposes, the Church obliges us to envisage) to a "new heaven and a new earth, the place where righteousness will be at home" (2 Pet. 3:13). "The heavens are the work of your hands; all will vanish, though you remain, all will wear out like a garment; like clothes that need changing you will change them" (Ps. 102:25-26).

In contemplating a theory of everything, who has the vaster concept, the Christian or the astrophysicist? For the Christian, knowledge of the heavens is not expected to end with awe of the universe. Rather, the more that concept opens up, the more one has a glimmering of the power of God who makes all this by a simple act of his will.

Bibliography

Aquinas, Thomas. *Commentary on Aristotle's Physics*. Translated by Richard J. Blackwell, Richard J. Spath, and W. Edmund Thirlkel. London: Routledge & Kegan Paul, 1963.

_____. *Commentary on the Metaphysics of Aristotle*. Translated by John P. Rowan. 2 vols. Chicago: Regnery Publishing, Inc., 1961.

_____. *Exposition of the Posterior Analytics of Aristotle*. Translated by R.F. Larcher. Albany, NY: Magi Books, 1969.

_____. *Summa Theologiae*. Edited by T. Gilby. 60 vols. New York: McGraw Hill, 1964-74.

Aristotle. *The Basic Works of Aristotle*. Edited by Richard McKeon. New York: Random House, 1941.

Conway, Pierre. *Aristotelian Formal and Material Logic*. Edited by Mary Michael Spangler. Lanham, MD: University Press of America, 1995.

_____. *Metaphysics of Aquinas*. Edited by Mary Michael Spangler. Lanham, MD: University Press of America, 1996.

D'Abro, A. *The Evolution of Scientific Thought*. 2d ed. New York: Dover Publications, Inc., 1950.

Davies, Paul. *The Mind of God*. New York: Touchstone Books, 1993.

de Bothezat, George. *Back to Newton*. New York: G.E. Stechert & Co., 1936.

De Koninck, Charles. "Abstraction from Matter: Notes on St. Thomas's Prologue to the *Physics*." *Laval Theologique et Philosophique* 13 (1957): 133-96; 16 (1960): 53-69, 169-88.

_____. *The Hollow Universe*. London: Oxford University Press, 1960.

_____. "Random Reflections on Science and Calculation." *Laval Theologique et Philosophique* 12 (1956): 84-119.

Eddington, Arthur. *Space, Time, and Gravitation.* New York: Harper & Row, Publishers, 1959.

Einstein, Albert. *The Meaning of Relativity.* Translated by E.P. Adams. 5th ed. Princeton, NJ: Princeton University Press, 1956.

_____. *Relativity: The Special and the General Theory.* Translated by Robert W. Lawson. New York: Crown Publishers, Inc., 1961.

Einstein, Albert, and Leopold Infeld. *The Evolution of Physics.* New York: Touchstone Books, 1967.

Feynman, Richard P. *Feynman Lectures on Physics.* Vol. 1. Reading, MA: Addison-Wesley Publishing Co., Inc., 1989.

French, A.P. *Einstein: A Centenary Volume.* Cambridge, MA: Harvard University Press, 1979.

Galilei, Galileo. *Dialogues concerning Two New Sciences.* Great Minds Series. Amherst, NY: Prometheus Books, 1991.

Gamow, George. *Thirty Years That Shook Physics.* Garden City, NY: Doubleday & Company, Inc., 1966.

Giancoli, Douglas C. *Physics: Principles with Applications.* 4th ed. Englewood Cliffs, NJ: Prentice-Hall, 1995.

Halliday, David, et al. *Fundamentals of Physics.* 4th ed. New York: John Wiley & Sons, Inc., 1993.

Hawking, Stephen. *Black Holes and Baby Universes.* New York: Bantam Books, 1993.

Heisenberg, Werner. *Physics and Philosophy.* New York: Harper & Row, Publishers, 1958.

Ingardia, Richard. *Thomas Aquinas: International Bibliography, 1977-1990.* Bowling Green, OH: The Philosophy Documentation Center, 1993.

Keeton, William T. *Biological Science.* 5th ed. New York: W.W. Norton & Co., Inc., 1992.

Lederman, Leon. *The God Particle.* New York: Dell Publishing Co., Inc., 1994.

Levine, Joseph S., and Kenneth R. Miller. *Biology: Discovering Life.* 2d ed. Lexington, MA: D.C. Heath and Co., 1994.

Lorentz, Hendrik Antoon. *Problems of Modern Physics.* Edited by H. Bateman. New York: Ginn & Co., 1927.

Miethe, Terry L., and Vernon J. Bourke, eds. *Thomistic Bibliography, 1940-1978.* Westport, CT: Greenwood Press, 1980.

Newton, Isaac. *The Principia.* Translated by Andrew Motte. Great Minds Series. Amherst, NY: Prometheus Books, 1995.

Smith, Vincent E. *The General Science of Nature.* Milwaukee, WI: The Bruce Publishing Company, 1958.

_____. *Philosophical Physics.* New York: Harper & Brothers, 1950.

Smith, Vincent E., ed. *The Logic of Science.* New York: St. John's University Press, 1964.

_____. *The Philosophy of Physics.* New York: St. John's University Press, 1961.

Weinberg, Steven. *Dreams of a Final Theory.* New York: Pantheon Books, 1992.

_____. *The First Three Minutes.* New York: Bantam Books, 1984.

Index

abstraction, 69-71, 73-75
accelerated motion, laws of, 16, 36,
    81-82, 172-74
acceleration, 40-41, 43-44, 57-58
acceleration, angular, 56-57
acceleration, centripetal, 57-59, 61-
    62
Achilles Paradox, 71-73, 81, 104-13,
    129-31, 139-40
Alexander the Great, 119
analogical knowledge, 165
Anaxagoras, 116, 122
anthropic principle, 194, 195, 198
Apostles' Creed, 1, 5-7, 7-8, 196-204
Aquinas
    on degrees, 53, 77
    on geocentric theory, 29, 197
    on spontaneous generation, 2-3,
        11, 16, 201
Aristotle
    on geocentric theory, 29, 197
    on natural motion, 21, 31, 67-68,
        73, 182-83
    on spontaneous generation, 2-3,
        11, 16, 201
art/science
    common meaning of, 83-85
    form of, 97
    genesis of, 10, 73-74, 83-84, 89,
        200
    need ordered universe, 10
Augustine, Saint, 119

Barrow, John, 194, 200
beauty, 166
big bang theory, 4-5, 15, 194, 201

cause, universal, 3, 11, 162-63, 168,
    201, 203-4
causes, four, 115-119, 123-24
Cavendish, Henry, 65-66
chance
    definition of, 11-13, 15, 124-26,
        134
    and free will, 126
    under God's power, 10-14, 126,
        134, 163-64, 168-69, 198-99,
        201
    and modern science, 14-17, 19,
        133-34, 191-96, 198-99
    not determinism, 15, 134
    opposed to ordered universe, 14-
        17, 133-34, 191-96, 198-99
    restricted to planners, 125, 134
    unpredictable, 125-26, 127, 128,
        134
change
    and motion, 104, 116, 117, 119-23,
        136-37
    not infinite, 156-57
    principles of, 119-23
    substantial, 121-23, 136-37
chemistry, related to physics, 118
Christian faith. *See* faith, Christian
Columbus, Christopher, 53, 77

universe, order in *(continued)*
  unchanged by new ideas, 19-20,
    26, 32
  See also universe

vector, 40, 48-50, 52
velocity, 39-40, 41, 43-47
velocity, angular, 56-57, 64
void, 147, 177

weight, 59-60, 62
weightlessness, 66, 80
Weinberg, Steven, 95, 192, 193, 195,
    200, 201
Whitehead, Alfred North, 200
Wiener, Norbert, 38, 200
will, free, 126, 163, 164, 168, 169-70

Zeno, 71-72, 104-13, 116-17, 156